11048269

A HISTORY OF
DEMOCRACY IN EUROPE

A HISTORY OF
DEMOCRACY IN EUROPE

Edited by Antoine de Baecque
Translated by Nicholas Y. A. Bradley

SOCIAL SCIENCE MONOGRAPHS, BOULDER
DISTRIBUTED BY COLUMBIA UNIVERSITY PRESS, NEW YORK
1995

This book was published with the assistance of a subsidy from The French Ministry of Culture

CONTENTS

5

INTRODUCTION

This book was inspired by the bicentenary celebrations of the French Revolution. For the bicentenary was to coincide with the most unexpected and far reaching commemoration: further revolutions. The obvious answer is that the liberation movement in Eastern Europe was a revolution against the revolution (since the Communists, officially, had usurped the myth of 1789-1793 under the shadow of 1917), so it might be called a *de-revolution*, or even the sometimes used neologism of "revolution" mixing the words revolution and reform... Possibly. Yet everywhere there emerged similar demands, stemming directly from the turning-point of 1789: democracy, in words (the Declaration of Human Rights) as well as in deed (universal suffrage and pluralism of political opinion).

Thus 1989 marks a watershed in European History; almost every state and above all their people henceforth recognized that public life must be based on Democracy.

It was a principle that found its application in the spring of 1990 with free elections in a large part of Central and Eastern Europe. In a way, it took two hundred years for Europe as a whole, simultaneously to show its wish to live not under identical regimes, nor according to similar political practices, but trusting its destiny to the same democratic ideal and thus to act. It probably took such a long time because, from the start of the French Revolution, the democratic ideal, in its institutions and application, was ambiguous: the fact that power was seized by force, that the representative system was weakened by lack of popular support, that wars had to be fought and exceptional powers given to factions, undermined political principles which were supposed to guide it. Yet, in each country at a different pace, with variations in ways and means, democracy progressed everywhere, until it appears today as the only political and social system possible.

This statement can sound naive, even simplistic. First of all because, as will be shown here, the forms taken by the rebirth of Democracy in Eastern Europe were manifold and we shall try to throw some light on the phenomenon. Similarly the passage to democratic regimes some fifteen years back was different in Spain and Portugal, and the development of democratic practices in the French countryside and English cities in the 19th century occurred in a gradual and uncertain fashion. Not to mention the crisis affecting Western democracies in the 20s and 30s. This History of European Democracy is an attempt to unravel the complexities of the growth of democratic regimes, taking into account their regional and cultural variety. To understand the process this is necessary; different traditions made for democratic restoration happening almost spontaneously in Czechoslovakia or even Poland; while it is still problematic in Romania and the Soviet Union, perhaps also Poland (which belongs to two types). The impact of national claims, sometimes of nationalistic ones is also visible here and there, intertwined with the ideal of Democracy.

The suddenness of the return to Democracy is deceptive, since it is tempting to conclude from it that Democracy is the obvious choice, the only regime under which civilized man can live. As if Democracy, a moment of balance in political life, had no History. We have become so used to the idea that our comprehension is warped, this is why it is necessary to study its genesis. Indeed a long familiarity has allowed democratic principle and its practice to be assimilated into our political culture so fully that it frequently gives rise to indignation at the discrepancies between high principles and their application, but it also tends to obliterate intellectual and historical preconditions for the rise of the democratic ideal. It is as if the sense of European identity, first in the West, later in the East, had become identical with Democracy itself. The constant weakness of the democratic discourse lies in ignorance of its specific History. This book is an attempt to fill a gap; there are collections of documents (most of them recent) on Human Rights, but there is no systematic study (spanning two centuries) in a geographical setting (in Europe) to explain the reality of democracy, the interpretations it was given at various times, or its regional traditions and relevance to day. An overall picture of the various facets of the same political concept, under sometimes conflicting interpretations, can present the democratic ideal and practice with something of more value than mere propaganda; it will be intellectually satisfying. The time has come to tell the story of Democracy for the benefit of future readers.

It is clear that the return to Democracy, in its mysterious intricacies is above all a historical process. "Democracy made its appearance at a given time, it was acquired through a break with a well ordered hierarchical society, ruled by principles that were considered as natural, and the peoples which at the moment are trying to shake the totalitarian yoke are engaged in creative work once again." as Claude Lefort wrote in 1989. Thus in freeing themselves from communist regimes which purported to bring History to an end by erecting a new world, the populations of Eastern Europe have thrown a new light on a dual aspect of History. They proved that they have now stepped into History, breaking the barriers that were isolating them; and they revealed our ignorance of the nature of the principles we live under, which appear "natural" (as once the old order seemed natural) and are in fact a moment of historical equilibrium. The return to Democracy in Europe is also a return to History: a democratic regime by its acceptance of conflict, which is subjected to bargaining and rendered harmless, is essentially part of a historical society.

This is the reason why there is a need for a vast European fresco of the History of Democracy spanning two centuries. In just over four hundred pages, which represents a challenge... or even a first draft of a historical process approached in a specific light. If basically Democracy means "Entering History" this book can be seen as one of the ways of retelling the story. There will be a cross examination of two kinds of documents: those which describe and explain Democracy in European democratic societies; others including a collection of manifestoes, programs and analyses serving as landmarks in the evolution of Democracy. Encompassing two hundred years, we have here about twenty accounts of the evolution of Democracy and its traditions in each European country, as well as nearly two hundred various documents, to support the analytical approach of the phenomenon. Above all it is useful to replace the events in their historical context; the historical development will be studied in the light of sources not easily available (an anthology) without neglecting the techniques of interpretation.

In this enterprise Democracy is a precondition more than a pretext. As can be observed in the interrelation of dates applying to each European country, only through Democracy can the sources be uncovered in their rich variety. There are many different kinds of democratic regimes, going from the Bonapartist form to social-democracy in France for example, which brought the same variations in contrary movements; the chronological vagaries of its various tendencies are impressive — it took over 70 years to generalize universal suffrage, and almost 50 years to give women access to the ballot box; and it is difficult to assess the effect of institutional changes in the regions. Thus more than a given notion, Democracy is an accretion of reforms, and though all components are essential, it grew through repeated experiments and seemingly contradictory analyses which were each one of them a vital ingredient in the final balance of the institutions, the development of the theory and the search for practical ways of enforcing it. Such a survey has been attempted here.

Antoine de Baecque

THE THEORY OF DEMOCRACY

Philippe Raynaud

Some 45 years after the defeat of fascism and national socialism, and in view of the collapse of communism and revolutionary ideologies, the political and social systems which appeared in the last two centuries in Europe and America have been newly legitimized, to such an extent that it is not easy to understand their violent births. To understand the initial precariousness of the present regimes the best way is probably to try and imagine the idea of Democracy that the founding fathers had in mind, before giving an account of the challenges facing Western society early in the last century.

Late in the 18th century, the word "Democracy" applied to a specific political regime: according to the Encyclopedia, Democracy is simply a form of government, with sovereignty given to the people as a body. A large majority of the theorists of modern political philosophy presents Democracy in this sense as belonging to the past (small city-states in ancient times) and, above all, its legitimacy in principle is doubtful. The kind of citizenship that evolved in classical Greece seemed out of place in modern Nation-States. Democracy requires both simple morals and uncomplicated social relations as well as an exaggerated emphasis on military valor. Even if this political arrangement is good for "virtue," it seemed best in those days to consider, like Montesquieu, that the growth of "trade" in modern societies constitutes an advance that was undreamt of in democratic city-states, since commercial relations are conducive to richer social exchanges and gentler manners. The democratic principle also meets with criticisms of an "elitist" kind: the wish for rational government brings about a certain distrust of the people which can be easily swayed by prejudice, and therefore tends to either " enlightened" absolute monarchy or a representative parliamentary regime. Yet on the other hand the extent of these reservations towards the political ideal of a reestablishment of democracy can only be understood if one takes into account the egalitarian aspirations of the Enlightenment. An attack on prejudice requires a firm belief in universal reason or "common sense," just as the legitimacy of existing institutions can only rest on their ability to serve the common good or to safeguard public security. While the preconditions to popular representation imply a certain amount of democracy, as the people is supposed to be at least capable of choosing its representatives.

In a way the history of the two great Revolutions of the late 18th century throws into relief the ambiguous relationship between modern politics, especially the liberal approach, and democracy. The more perceptive of the founding fathers of the American Republic or of the French Constituent deputies were unanimous in judging the classical principles of democracy as a thing of the past and of doubtful value. The editors of the Federalist who supported the principles of the Constitution advocated at the Philadelphia Convention sought to create a great trading Republic, not a Democracy: the Republic they envisaged was not the lesser of two evils to their mind but rather a higher political form that was made possible by the means of representation of the people and above all by drawing on a variety of talents and interests as the natural basis of progress. In spite of the many differences between the French revolutionary process and the creation of the United States of America, the citizens of 1789 were not very different in their way of thinking from their American precursors: they also wanted to have a representative government, the only suitable choice for modern society, as it was based on expanding trade and full employment. The two great Revolutions of the late 18th century were in the main liberal revolutions whose aim was to guarantee and widen the scope of "rights" and freedoms which existed only in so far as a private sphere of interest had been recognized, the autonomy of which was increased by freer economic activities and a loosening of the hold religion had over society.

Yet it should be observed that, in both countries, the revolutionary process was accompanied by profound changes in the liberal political culture that can be described as democratization of liberalism.

This happened in American politics, as it developed after the war of Independence until the Constitution was adopted. Recent American historical research has shown that the men behind the American Revolution, far from being "moderates," were the heirs of English Liberals (whigs) who stood against the Monarchy. The latter's aim was to safeguard the "English Constitution" evidently, with its numerous traditional components (an Established Church, a ruling aristocracy, the monarchy) whose supporters often invoked the classical ideal of a "mixed political system," based on a combination of monarchical, aristocratic and popular elements; but the most radical among the Whigs stressed the "democratic" aspect of the English government by emphasizing the power and protection it gave to the popular section of society. While they recognized the class division as a fact of life, they thought the outstanding advantage of the English Constitution was to give a substantial political weight to the people (through the Commons) which curbed the power of the aristocracy and above all of the government. These ideas attracted a lot of interest among American settlers, and after the struggle for independence they acquired further significance. The original feature of the American political experiment derives from the specific problem facing the settlers, which gave rise to a new attitude towards representation. In their opposition to the taxes raised by the English Parliament, the Americans made use of traditional liberal claims: "no taxation without representation." While from the point of view of the mother country, the colonies' inhabitants were represented in Parliament in reality, just as the other British subjects who were not all given the right to vote. Logically American claims tended to tighten the bonds between Parliament and its electorate, as well as widening the basis of representation and taking into account the electorate's interests, while keeping a sharp eye on the legislative body to prevent any encroachment on popular sovereignty. The young American Republic's institutions, from the first constitutions of the States to the one adopted by the Union after the Philadelphia Convention (1787), reflected both some similarity with the English institutions and a new tendency to strengthen the popular element in "government" From the English tradition the United States retained mainly the system of balance of power (checks and balances) as guaranteeing freedom since, through them, "le pouvoir arrete le pouvoir" (power puts a stop to power) in Montesquieu's words. This is the reason why most of the States and the Union itself retain the two chamber system, while trying to maintain a balance between legislative and executive powers. However, the tradition underwent a considerable change as the notion of mixed political system was removed from that of balance between permanent social forces while all institutions acquired a popular basis: the federal Senate represents the states of the Union, but it is not an aristocratic Chamber, the appointment of the President is indirectly dependent on the American people and the interests put forward by the interplay of various "factions" are ceaselessly changing under the influence of what Tocqueville called the "equality of social conditions." These political innovations arose in a society unlike any other at the time, that of the English colonies of America, with few differences in hierarchy, hardly any "aristocracy," and where the numerous Churches made for religious tolerance. The reforms enacted by Jefferson and his friends (the abolition of primogeniture, "disestablishment" of the Churches) ensured the stability of this fundamentally egalitarian social structure on which rests the American democratic experiment.

From the point of view of the tasks that the Revolution had to accomplish, France found herself in a situation quite contrary to that of America: centuries of aristocratic rule and absolute power had left deep marks, but this was the reason why a clean break with the Ancien Regime had to be made, thus giving it a universal appeal which reverberated all over Europe in the 18th century. These original features of the French political development gave the French concept of representation its characteristics first of all, but also played a major part in the set of phenomena which are usually defined as "Jacobin."

The National Assembly in 1789 was in a situation exactly opposite to that of the American Rebels fifteen years earlier; the latter had to fight against a powerful Parliament, drawing its authority from a modern concept of representative mandate and from a largely traditional electoral system. This is the reason why the Americans had to endeavor to widen and rationalize the way of selecting representatives, as well as insuring that the representatives' interests would be taken into account and be given control of the legislative body. On the contrary the French had to free themselves both of the system of the coercive mandate (deriving from the consultative character of the etats generaux) and of the crumbling legacy of the old "Constitution." Hence the combination of a voluntarist and "geometrical" reconstitution of the body politic, the great emphasis given to the "general will" and the tendency to assert the full sovereignty of the legislative power. The "Jacobin" experiment from the founding of the club to the days of "Terreur" finally gave a new meaning to something that could have been merely a "continental" version of liberalism. The "Jacobin" process effected a transfer of the sovereign power of the "nation" from the representatives to the "people," but at the same time it required the people to undergo a moral and political regeneration, while widening the scope of Human Rights to include all the "paupers'" needs. Jacobin democracy therefore brought into being a new figure: in a search for egalitarian progress the struggle against the Ancien Regime coincided with an exaltation of a new kind of citizenship, and the praise given to revolutionary vigilance or even violence was part of a project aimed at creating a New Man and raising the awareness of what would soon be called the "social question."

Eighteenth century philosophers understood democracy in two ways: as the destiny of modern society and as one of its possible forms. On the one hand, the experience of revolutions in this century in no way contradicted any objection that had been leveled at democratic political systems, whether by traditional or liberal theorists, rather it seemed to confirm the advantages of a representative system. Yet on the other hand, after the French

Revolution, and equally in North America, societies seemed prey to a new and manyfold restlessness, in which a desire for equality played a major part. Such is the puzzle confronting liberal thinking: the realization of its program brings about not only a reduction of power for the State in favor of the regulations appearing spontaneously in the field of relations between individuals, but also gives rise to the hope, may be illusory, that society can enjoy full control over itself. As for the most fervent supporters of the rule of the sovereign "people" such as Michelet in France, they expect from the new system a great deal more than increased influence in government for the laboring classes.

The best guide to grasp the new meaning given to democracy is undoubtedly Tocqueville, whose book *Democracy in America* gives both a matchless description of life in America and a theoretical analysis of the kind of society that was created there. Tocqueville introduced a new element in liberal thinking: he was the first to understand fully why a liberal political program could not be realized if there was no departure from the compromises achieved between the old aristocratic society and modern trends, as embodied in the "English Constitution" or, in France, in the 1814 Charter. Liberals at the time of the Restoration, such as Guizot, Remusat or Royer-Collard knew full well that the new society could not reject completely the principles of the French Revolution, and that it contained the seeds of sometimes radical egalitarian aspirations ("democracy is in full spate," in the words of Royer-Collard); but they remained committed to a system which Tocqueville was perceptive enough to dismiss as impossible. Guizot and his friends saw modernity in granting equality before the law to all citizens, but political rights would be the privilege of an elite, which though mobile was comparatively small, that of "capabilities," that is to say the forces in the new society proving to be the most dynamic and the most concerned in preserving social order. Dogmatic Liberalism from the start had a "conservative" connotation, which was expressed in the notion that the rise of the "middle classes" was the final goal in the search for equality that had characterized European History from the first struggles of the Tiers Etat up to the Revolution. Liberalism is also present in an almost "centrist" political ideal, half-way between the reactionary dreams of counter-revolutionaries and the egalitarian claims made by Republicans and the more radical Democrats, such as are associated to Liberals' minds with the 1793 Terror. Tocqueville, while being in part a follower of Guizot and Royer-Collard, methodically proved that democracy, in reality, represented the true goal of Liberal demands. *Democracy in America* retained Guizot's idea that the Revolution which made citizens equal before the law and gave them political freedom was the central aspect of modern European History. It said: "The gradual development of equality in social conditions is therefore a providential occurrence, in all its main characteristics: it is universal, lasting, every day more independent of human influence; every event and every man help its development." Yet this picture of providential intervention in the rise of "equality of conditions" is different from that of Guizot in three respects: Tocqueville saw any attempt to stop the growth of egalitarian aspirations as bound to fail, he distinguished between democratic and revolutionary spirit and above all he showed how closely linked were the democratic principle of popular sovereignty and individual emancipation dear to Liberal thinking.

Tocqueville demonstrated how futile were the hopes of the Conservatives to safeguard the unequal distribution of wealth from democratic claims, since in his philosophy the cause of equality was invincible. It represents one of the most vibrant themes of *Democracy in America*: if "equality of conditions" is the principle behind modern democracy, it is because it does not imply "real" leveling of men as regards riches or power so much as a relativizing of hierarchical differences, whether public or private, under the impact of the abstraction. As the best recent commentators of Tocqueville have pointed out, the passage which throws the most light on this idea is undoubtedly the chapter on relations between master and servant, in the second part of the book. Naturally this is by all means an unequal relation, but it derives new meaning from a context in which equality is the rule and nothing guarantees the social standing of each individual: "When conditions are almost equal, people are for ever changing places; there is still a class of servants and a class of masters; but they are not always made up of the same individuals nor above all of the same families; there is no more fatality in commanding than in obeying... When most citizens have lived under similar social conditions for a long time, and equality has long been a recognized fact, public feeling, completely impervious to exceptional cases, ascribes to the value of man in general limits above and below which is difficult for a person to remain for long. Though wealth and poverty, the condition of master and servant, may accidentally create a large gap between two men, public opinion which is based on the normal course of things, brings them closer to the common level and gives them a kind of imaginary equality, in spite of the actual inequality of their conditions."

Thus equality is an imaginary bond which does not preclude inequalities in actual fact: this lasting discrepancy between the promises of progressive thinking and reality is the ground for bitter attacks against democracy, and in the first instance the socialist criticism of "formal" equality as it exists in bourgeois society. Yet the egalitarian principle nonetheless is not without a remarkable impact on society, especially as regards the changes in relations between masters and servants. In traditional, "aristocratic" society, differences in status were seen as unbridgeable and almost natural, but the paradox was that this could be accompanied by familiarity between the classes, which was made easier by the fact that each one knew that the social hierarchy was not in balance; in a democracy, on the contrary, contractual links make for more neutral relations, while the fact of equality "in abstracto" encourages a reaction of distinguishing themselves among the upper classes, all the stronger when inequality is more precarious. Tocqueville thus shows how equality is a breeding ground for two apparently contradictory passions: each advance on equality increases the character of illegitimacy of the remaining inequalities by smoothing the way to a gradual progression of egalitarian demands as regards the whole spectrum of human relations, while simultaneously, awareness of equality increases reflexes of "elitist" defense in those who feel threatened by the growth of democracy. This is why, while Tocqueville rejected any idea of either going beyond democracy or returning to the traditional or aristocratic social relations, he gave us an insight into the negative attitudes prevailing in an egalitarian society. Since modern democracy is social rather than political, it can combine a burgeoning of the most radical tendencies with a front of moderate political institutions of a representative kind. Yet at the same time democracy is the scene of passions which can turn against it: socialist criticism of purely formal equality, just as much as "elitist" theories, are a direct result of the democratic experiment.

A study of American society, in which democratic principles can be applied to the full, since they are not hindered by the old aristocratic structures, gives a rather comforting answer to the perplexities of some who, without being counter revolutionaries, feel disquieted by the rise of egalitarian claims. If advances in equality are accompanied by revolutionary troubles, subversion and anti-social passions, it is not due to the nature of democracy but to the particular conditions in which it appeared in France: it is not so much the "democratic spirit" which is at play here, but the "revolutionary spirit," born of the clash between the aristocratic world and Revolution, and which egalitarian progress can help to overcome.

More than a political system, modern democracy therefore is above all the expression of a wholesale change in society, replacing the old hierarchical relations with the notion of equality. Nevertheless a direct consequence of this is the presence of the political principle of popular sovereignty in the modern social system. This principle is somehow the natural accompaniment of equality and individual autonomy: the rise of democracy is not only a result of increased complexity in the division of labor, it is also observable in greater autonomy for the individual, who self-governing in his private life, demands the same freedom in the area of politics. Moreover modern democracy only spells out what in most societies is hidden by traditional hierarchical relations:

"The principle of popular sovereignty, always present to some extent in most human institutions, usually lies buried there. It is not acknowledged even if it commands obedience, and if sometimes it happens to come to light, it is quickly driven back into the gloom of the sanctuary...In America, the principle of popular sovereignty does not remain hidden or unproductive as in some nations; it is inscribed in social customs, in the Law, it can freely expand and reach unhindered its ultimate consequences."

One of the main distinctions of Tocqueville's analysis is to show the gradual emergence of the idea that democracy is much more than one of the possibilities of liberal development in Europe: democracy is both, as a social process, the foundation of modern History, and, as a political principle, it accompanies individual emancipation. Yet, on the other hand the growth of democratic civilization was marked by unheard of strife, and the history of the 20th century as a whole seems to give the lie to the optimistic declarations of the humanitarian prophets of the previous century. The challenges that confronted democratic societies are part and parcel of our understanding of them.

Even though its advance seemed irresistible to the more clear sighted observers, democracy was always the butt of violent attacks as a principle, some of this criticism laying the foundation for the "totalitarian" movements of the 20th century. This does not mean, however, that the history of democracy can be reduced to a struggle against the obsolete remains of aristocratic and religious societies. The fiercest opponents of democracy are its heirs and in the end they often contributed to the reform and stabilization of societies born of the 18th century revolutions.

If one examines the counter revolutionary ideologies springing from the tragedies of the Great Revolution, it is obvious that present day political theorists share with it many terms of reference. However they might wish to rebuild the Ancien Regime, such as de Maistre and Bonald were in reality far removed from the world to which they claimed to belong. Criticizing "abstract" revolutionary principles in the name of History, they were helpless on the intellectual level in the face of a stabilization of bourgeois society which sealed the historical success of the Revolution, They devised a political system aiming at the reestablishment of an organic social order, but they were in fact passionately fighting for the revolutionary ideal of regeneration, and this led them unwittingly to a "revolution in reverse," not to the "opposite of the Revolution." This explains why a portion of the inheritance of the counter revolutionary theory was passed on in all legitimacy to the "left," through a gradual development in some of its best representatives, such as Lammenais and Ballanche, but also through explicit criticism of revolutionary abstractions, made by emerging socialist thinkers, in imitation of traditional thinkers.

Attacks made by the Socialists against modern democracy are undoubtedly the most effective of all and still difficult to ignore. They were directed at the idea of democracy, not merely bourgeois society and its injustice. Such was the attitude of the early revolutionaries, "enrages" or disciples of Baboeuf. They advocated resistance to the "abstraction of Human Rights," in the name of the needs of men in real life and the measures they put forward (such as a tax on foodstuff by the maximum) owe as much to the traditional "police state" of the Monarchy as to "direct democracy." The phenomenon is even more visible in the greatest French and German theorists, as they were fully aware of the urgent need to break with the "political illusion" (Marx) of the Revolution and the emerging democracy, in order to solve social problems. Others suggested to give prominence to the "social Constitution" (Proudhon), or to go beyond the "lawmaker's" mentality present in the French Revolution (Saint Simon). Yet socialism can also be understood as a offshoot, or a "dialectics" by-product, of the democratic movement, in so far as it rests on conscious control of the future of society by itself. This continuity is striking in the English tradition: the emerging labor movement was intrinsically linked with the democratic ideals which became famous after the French Revolution, socialist ideas were championed both by Human Rights theoreticians and by the descendants of Utilitarians, and Charterism mixed social claims and demands for political reform. Even if it is of a more complex character, the link between the socialist idea and democracy was also present in France and in Germany, as was made evident by Louis Blanc's devotion to the Jacobin tradition, as well as Marx's attachment to the Republican ideals of his youth. As the founding fathers of Sociology saw full well, Socialism was the fruit of the Enlightenment and its dialectics which can be given two different interpretations: as an attempt to restore modern society in its unity that was lost with the rise of a liberal economy (Durkheim) or as the end result of the ambiguities of modern concepts of Human Rights and equality (Weber). The development of the Welfare State in the 20th century is a proof that liberal democracies could to a certain extent accommodate the demands of their socialist opponents.

The great divide between the present day and Democrats or Humanitarians of the last century lies in the disillusions experienced in recent times: two World Wars, the rise of totalitarian systems and the disasters of the post-colonial era put paid to the notion of human societies advancing serenely towards freedom and democracy. However, this does not mean that to be up to date we must give up our perception of a fundamental break achieved in the late 18th century. The tragedies occurring in this century were a consequence of the changes in political life that took place then: modern wars derive some of their violence from the traditional idea of balance of power having been discarded, while totalitarian regimes were born of disrespect for democracy and also an attempt to realize the ideal of unity and transparency which is part of it. In this sense, even if making democracy work will always be a difficult and hazardous task, contemporary European History can only be the History of democracy.

THE PRACTICE OF DEMOCRACY

Paolo Pombeni

Since World War II democracy, in the sense of government by
the people, has known such progress in a large part of the world
that it has come to be regarded as the natural outcome of all
political development. Even its critics see it as unavoidable. "To
day, in many nations, democracy has given way to dictatorship,
and it is discredited everywhere. Is this only a temporary setback?"
This bitter statement, was written in 1934 by J.A. Hobson, a
Liberal English publicist who was well-known for his study of
imperialism. He was one of a large number of observers made
uneasy by the helpless attitude of Western political systems as they
were confronted by the rise of fascism. Tocqueville had become an
institution and everyone accepted his judgement that democracy
was inassailable. In 1867, Robert Low, a proud right wing Liberal,
could exclaim during the debate concerning Electoral Reform in
the British Commons: "Monsieur de Tocqueville maintains that
democracy is unavoidable, and the question is not whether it is
good or bad in itself, but how we can make the best of it. Here ...is
the reasoning of a coward, and I hope this Chamber will not allow
itself to be influenced by it." Yet in 1911, the Italian right wing
Liberal Sidney Sonnino, warning his allies that they should not be
too hopeful about retaining restricted suffrage, encouraged them to
be prepared to survive in a system of open political competition

and wrote: "The most urgent political problem is, as Tocqueville said, to protect society from demagogy through a better organization of democracy."

Yet in concrete terms what did this irrepressible ascent to democracy in 19th century Europe consist of? The answer is not simple, nor an explanation of the process of decline between the wars. Though there was a great deal of talk about democracy in the course of the 19th and 20th centuries, the word remained shrouded in ambiguity. There is a simple definition, according to which democracy is self-government in a society made up of free and equal citizens. Yet such a society could hardly exist, as is shown in political science books of the 19th century, except in America, or rather in the early days of America: there, due to lack of History, (therefore lack of feudal ties as a legacy of History) together with wide opportunities of making a private fortune, there was ground for describing society as made of free and equal individuals, who took self-government as a natural fact. As we know, Tocqueville outlined this; yet the lesson was well remembered as a fundamental creed and American society served as a model. A writer such as Emile Boutmy, thought likewise; in 1871 he established the *Ecole libre des sciences politiques*, and therefore he already knew about the changes affecting American society under the impact of the immigration wave of the 1860's.

It was quite a challenge to devise a way to reproduce this perfect kind of society in Europe. To do so meant abolishing a rich historical past, a past which leaves behind the political society (or in front, depending on the angle) a civic society with many layers, institutions, classes, scales of values and in constant flux. The Jacobins, at the time of the French Revolution, addressed themselves to the problem and declared that the political society was under obligation to promote a classless civic society to support it. This ambition suffered from being associated with the Terror and a dictatorial rule.

Apart from this tragic historical experience, what form could democracy take? Naturally a system in which men enjoying liberty and equality govern themselves... One condition, however, that there is agreement on two points: who is really free, and what term of reference can be given to the notion of equality? Another question: if some subjects are deprived of freedom and equality, shall they be kept outside the democratic system of politics, being unable to take part in it? Rather is it not necessary, for the system to be really democratic, that it makes those who are not yet free and equals so? The practice of democracy in Europe must be examined in this light and according to concepts which have long exercised the minds of political leaders and were expressed in a wide variety of ways.

In the Constitutions which came into general use after 1830 the meaning of self-government by "free and equal citizens" was a representative system in which all subjects fulfilling the condition had the right to vote. In a few cases it was thought that the system was only applicable where there had previously been a diffuse kind of self-government, in countries where local or traditional communities had been a training ground for learning the discipline of constitutional power which could later spread to the whole nation. Great Britain was the customary reference in this respect in all the writings of European authors who made a myth out of it; yet it is far from certain that the British leaders were aware that their system implied such self-government and constitutional representation. On the other hand, it is true that in this country an exceptionally high rate of political participation and high quality in political leaders were a direct consequence of this wide practice of "political virtues" in the 19th century.

This has to be born in mind in order to understand why Great Britain, with a restricted electoral system and no universal suffrage until 1918, already appeared in the 19th century as exemplary. In reality, here participation in politics was granted, not so much through casting one's vote as an individual, (long seen more as a duty than as a right in British political thinking) as through involvement of the citizen in the machinery of decision-making which went right through the various "communities," either territorial or intellectual, to which the subjects felt they belonged, whether they could vote or not. It was in countries where the community element of the political pyramid was regarded as belonging to traditional Ancien Regime customs, that the question of the principles of electoral reform seemed to be of paramount importance. French politics were intensely concerned with these in the period after the Revolution, until finally after decades of development the process of constitution stopped with the stabilization of the 3rd Republic. Early in the new era, France adopted universal suffrage (or was it a surrender?) turning all inhabitants into free and equal citizens, in reality it should be remembered that this law was accompanied by many safeguards, to prevent naive participation to elections.

The question of electoral systems anyhow remained the basic means of controlling the working of democracy. Of course, the interaction of democracy and universal suffrage collapsed in a spectacular way when in 1866 and again 1870, Bismarck, the Conservative, drafted two constitutions (for the Norddeutsches, later for the German Reich) providing for universal suffrage. It is a wonder that Bismarck postured as relying on popular wisdom and chose to have his actions ratified by referendum, as it were, in spite of critical international opinion... All the same, in so doing, Bismarck put an end to the relation between democracy and universal suffrage.

In any case, the opposite side, that is to say the sometimes ambiguous relation between universal suffrage and representation, was beginning to create a problem. While many critics, in the Anglo-Saxon system, emphasized the need to represent brains, not numbers, a similar concern was voiced all over Europe to some extent. It should be remembered that the representative system, everywhere, included two Chambers, and the High Chamber was supposed to redress the balance of representation which was weakened necessarily by the fact that the vote was given to subjects whose "freedom and equality" were as yet untried. In this sense, two famous incidents illustrate the turning points reached in 1870 and 1880: the 3rd Republic in France tried to create a Senate with distinctive characteristics which could act as an alternative to the Chamber of Deputies, while in England Lord Salisbury claimed that the Lords were better qualified to represent the nation than the Commons, which were only an expression of blind numbers.

The debate went on for years, for instance there was in 1911 a fierce clash in Great Britain between the Liberal Government trying to promote social improvements and the Lords who stood against them (the end result was that the Lords lost their equal share of legislative power and only retained the right of vetoing laws of which they did not approve). In 1947-1950 there burst another battle between the Commons enjoying a Labor majority and the Lords which were at a great disadvantage this time. In Italy the Senate experienced much frustration, as it was deprived of any political power, but still considered as useful in the Constitution and public opinion. The same could be said of the 4th Republic in France, whose Constitution failed to give the Upper Chamber strong characteristics which could have made it play a part in the question of representation.

From this point of view it could be said that the only instances of two Chambers having a balanced responsibility in decision-making are to be found only in the Federal-type systems, as in Germany for example. Here the Upper Chamber serves to exercise a function of temporary control on the government of member-states. To start with, Bismarck had given it a negative function to enable him to counter parliament (Prussia alone had 17 votes out of 58 in the Bundestat, that is to say that the Reich Chancellor, the Prime Minister in reality, could count on a third of the votes at any time...), but later it acquired a different influence, of a dialectical character.

It is clear, however, that in practice the two Chambers system proved to be a major failure in contemporary political life. Though it has been retained almost everywhere, it has neither given rise to a proper theoretical justification, nor has it been discarded.

THE PRACTICAL EXPERIENCE OF DEMOCRACY

"Over the post war period democracy, meaning popular self-government, had spread across the majority of countries and could be viewed as the natural conclusion of political evolution. Even those opposed to it, saw it as inevitable. Today, in several countries, democracy has been replaced by dictatorship and is generally being discredited. Is this just a temporary set-back...?" This bitter observation, was written in 1934 by J. A. Hobson,[1] a

---

[1] J.A. Hobson, *Democracy and a Changing Civilisation*, London, 1934.

well known British liberal writer and thinker whose name is closely linked to his study of imperialism. He reflects the views of many people deeply disturbed by the reaction of western political structures to the fascist threat.

Tocqueville had been the *auctoritas* who progressively succeeded in convincing western political opinion of the inevitability of democracy. In 1867, in the British House of Commons, during a debate on electoral reform, Robert Lowe a staunch right wing liberal declared: "Monsieur de Tocqueville states that democracy is inevitable and what we need to ask ourselves is not whether it is good or bad in itself but how we might most easily adapt to it. This is [...] the thinking of a coward, which I hope will not influence[2] the House." Yet in 1919, the right wing Italian Liberal Sidney Sonnino appealed to his supporters not to cling to the illusion that they could keep limited suffrage, but on the contrary, exhorted them to prepare to survive in a system with open political competition. He wrote: "The most serious political problem today is, in the words of de Tocqueville, to defend society from demagogy through a more efficient organization of democracy."[3]

What exactly was this irresistible tide of democracy in Europe during the 19th Century? There is no simple answer, nor an explanation to its sudden decline in the inter-war years. For although democracy was discussed a great deal during the 19th and 20th centuries, the exact use of the word itself is often very ambiguous. A simple definition of democracy involves the self-government of society by free and equal citizens. Yet this sort of society could only exist, as suggested by 19th century political scientists, in America, and even then America in its early days, when the *absence* of a past (hence the absence of feudalism as a product of history), as well as ample opportunities to make a

---

[2]Quoted by J.W. Burrow, *Whigs and Liberals. Continuity and Change in English Political Thought*, Clarendon, Oxford, 1988.

[3]S. Sonnino, *Scritti e discorsi extraparementari 1870-1929*, Laterza, Bari, 1972, vol. II, p. 1590.

fortune, meant that it could be maintained that these were free and equal people for whom self-government would have been a natural reality. This of course is what Tocqueville expounded: yet the reverberations of this message, in its very essence, would echo for a long time after. For example an author like Emile Boutmy, founder of the Free School of Political Science in 1870, who therefore would have been aware of the consequences of change in the American scene due to the massive waves of immigration in the 1860's, still continued to base his ideas on this fundamental premise.[4]

It was therefore no easy task to work out how to reproduce this perfect society in Europe. The vast legacy of history would have to disappear, a legacy that left political society behind, (or against it depending on one's point of view) a secular society with many layers, institutions, hierarchies and value systems; full of tension and competition.[5] The Jacobins during the French Revolution of course tried to take the bull by the horns, proclaiming the right and duty of the body-politic to develop in its own interest a homogenous secular society.[6] Yet subsequently these aspirations could not be disassociated from the Terror nor from the dictatorial use of power.

ELIGIBILITY TO VOTE

Apart from that tragic experiment, what form might democracy take? The answer of course rested on a system where free and equal men would govern themselves.... On condition however that two points are clarified: who is truly free, and in

---

[4]E. Boutmy, *Etudes de droit constitutinnel. France-Angleterre-Etats-Unis,*Plon, Paris, 1885; and *Elements d'une psychologie politique du peuple americain,* Colin, Paris, 1902.

[5]R. Kosellek, *Le Regne de la critique,* Minuit, Paris, 1979.

[6]Lucien Jaume, *Le Discours jacobin et la democratie,* Fayard, Paris, 1989; and by the same author, *Echec au liberalisme. Les jacobins et l'Etat,* Kime, Paris, 1990.

what terms can one judge equality? Also, if some elements lacked freedom and equality, should they be excluded from the democratic system, unqualified to participate? Or else, to be democratic, should the system be responsible for making people as free and equal as possible? The institution of democracy in Europe has to be judged by this conceptual measure of the world, which for a very long time and in various and differing ways has haunted all political classes.

In the constitutional regimes which began to emerge during the 1830's, the self-government of *free and equal citizens* signified a *representative system* where every citizen who was eligible had the right to vote. With a few exceptions this system was felt to be the only worthwhile one in terms of fulfilling a diffuse *self-government*, where local or traditional communities provided the basic elements for a mental *habitus* and a constitutional apprentice-ship that would extend to the level of the whole nation. The mythical reference point for all European writing on this was Great Britain; yet it is doubtful whether the British system was so enlightened as to be predisposed to combining *self-government* with representative constitutionalism. On the other hand it was true that the exceptional rate of political involvement and the sophistication of its political classes depended without a doubt during the 19th Century on the widespread belief in the implemen-tation of these *political virtues.*

This has to be remembered to understand why Great Britain, which had a rather closed electoral system and which in 1918 belatedly introduced universal suffrage, was in the 19th century considered to be a democratic model. In fact, involvement in the political process was guaranteed, not so much by the individual's right to vote (which British political theory in any case had for some time felt to be a *duty* rather than a *right*) but rather for the individual's contribution to the political *decision making mechanism* which transcend the various *communities* (both territorial and intellectual) to which subjects, eligible to vote or not, might feel they belonged.[7]

Yet in countries where a community system of political hierarchy was a traditional element defined as the *Ancien Regime*, the question of the right to vote and regulating electoral activity was of primordial importance. These questions were at the forefront of French politics following the Revolution,[8] and continued to be at the center of debates right through its constitutional phase, in other words right up to the consolidation of the III Republic.[9] Even though France at its inception was converted to (or gave in to) universal suffrage, making all its citizens free and equal, at the same time it is only right to recall that this acceptance was ringed with countless qualifications which were supposed to stop any *naive* participation in the electoral process.

The question of electoral system was to remain, in any case, the most obvious and fundamental way of controlling democracy. Of course the link between democracy and universal suffrage suprisingly and symbolically was broken in 1866 and then in 1870 when Bismark the conservative drew up two successive constitutions (the *Norddeutsche* and then the German *Reich* constitutions) which allowed for universal suffrage. Bismark's hypocrisy in putting his trust in the masses is transparent, and an obvious explanation springs to mind that he needed their backing, in the

---

[7]For more on the British electoral system see E. Biagini, "Rappresentanza virtuale e democrazia di massa: i paradossi della Gran Bretagna vittoriana," *Quaderni Storici*, XXIII (1988); F. Cammarano, "Logiche communitarie e associanismo politico nella Gran Bretagna tard vittoriana; procedure elettoriali e "corruzione"," *ibid.*, on the specific point, F. Cammarano, "National party of Common Sense," *Strategie del conservatismo britannico nella crisi del liberalismo 1885-1892*, Lacaita, Manduria, 1990.

[8]P. Gueniffey, "L'organisazzione della candidatura durante la rivoluzione francese," *Ricerche di storia politica*, V, 1990.

[9]On this very important point I was privileged enough to attend the elucidating classes of Pierre Rosanvallon during my stay at EHESS in January 1990.

form of referenda, for those political acts that might be frowned on by the international community.[10] Nevertheless Bismark thus heralded the end of the democracy/universal suffrage binomial.

TO A TWO HOUSE IMPLEMENTATION
OF DEMOCRATIC REPRESENTATION

In any case, the opposite side of the coin or in other words the often ambiguous relationship between universal suffrage and representation, already presented a problem. Cries were heard in the Anglo-Saxon system for the need to represent *brains not numbers*; similar preoccupations were voiced more or less everywhere in Europe. Far too often we forget that generally the representative system took the form of two chambers, and that the Upper House was meant to have a corrective and balancing role for weakened representation that inevitably seemed to emerge from a system which gave the vote to subjects whose *freedom and equality* were not always apparent. There are two famous episodes illustrating this in the crucial 1870's and 1880's: the attempt by the French III Republic to create a Senate with its own specific make-up and a potential role in opposition to the House of Deputies, and in England the warning given by Lord Salisbury about the House of Lords being more able to represent the nation than the Commons since the latter was no more than the alchemy of numbers.[11]

Of course the debate did not end there. One should remember the fierce struggle in Great Britain in 1911 which pitted a Liberal government desirous of social reform against a House of Lords who were not. This confrontation ended with the abolition of legislative parity between the two houses and a reduction in the

---

[10]One would consult L. Gall, *Bismark*, trad., Fayard, Paris, 1986; M. Sturmer, *Regierung und Reichstag im Bismarckstaat 1871 bis 1880. Casarismus oder parlamentarismus,* Droste, Dusseldorf, 1974.

[11]J.M. Mayeur, *La Vie politique sous la Troisieme Republique*, Le Seuil, Paris, 1984; P. Marsh, *The Discipline of Popular Government: Lord Salisbury Domestic Statecraft*, Harvester, Hassocks, 1978.

power of the Lords to veto laws they did not approve of. Again there was further conflict in 1947-1950, this time heavily weighted against the House of Lords, involving a House of Commons with a Labour majority. One can also look at the many upheavals in the Senate of the Italian kingdom. Although it had no political power it was thought to be useful for constitutional matters and for its soundness in terms of political culture. One could also look at the example of the constitution of the IV French Republic where once again the second chamber was not given a specific role but which, in a pragmatic way, settled questions of representation.

So it could be put forward that the only system where the two chambers have shown a dialectical function when making decisions is the federal one: in the case of Europe in Germany. There the second chamber's role is to have temporary control over member state governments. Initially, of course, it was an instrument of antirepresentative manipulation put in place by Bismark for his own purposes — Prussia alone had 17 votes out of a total of 58 in the Bundesrat — in other words the Reich Chancellor, who in practice was the Prime Minister, from the start had a third of the votes at his disposal. Yet with time it was to start to have a greater dialectical influence.

Yet one has to admit that the two chamber system has been one of the biggest failures of modern democratic practice. Certainly it has been preserved almost everywhere, yet without having any sound theoretical basis, nor being eliminated from the political stage. Basically no political system has dared state openly that it would be unjust, apart from majority representation, to have any other type of representation: representation by the "best" has become increasingly suspect, for who are they? Even the fascists did not venture in this direction. An assembly of "specialists" would also have its problems, for who would appoint and select them? As for "corporate" representation this was not very convincing. Hence two chamber democracy continues, linked to a functional system of dual control that sees the time-consuming decision-making process as a safeguard which provides the opportunity for outside public intervention (also of pressure groups) within the legislative mechanism.

PARTY DEMOCRACY

In contrast the only institution which seems to have acquired a fundamentally representative role, hence a democratic force, unforeseen initially, is *government*. When one thinks of this, ones thinks immediately of the experience of General De Gaulle. He himself was the end product of a long process of change, although perhaps the only one with the courage to attempt to rationalize a phenomenon that already had a long history.[12]

It was Benjamin Disraeli and William Gladstone who in the 1870's made elections a referendum, a testing ground for the popularity of the government and its leader, or on the contrary in favour of the opposition leader, that of the opposition who already *in petto* would be voted the new head of government. Subsequently in British history, this unstated presumption was to become a canon rule.[13] Yet in a limited but general way this fact became a norm all over Europe: *government* became the ultimate objective of the electoral struggle, the focus of democratic rivalry. In so doing, a dynamic system of representative appointments, concentrated on government, was established. The question of having a *democratic government*, in other words having electoral support and knowing it was subject to this, became more important than having democratically elected parliaments. Furthermore, increasingly more emphasis was given to the nature of the direct appointment of an *opposition*, which does seem to be one of the main characteristic of contemporary democracy.

Out of this system of dependency of government on electoral competition, issuing from England at the end of the 19th Century,

---

[12]On De Gaulle, see J. Lacouture, *De Gaulle*, 2, *La politique*, Le Seuil, Paris, 1985; L. Jaume, "De Gaulle dans l'histoire francaise et la souverainete," *in l'Etat republicain selon de Gaulle, Commentaire*, n. 51, automne 1990.

[13]The first person to have put this point in doubt is paradoxically Margaret Thatcher who by resigning in November, 1990, following an internal split in the party rather than a general election, gave the party the role of appointing the Prime Minister which had previously appeared to have been lost to the electorate.

the role of political parties was to become crucial, as underlined by Max Weber.[14] It was feared it would not always be feasible to guide huge sections of the population in such complicated matters without providing a political framework for society. Straightaway this raised new problems which were studied by numerous political theorists such as Leibholr[15] in the German Weimar Republic: for if a party system guides the choice of the electorate, even organizing putative choices, how could the notion of *sovereignty* be maintained in the new democratic system? Would this be governed by the representative nature of the political parties who would be a sort of people's delegate, rather than a charismatic individual leader? How in fact could the identity of the nation and its representation be preserved?

In many ways it is useful to use an analysis of fascism to deal with what was to become one of the fundamental expressions of every democracy: the contemporary party as a *mould*.[16] But fascism though it portrayed itself as the scourge of *multi-party democracy* which it saw as an electoral farce lacking any deeper validity, nonetheless built its own political system on the basis of a party. On the contrary it proclaimed its own party as an institutional phase that would lead to the creation of a society of free and equal human beings. It was a perverted form of democracy in the sense that it had to operate within the limits of a single party, but without the relationship that links the electorate to the opposition of different parties.

In the fascist system it was in fact the party that instilled political education and made men *citizens*, worthy to take part in public life, therefore those outside the party were refused political rights. It was also the party that was in charge at least in theory,

---

[14]D. Beetham, *Max Weber and the Theory of Modern Politics*, Blackwell, Oxford, 1985.

[15]G. Leibholz, *La rappresntazione nella democrazia*, trad. Italian, Giuffre, Milan, 1989 (German editions 1929 and 1960).

[16]Paolo Pombeni, *Introduzione alla storia dei partiti politici*, Il Mulino, Bologne, 1990, 2nd. ed.

of choosing leaders, so confirming at the same time the aristocratic nature of the elite, together with their openly aristocratic status. So the Italian fascist theoretician, Sergio Pannunzio, in 1928 could straightforwardly state that: "Yesterday's right was the voting slip (the voting slip that every Italian elector received before the poll), the present right is the party card... The card is the symbol of an organic political system, of which each constituent part although unable on its own, judges and weighs everything in relation to its membership."[17] These words were part of a totalitarian program, yet could very well have been used, out of context and without mentioning its provenance, of the reality of post war democracy. Fascism of course introduced something new into the party system, the idea of a one party state, with the party being at pains to avoid being seen as a catch-all which could undermine the concept of sole sovereignty which seemed an indispensable characteristic guaranteing the survival of an organic state. Consequently, from a fascist perspective, democracy in terms of competing parties struggling for control of the system, would have appeared as a denial of the sovereign will, which was a fundamental requirement of the modern state.

Fully to grasp the problem that this posed we must look at the theory of parties in Liberal European constitutionalism where the party was seen essentially as the embodiment of public opinion, sometimes of necessity with a single objective (for a "philosophical" party two truths can not coexist),[18] sometimes of necessity pluralistic (arguments by factions leading public opinion to enunciate politically a middle road). At all times however the parties have a purely functional *service* dimension which allows ambient public opinion to express itself. The existence in the constitutional sphere of legitimate groups operating on the basis of patronage and obedience while using mechanisms outside public

---

[17]S. Pannunzio, "Scheda e tessera," *Il Popolo d'Italia*, 14 January 1928.

[18]Th. Schieder, "Die theorie der parteit im alteren Deutschen Liberalismus," taken from *in Staat und Gesellschaft im Wandel unserer Zeit*, Oldenbourg, Munich, 1970, 110-132.

scrutiny (social, cultural and ethnic links etc.) would be unthinkable in such a system. Yet following the arrival of voting organisations which relied on prior decision making of a semi-constitutional nature (the first organized party being the *Birmingham Caucus*[19]) on the political scene in Britain, consultation became the norm in politics, concerned with the explicit manipulation of the political body such as the electorate based on the presumption of autonomy of its membership.

How could there possibly be democracy when the context could not possibly offer open competition to free and equal citizens, but was rather an amalgam of confused electors, often uneducated, suddenly having access to the electoral market?. What factors could transform them into prime movers in a democratic system? What training could enable them, despite everything, to contribute to the smooth running of the system and not to its demise? James Bryce, the famous American political theorist of the end of the 19th Century, was forced to admit that these qualities were present in the *party-machine* since, in America, "the spirit and strength of the party are as essential to the action of the government machine as steam is to the locomotive." This was to admit to the defeat of democracy as dreamed by the philosophers of the Enlightenment and put into practice, with some problems, by the French revolutionaries.

Yet this realization, that was beginning to gain currency among the scientific community, remained relatively isolated; the European systems, with the exception of the British system, continued after the First World War to be very closed, if not downright hostile, to these "Euro-American" parties, where the cohesion of the *political machine* was not so much guaranteed by the expedients of *constitutional tinkering* directed at reaching the summit of power, as by the transformation of political ties in pre-existent cultural or institutional structures (class and religion being the most widespread).

---

[19]Paolo Pombeni, "Ritorno a Birmingham. La "nuova organizzazione politica" di J. Chamberlain e l'origine della forma partito contemporanea (1874-1880)," in *Ricerche di storia politica*, III, 1988, pp. 37-72.

In fact Bryce at the age of 82 wrote in despair: "Must there always be political parties? Nobody has yet succeeded in showing how a parliamentary government might operate without them," adding that even though "sociologists continued to denounce parties" nobody knew what to do about the initial question.[20] Yet it is also clear that experiments on the electoral system, where the decisive role of parties would be decided by proportional voting, were in a way felt to hamper the constitutional system. In Italy a proportional system was introduced in 1919 but was manipulated by the Liberals to such an extent that it lost its vitality: as a result not only did it fail to retain the old balance of power but also to create a new one.[21]

COUNTERWEIGHTS TO PARTY POWER

The reaction of democracy to party manipulation is emphasised by the shift over the question of freedom and equality from the political to the social field. The problem was therefore, on the one hand, to recognize a social equivalent to the political deed required for universal suffrage, and on the other to attempt to organize the integration of ordinary society in politics, totally separate and independent of traditional layers.

On the former, it is important to note that the development of a *Welfare State* in Europe between 1900 and 1950, occurred distinct from traditional ideas of charity: the question was no longer one of support for the poor but a *redistribution of wealth*, in other words *a democratic strategy* in the true sense of the word, seen more and more as the reverse side of the coin for citizens who were no longer free and from whom the state required extremely onerous commitment and service which might only be considered in time of war. Democracy thus is felt not so much in terms of access to competition in the political field but as the rise

---

[20]J. Bryce, *Les Democraties*, French trad., Payot, Paris, 1924.

[21]M.S. Piretti, *La giustizia dei numeri. Il proporzionalismo in Italia 1870-1923*, Il Mulino, Bologna, 1990.

to a certain level of equality of opportunity, at least in terms of experiencing a general basic level of well-being.

In this shift of the scope of democracy, the political system was forced to find new corporate spokespeople. It is interesting to observe that during as well as after, the building of the welfare state, in the inter-war years there was a shift in interest towards trade unionism, no longer perceived as a functional moment in industrial relations but as a new representative system and form of organisation of society.

European culture which began to take into account the *body politic*, identified the union, and not just the party as an essential element in the theory of social institutions. In the same way the corporative slant of fascism took this proposition up, even though, at least with the Italian fascists who fundamentally tried, albeit in a confused way to give expression to these ideas in the institutions, corporate aspirations remained subject to the political actions of the party.

Today, when there is clearly a crisis of trade unionism,[22] it is hard for us to understand the threat that this posed, in its various forms and at different times, to party democracy. However, through the various stages of the British labour movement, certain features of Weimar, the Italian and French constitutions of the 60s, it really seemed that a new structure of "democratic" political representation could from then on be embodied by labor organisations.

Yet in the end it is the party system that has come out on top: either in an *absolute* way as in Italy or like in France strictly controlled and evolving from structures of *new sovereignty* that are legitimized by the mechanism of nominational plebiscite. The Party form has come out on top as the most democratic form because it brings together the guarantee of a measured education of the electorate (where all are free and equal, but society is made homogeneous by focusing on the political expression of differing views) and control of the machinery for selection of the political elite. Once these two dynamic requirements are in place then it is possible to introduce further questions, such as the redistribution

---

[22]P. Rosanvallon, *La Question syndicale*, Calmann-Levy, Paris, 1988.

of wealth, complementary forms of representation (for example the unions) and the existence of new forms of sovereignty.

In this field, Europe has experimented in various directions and experienced different historical paths, yet the general constitutional order which emerged from the traumatic experience of fascism has culminated in democracy and the parties being inextricably linked. Not just because in countries such as Italy and Germany (or at least to some extent in France) the parties as organizations had meant *democracy in exile* surviving during the period of totalitarianism, but also because the relationship between a complex modern state and choice of government by all the electorate was felt to be impossible to achieve, without institutionalized cultural political integration which the party system provides.

In some cases the power of this partisan mediation has been reduced or limited by the obligation to use referenda, or because of the existence of simple dual party systems such as in Great Britain, or direct election of a President by universal suffrage (as in France). But at the same time, in certain cases, as in Italy, the farming out of political life among the parties has become so very formalized that the continued existence of the State institutions themselves has been put into question.

So the sad comment of venerable Bryce once again is true: democracy in motion, stalled by inter-party manoeuvring, seems to have failed, yet other than such manoeuvring, nobody, apart from in their dreams, seems to know how political life might be made more democratic.

NATIONALISM VERSUS DEMOCRACY

Jean-Yves Guiomar

Sticking to a strict interpretation of the term, democracy, prior to the 20th century, existed only in a few countries of Europe and only for brief periods; as for nationalism proper — chauvinism and the wish to dominate —, it only truly showed itself after 1880. So these notions need to be understood to refer to extensive trends, principles which would become progressively embodied everywhere in political and social reality.

All that involves the people, in terms of political and social relationships will be referred to as *democracy*; the social body in its objective, synchronic reality: a group of people joined by the fact that they are bound by the same sovereignty, spread over a fixed territory, differentiated by sex, age, way of life, wealth, profession and social status. From the political angle this social entity is organized around those who govern and those who are governed, either belonging to specific hereditary groups (traditional monarchies) or else from their own group (representative systems). Apart from this criteria all peoples are seen to be the same, whatever their system and can be compared to each other. Democracy is the movement whereby objective realities of the social entity and interests of the individuals are increasingly taken into account by the political institutions, the governed increasingly controlling and influencing those who govern, competing for a say

41

in decision making which affect them, above all raising taxes and
control of public spending. *Democracy* implies the supremacy of
home affairs over foreign policy.

As for *nationalism*, it relies on the preeminence of peoples as
ethnic and/or linguistic groups, organized around a common
history, a distinct branch, a sense of community which prevails
over distinctions mentioned above. The diachronic, historical
dimension consequently is of the utmost importance. The *contract*
is made not with the living but with previous generations, however
far back one might need to go. According to this criteria, peoples
in an absolute way are, qualitatively different from each other and
can not truly be compared. Its first principle being the insurmount-
able difference between peoples, *nationalism* implies the
predominance of foreign policy.

There is the familiar contrast between two types of idea of
nation, one French and the other German, which support our
definitions of *democracy* and *nationalism*. Charles-Henri Pouthas
clearly outlined this opposition when he writes that the French
concept of nation arises from "the rationalist principle of natural
law, therefore like reason it is both an individualist and universalist
concept. Because of this it is linked to liberalism where is would
become a source of additional reference in international law. So it
relates to the principle of sovereignty of the people."[23] In
opposition to this controlled and politically interconnected
structure, Pouthas sets out the German view, based on Herder and
the organic view of peoples, formed not by the free aggregate of
individuals but by a sort of unconscious and indelible branding, the
product of generations.

It is not certain that this famous opposition could stand up to
analysis, yet this in itself would need a separate essay. Let us here
simply remember that it only really became important after 1870
and that it owes much — if not all — to the ferocity of Franco-
German antagonism between 1871 and the Second World War. Yet
to understand *both* democracy and nation it will be necessary to go
further back in time.

---

[23] *Les Revolutions de 1848 en Europe*, CDU, 1952.

THE THREE STAGES TO BECOMING A NATION

If the democratic movement can uncover distant ancestors in for example the medieval communal movements, and if nations existed well before the middle ages, it seems preferable together with numerous authors, to take the 18th Century as the real starting point of these two movements, when throughout Europe, with differing degrees of intensity, political and social systems, as well as international relations instituted at the time by absolute monarchs, were systematically put into question and the *ancien regime* following the French Revolution began to crumble. It was then, and only then, that politically the factor of nation and in particular language became important.

Three stages can be distinguished: the first runs from the end of the 18th Century to the "people's spring" of 1848, the second went from the failure of 1848 to the end of the century and finally the 20th Century.

The first stage was the blossoming of the nation, everywhere associated with political liberalism (the struggle to set up constitutional regimes, the extension of suffrage), with individual freedom (freedom of movement, expression, of the press) and social progress (progressive elimination of obligations and duties rooted in feudal times). This association undeniably resulted in progress: the gradual establishment of a representative system in France from 1814 to 1848, the development of English parliamentarism in 1832, the creation of Greece in 1832 and above all of Belgium in 1831, with a liberal constitution establishing real control of the representatives on public finances and especially over the war budget; a constitution which would become a model for many nations. This stage was little troubled politically by cultural problems, yet a French diplomat Paul de Bourgoing, was to note with apprehension in his book entitled *Les Guerres d'idiome et de nationalité* published in 1849, that since the 1840's a strange fact underlines and dominates all events: peoples of different languages are going to war and have a tendency to form different nationalities. This basic characteristic of the principle of nationalities would become an important element in the second stage.

This second stage was dominated by the creation of a united Germany and a united Italy, which joined, above all Germany, Great Britain and France, the great powers, in leading Europe, but also saw the creation of Romania (1861-1878), Bulgaria (1878) and Serbia (1878). This second stage in some ways continued the trend of the first: the national factor was still seen as having positive values, of hope for individual freedom and social progress, yet the power of the state and military factors were to become preeminent over that of the people. Already by the end of this period, sudden outbreaks of violence were to occur in France, Germany, Italy and even Great Britain. The Balkan wars of 1912-1913 with 300,000 dead were not a novelty. The small nation states, products of the principle of nationality, as proxies of the great imperial powers would mirror on the ground their interests, be it at the congress of Berlin in 1878 or the treaties which marked the end of the First World War, as the only interests worth being taken into consideration.

The outcome was that even though universal suffrage became common everywhere, and the majority of people saw marked improvements, the third stage, the 20th Century, was in fact dominated by tensions, dreams of dominance over others by the great powers such as Germany and Italy as well as small eastern European and Balkan countries. Even though it rode on the tide of nationalism, the movement went much further than nationalism proper, as can be seen in the ideas of Arian German superiority, Mussolini's references to the Roman Empire and the Bolshevik continuation of the basic concerns of the Russian Empire, now subordinated and identified with those of the world proletariat.

Hence following the Second World War, and despite the strength of patriotic feeling which was generated by resistance to the nazis and their stooges, public opinion everywhere tended to favour supranational avenues, even if recently there seems to be a resurgence of nationalism in the east following the collapse of the Soviet Empire.

These three stages are linked to the economic development of Europe. In fact from east to west capitalism developed very differently both in quantitative as well as qualitative terms. In the west — in Great Britain, France, in the Rhine countries and even in northern Italy —, from the end of the 18th Century and the second half of the 19th Century a financial and industrial capitalism became established, developed by the middle classes who took over control of society. The further one went eastward the less power the bourgeoisie held, and the development was accomplished by what is called the *Prussian way*, set in place, as in Meiji Japan, by the former aristocrats and the state. At the far end of the continent, Russia was an exception, changing brutally from the rule of the aristocracy to a new social class that was both peasant and technocratic. The Soviet Union embodied the desire to jump a *stage* of capitalism whatever it involved, and belief that as a consequence, since exploitation and dominance no longer existed, the problem of nationalities would automatically be resolved by the setting up of equal and brotherly relations between the peoples of the former Tsarist Empire.

Out of these differences in development it follows that the problem of nationalism during the middle of the 19th, and in the 20th Century, would arise basically in politically fragmented and unstable areas, that were stagnating as with the Habsbourg Empire, or in decline like the Ottoman Empire or through subversion, for instance the Russian Empire. If the movement in the west towards *democracy* has succeeded in developing in a relatively clear and sustained way, so studies based on constants and homogenous factors from one country to another can be made, a *nationalist* trend has been enunciated in very confused and muddled terms, with words such as people, motherland, nation, state, nationality, language, dialect, popular culture etc. having different if not opposite meanings depending on where and who used them. It would seem that where homogenous countries lacked a strong enough class or social group to lead then, so virulence of the discourse which exalts the nation, its history, the power of its language, the ancestral virtues of its rural population etc. increases as well.

THE RIGHT OF PEOPLE TO SELF-DETERMINATION
AND THE PRINCIPLE OF NATIONALITIES

One can not emphasise enough what a major turning point was the failure of the 1848 revolutions all over Europe. The promise of the "people's spring" was fully consistent with two fundamental principles: the right of peoples to self-determination and the principle of nationalities. If in the ensuing history of Europe *nationalism* came to imply everything which was hostile to *democracy,* it was as a result of this turning point. But of course the failure of 1848 forces one to question the underlying relationship between the two principles, for it would be wrong to ascribe this defeat solely to aristocratic reaction. No doubt one must try and understand whether there was not, in the principles themselves and in their relationship, something which made them powerless to succeed, each in order and both together. Let us begin by redefining them.

The right of peoples to self-determination refers to the right of a people not to be dominated by others, whether *internally or externally*, where its vital interests are concerned and the right to provide itself with institutions that it feels are useful to these interests. It is therefore quite understandable that such a principle, already in force since the 16th Century and the struggle against the Spanish in the Low Countries, a veritable testing ground for European liberal democracy, really came to the fore in the 18th Century: it was a time when, under the impetus of forces linked with the rapid growth of towns, trade, and industry, society began a struggle against the absolute domination of a caste isolated from the majority of the social fabric and linked to the survival of a traditional rural existence. The main point was that this principle in no way depended on the native or foreign character of these castes; fundamentally it refers to the internal organisation of the social fabric and especially the ruled/ruler relationship which had to be completely changed, drawing on the example of the French in 1789 against the Bourbon king and the aristocracy.

Quite different from the principle of nationalities which made out that each people as a whole is distinct in origin and qualitatively different, pushing to the fore what Claudie Bernard, in a suggestive essay on *Le Chouan imaginaire*,[24] called the relationship between "Sameness" and "Difference." According to this principle the dominion from which they have to free themselves is obtrusive, resulting from conquest, presented in terms of a foreign power which, for its own reasons, stifles every form of expression of the *national spirit*, which has to be recovered in its unaltered purity, the same as prior to the conquest, through the process of liberation. The conflictual nature of the relationship — ruled and ruler, is therefore solely or mainly based on the fact that one and the other belong to different ethnic groups, hence the idea that the conflict will disappear once the rulers and ruled belong to the same nation (nation being at the time an equivalent for nationality). The outcome of this principle is: one nation, one state.

Yet in the reality of the historical process the distinctions between the two principles are somewhat blurred and unsynchronized, and are not as clearcut as, due to hindsight, they have been portrayed. It is easy to portray *democracy* and *nationalism* as conflicting notions when seen in the period of the third historic stage mentioned above and whose buds were present in the second stage (whose seeds could be identified in the first). Yet in the period from the end of the 18th Century, up until 1848, what was common to both principles and what was to become antagonistic were closely interwoven. Subsequently, and even now, almost everywhere, this confusion has become so widespread that the two principles are often mistaken for each other, so analyses which are so necessary to understand anything, are often felt to be somewhat clumsy.

To try to shed some light on this matter let us look again at the 18th Century. It is possible to say that this century was the mother of *democracy*. Political sciences, public law (Locke, Montesquieu and Rousseau), criminal and civil law (Beccaria; the French lawyers such as Pothier and Aguesseau who heralded the Civil Code,); sociology, political economic and administrative sciences (Montesquieu, Adam Smith, the German universities above all Halle and Gottingen); social interaction (Voltaire, the

---

[24]French University Press, Paris, 1989.

encyclopedists, Kant); History as a place where human destiny can be found (the British historians Hume and Gibbon, and for the French Voltaire); socialism (Malby, Rousseau, Babeuf, Buonarroti) etc. The way was clearly marked and would lead to Tocqueville, Marx and Max Weber.... In terms of concrete achievements there were English developments such as ministerial responsibility, accepted by the end of the century, and French advances in national sovereignty, representation and equality in law.

However in terms of *nationalism* the legacy of the 18th Century is on a par. This is much less commonly known despite the numerous studies made since Ernst Cassirer's (1932) *La Philosophie des Lumieres*, made the serious mistake of seeing romanticism (a fitting term for confusion) as the starting point of this line of thought, although it did no more than exploit and give it force, giving more importance to its celebration than to its understanding. All the countries of Europe (not only Herder's Germany which in fact took the lead from England and France) were to discover fabulous hidden urns containing information about their history, records and accurate sources for the language, anthropology, ethnology, aesthetics, literature and folk songs of the past. The discoveries at Pompei and Herculanum, the taste for the Middle Ages, the spread of neo-Gothic, the wave of fossil finds, the Celts (in Britain and in France), the Germanic tribes (the Saxons for the British and the Francs for the French while the Germans were carried away by Arminius), the Iberians, the Slavs, the foresight of the Indo-European linguistic group; these are some of the important results reached during the century of the Enlightenment which was far removed from an epoch of cold and abstract reasoning. The energy of the physiologists, the theory of the *chain of beings* from the disciples of Leibniz, are the origin of the organic concept of the nation, which in the 18th Century was not particularly a German idea.

Hence the reason why, when the masses began their emancipation, the facts involved owe as much to the principle of self-determination of peoples, in keeping with *democracy*, as to that of nationalities, which is of *nationalism*. In fact it would seem these two principles operate jointly without being specifically analyzed or singled out by the protagonists, until the middle of the 19th Century.

MOTHERLAND, NATION, AND STATE

The French Revolution is at the origin of these notions. From 1789 to 1791, with the transformation of the estates general to a National Assembly. The problem of the principality of Alsace, the status of Avignon and the earldom of Venaissin and the principle of the right of self-determination were vigorously taken on board. Drawing from the works of Montesquieu and above all Rousseau, as well as the physiocrats — dressed up by the ever so clever Sieyes — they dealt both *at the same time* with the self-constitution of a people, in no way based on historical foundations and ignoring ethnic connotations, and uphold the consequent basic right of this people to provide itself with the necessary institutions, its authority stemming from national sovereignty, declared by its representatives.

Like a trail of gunpowder the movement spread everywhere, to Holland, Germany, Italy... Patriotism, which bonds citizens together against the foreign oppressor — not in an ethnic sense but simply politically — kindled their energies. But in these countries, unlike France, the middle class were weak, the rural masses, dominated by traditional catholicism and piety, remained quiet, except in rare cases. Very quickly patriots were in a minority, caught in the dilemma of either joining the victorious armies of the French Revolution or finding an autonomous path to liberation with all the dangers that this might imply. This was the case of the Belgium patriots, the Dutch, the Swiss, the Rhenians, the northern Italians... At a time when the Greater Nation had reached its peak in Europe, the course of action for the patriot was very limited. It was also limited for the French patriot who remained true to the principles of 1789 and who had successfully defended them in 1793.

It was elsewhere[25] suggested that we distinguish between three propositions: *motherland, state and nation,* since the traditional coupling of state and nation does not stand up to analysis; it does not permit highlighting the specific nature of patriotic feeling and leads to complications which might be dangerous in distinguishing *good* national sentiments of a defensive nature and *bad* nationalism of a chauvinistic and aggressive nature. So for example, in France after Boulanger the situation seemed relatively clear — even though the birth of this left wing movement was slightly worrying — in the first half of the century the situation was far more complex with staunchly nationalistic republicans. These three propositions should be defined in a similar way to how they were felt by the participants of European history at the end of the 18th Century.

Nation is an all embracing word, a cultural operator, a product of an assumed past, of a variety of values which run from language to literature and to the "genius of a people." A symbol and source of symbolism, it is felt to be the keeper of sovereignty and confers legitimacy on the state.

The *State* is the ultimate instance of command and implementation, the executive organ of the law which aims to rationalise the future of society, to arbitrate between the various or contradictory interests of its members. It is also the state which controls the armed forces which might defend it against another state.

Motherland is the social body made aware of itself, working freely in the present to reshape the constituent parts of society with a view to achieving justice and brotherhood, taking in the national conscience which leads to openness and rejects what reinforces social or institutional opposition to progress. It is the instance through which the new members of a social body, be it by birth or immigration, acquire a place within it which is not completely defined *a priori.*

The development of European states (and others) since the middle of the 18th Century would depend on how these three principles interacted with each other. In terms of *motherland* exceeding openness; in terms of state maximum closure. The

---

[25]*La Nation entre l'histoire et la raison*, La Decouverte, Paris, 1990.

association motherland-nation favours what earlier was called *democracy* and has the hallmarks of a universal doctrine; linking nation with state tended towards what was called *nationalism* and has a tendency to exclusivity.

Yet it has been suggested that the French Revolution in its initial stage (1789-1793) succeeded in joining motherland and nation, opening a line of thought that later in France as well as all over Europe, would be an inspiration to those fighting for freedom and equality. But because of French military expansion, the creation of the Empire and then the defeat of France in 1814 and 1815, Europe following the Napoleonic Wars was made up of states characterised by a strong association of state and nation, which confirms the fact that despite the initial aspirations of its promoters, the principle of nationality would from then on be used by the state to its own advantage. Those Ancien Regime states based on property, above all Germany and Italy, would develop in this way over the following century. This was much less so for the Habsbourg Empire which could not manage this transformation and consequently guaranteed its own demise. As for the United Kingdom, atypical in every way, it cannot be characterized in this way.

At the Congress of Vienna in 1814-1815, neither the right of self-determination nor the principle of nationalities (already strong albeit unvoiced), nor even the organic concept of a national state, were taken into account. Worse still, at the Congress of Verona in 1822 the upholders of the Holy-Alliance stated that no people had the right to modify its institutions, even with the agreement of its sovereign. This was the moment when Great Britain finally broke ranks with the Holy-Alliance, laying down the principle of non-intervention which France supported. This principle, which is an avatar of the right of self-determination, would be upheld in 1832 in the defence of the newly created Belgium state against the king of Holland.

It was in reaction to this situation that all over Europe supporters of *democracy* and *nationalism* united in patriotic movements. These movements developed after the Empire as secret societies such as Charbonnerie, which was created in Naples in 1806 as an off-shoot of the association of Bons-Cousins, formed at the end of the 18th Century in Franche-Comte and enjoyed the support of Murat, later returning to France with the Restoration. A huge network of fraternities, still relatively unknown, can be guessed at: the Enlightened of Bavaria of the 1780's which returned as masonic lodges (the Friends of Truth). Buonarroti, energetic heir to Babouvism, tried to form a federation of societies in Switzerland, Brussels and Paris. From 1813-1815 among young Germans and in Prussian patriotic movements, civil servants and soldiers in the kingdoms of Italy and Naples, within the Spanish military, among Belgium liberals and catholics, everywhere demands were made for political freedom, civil equality and to varying degrees social justice, and the aspiration for unity and national independence which were to become inextricably linked.

Yet the movements were complex and multi-faceted and many aspects are still scarcely known. On the right were liberals and spiritualist republicans for whom race, history and the national language fed hopes of freedom. This gave prominence in France among others to Guizot, heir to Malby, also Savigny the head of the German school of customary law, Augustin Thierry whose point of departure was the *seminal theme* of conquest, Michelet who dipped into customary law *via* Jakob Grimm and Quinet who translated Herder and, like Michelet, was influenced by Cousin. On the left the influence of the *nationalist* line was weaker, in fact almost non-existent, the dominant concept was not that of national sovereignty but of popular sovereignty, which is far more difficult to embody in institutional terms because it detracts from the important concept of representation, impugns political legitimacy and stresses direct worker democracy.

Aroused by poets and artists — the plays and poetry of Schiller, the works of Heine, Leopardi, Petofi, Goya and Delacroix...—, against the Russian ogre guilty of atrocities in Poland, against the despotic Ottomans and the war of liberation in Greece, against selfish Albion and the suffering in Ireland, the liberal tidal-wave continued to rise throughout the first half of a century in which in France the Bourbons were victorious in 1830 and the Orleans monarchy in 1848. In the same year the focus was on the Habsbourgs. Germany, Italy and Hungary could not develop as long as the dynasty continued to reject political change and maintained its vice-like control of the national question.

Even so the movement failed everywhere. The weakness and lack of unity of Liberalism — 1848 was an urban uprising, carried out by the liberal middle and upper classes —, the opposition between the various nationalist movements — especially within the Hungarian state between the Magyars, Slovaks and Romanians —, compounded their defeat in the face of conservative forces. This failure, in a seminal way, split the *democratic* and *nationalist* tendencies. The idea of a prosperous nation inspired the creation of states based on the alliance of the military aristocracy and the conservative middle class with limited suffrage.

It would appear that the right of self-determination — a complicated and, even from the start, perhaps contradictory notion — strengthened the principle of nationalities, which of itself contributed to the creation of states that relied on the worship of nationalism, in the narrow sense of the word, and conducting international relations by means of conflict. At each stage of this evolution the *democratic* tendency lost some of its force to the advantage of the *nationalist* argument. Over this period an exchange of values occurred that changed their meanings. Hence for example Fallersleben, who in 1841 composed *Deutschland uber Alles* was a Liberal and a German patriot; in the 1860's he began to work for the Prussian state. The "right of nations to self-determination"[26] which was proclaimed in October 1918 by the Slovak National Council illustrates how far this transfer from one to the other was possible.

Even so the wish for democracy which is at the heart of the right of peoples to self-determination, was not totally extinguished. Although it was constantly being sapped and oft suppressed over the last two centuries, the 17th Century call, central to its criticism of the old order, for peace between the citizens of every country and peoples through justice, was kept alive.

---

[26]The complete text of this proclamation is quoted (together with several other similar texts) by S.J. Kirschbaum, in *Slovaques et Tcheques, L'Age d'homme*, Lausanne, 1987, p. 152.

Today it would seem that this demand has been vigorously taken up in Eastern Europe, pitting the *democratic* and *nationalist* tendencies against each other; allowing for alliances and underlining their contradictions. None of the states that emerged at the end of the First World War have found stability (therefore unlike the Second World War it can not be said to have finished). They all went from authoritarian regime, following the State-Nation line for the benefit of the State, to communist dictatorship which aims at achieving the union of motherland, nation and State. This union which should work for the benefit of the former, quickly evolved to the exclusive benefit of the latter, where all three ideas became mixed up. This is why in the Soviet Union, as in the former Popular Democracies, the divisions of the *nationalist* tendency were deemed to have been resolved.

Whether in homogenous countries such as Poland, Hungary or Bulgaria, or in those countries with several nationalities such as Czechoslovakia, Yugoslavia, Albania or the USSR — Romania is somewhere in between — a complicated and dangerous task consists of redefining these three instances: motherland, nation and State. Shown for example by Slovakia which is on course for separation from Bohemia, Slovenia which declared itself independent and sovereign on the 26 December 1990, the Baltic Republics, Georgia and Armenia, on the way to secession, the whole geopolitical order of Eastern Europe is beginning to change. Even if conflicts can be contained by negotiation, there is in every present-day (January 1991) state and between those states, conditions which throws into sharp relief the main tendencies of the past. It remains to be seen how far in the short and medium term we manage to control what is the province of the long term. The nub is whether social and political forces can emerge, capable of giving the patriotic elements what they need to resist the temptations of magically *resolving* existing problems by setting up new nation States (ever smaller) or strengthening the old ones. While the latter might seem to provide an opportunity for greater contact, in reality it would only be a return to isolation with individual peoples trapped.

Clearly the problem hinges on the introduction of a market economy — its form and speed — that will put this part of Europe under conditions never previously experienced. These countries retain a large agricultural and rural population (and even the urban classes have not completely shed their old habits). They are the foundations of strong nationalist feelings, often associated with religion. Is there room for the development of a strong capitalist, nationalist, middle class? At present, in place of the fallen communist parties there is a tendency for a political and intellectual body formed by the *intelligentsia* to step in. These are a product of the people's spring and are influenced by the spirit of 1848, with strong religious connotations, as in Poland, or moral standing as in Czechoslovakia with Vaclav Havel.

So Eastern Europe once more faces as important a turning-point as in 1848, which was a disaster there. Will these countries be able this time to steer it towards the blossoming of relations between people-nation and state? This is the challenge.

We know a lot and at the same time very little about these questions. A lot because each European country has produced quantities of historical analysis, while the democratic movement and the question of nationalism have been the subject of many studies. Yet, in terms of nationalism, it is surprising to note that in contrast to the number of works which have been published, the results are very meagre indeed. There is on the subject a glaring lacuna in our knowledge. In our opinion the main thrust should concentrate on two avenues of enquiry:

— work at the level of concepts and tools of analysis; historians are loath to embark on this essential task. The work of the anthropologist Ernest Gellner, *Nations et Nationalisme*[27] for example gives a new and stimulating approach of this subject;

— a strongly international approach. This is difficult to implement because of the breadth of knowledge needed (hence the importance of multi-disciplinary and collective approaches), which alone can break away from the national study of history highlighting its own

---

[27]Published in 1983 by Basil Blackwell, Oxford, translated into the French by Payot, Paris, 1989.

origins (hindering truly critical study) and from supranational analyses giving an altogether far too rosy picture. Henceforth it is impossible to study the history of nations by splitting up their internal and external policies: they are two sides of the same history.

THE DEMOCRATIC REVOLUTIONS OF 1989

Rene Girault

"Qui l'eut cru; qui l'eut dit" (Who would have believed it, who would have foreseen it). This famous exclamation can today once more be used to portray the general feeling of Europeans following the huge democratic tide that engulfed eastern Europe in 1989. No doubt in a few years time historians will be able to calmly explain the *objective* facts of these countries' political, economic, social and cultural state that would inevitably lead to the final denouement; yet realistically, in 1988 and early 1989, nobody could have imagined the strength of the democratic movement nor the speed of its success; a success even more startling given that it was achieved without any large-scale revolutionary violence. The image of a ripe fruit falling from a tree comes easily to mind. The scale of change, its similarity across such a huge geographical landscape is cause for wonder: how and why did seven countries, united in a seemingly robust "socialist camp," experience such radical change.

The transformations that occurred did in fact involve seven states: East Germany, Bulgaria, Hungary, Poland, Romania, Czechoslovakia and the Soviet Union where it might even be worth distinguishing the various parts since the events in the three Baltic republics, in Moldavia, in the Caucasus and the Ukraine have their roots in this same democratic onslaught. We will not look at the Albanian nor the Yugoslav case, even though they have experienced the counter-effects of widespread change, since neither of these two states would radically change during 1989. Even so, limiting ourselves to those previously mentioned, more than 125 million Europeans out of a total of 500 million were involved, in other words one in four and that excludes the 200 million Soviet citizens living in European Russia. A peaceful revolution for such a great many Europeans: when has this continent witnessed, even though it has experienced many revolutionary somersaults, upheavals on such a scale?

THE DAWN OF THE NEW YEAR...

At the beginning of 1989 however, the situation in eastern Europe still appeared stable, even though in various places tensions and fractures showed that the system of so called "people's democracies" would soon have to accept there was a need for change. At the heart of this essential change were economic pressures together with social unrest. Each eastern European state had their own specific conditions of development, most importantly in terms of links between the towns and the country and the modernisation of their economies; yet, some characteristics were common to all. The burden of debt in the people's democracies was high, mostly accumulated during the 1970's in order to speed up internal growth, thus forcing governments to implement austerity measures to get the means to repay them; at the same time as their Soviet big brother was having to confront a severe economic crisis that made commercial trade more expensive or more unequal depending on the point of view one adopts. Almost everywhere, political masters and economic experts were confronted with the need for changes in the way nationalised industries operated so as to make them more competitive, which raised the recurring problem of their integration into a market economy. Also how would it be possible to improve the efficiency of the distribution system for industrially manufactured goods or the delivery of agricultural produce when the widespread practice of "graft," backhanders and theft operated to the advantage of many members of the political establishment? In general the calling into question of established economic procedures, in the name of an indispensable modernisation, put at risk the fragile balance of eastern European society that was only possible because of the overall egalitarian mediocrity of wages and the possibility for individuals to survive only through shady deals. Yet the peoples of these societies, long dissatisfied with their own standard of living, were not willing to pay the price of reforms conducted by the very same people who lived in the lap of luxury "in the name of the people's government." The suspicion of ordinary people to those in power, be it at local or at national level, made them want to have more say in the business of politics.

At the dawn of the new year 1989, the political situation in eastern Europe appeared confused. On the one hand in Poland, Hungary and the Soviet Union the traditional powerbrokers were under pressure from opposition within the communist party or outside, intent on extending freedom and keen on demanding more democracy; on the other hand in Bulgaria, Czechoslovakia and the DDR the ruling communists appeared to be still strong enough to resist any democratic movement. Thus in January 1989 discussions began in Warsaw between the government team led by the minister of the Interior General Kiszczak, a close collaborator of General Jaruzelski, and the leader of Solidarnosc Lech Walensa, to prepare a new constitution which would at last allow elections that would reflect public opinion; the round table taking place in February ended with an agreement on free elections, even though the communist party obtained guarantees of "minimum" representation. In Hungary within the communist party, supporters of the reformist tendency gained the upper hand during the plenum in February and laid down the principle of a gradual transition to a multiparty system, free elections by the end of the year and a new constitution by 1990. In the Soviet Union the start of the election campaign for a new Supreme Soviet, which would at last become a true legislative chamber with free debates and pluralistic voting, reflected the widespread desire for real democracy and showed the Soviet citizens as active and politically aware as anywhere. From January to March (the elections took place on the 26 March) the authorities had to tolerate the "excesses" of the press and television, in other words the true implementation of glasnost; elections with results of 98.9% a foregone conclusion were a thing of the past. These three countries were to form a dynamic tendency for democracy within eastern Europe.

Consequently the harshness of repressive actions in both Czechoslovakia and Romania appeared even more intolerable. In the latter half of January demonstrators in Prague were dispersed with truncheons and the opposition leader Vaclav Havel was once more sentenced to nine months in jail. In Bulgaria, the head of the Communist Party and head of state Todor Jivkov, a political old-timer, still felt secure with the strength of his own personal power; he still held the reins of the party to the extent that it was a family concern. In Romania the reign of terror that the infamous Securitate implemented allowed the implementation of another "brilliant" idea of Nicolae Ceauşescu the Carpathian communist tyrant: the destruction of country villages to force their inhabitants to taste the advantages of urban life, even though unwillingly. The despotic nature and sycophantic adoration of the master and his wife, placed Romania on the lowest rung of the scale of freedom. His regime appeared a model of rudderless megalomania and was denounced by most of the other "fraternal" states, foremost of these the Soviet Union. The DDR by comparison attracted very little outside attention, since it was held to be economically developed, efficiently governed politically by authorities who were quite willing to strike against their opponents. A striking impression was of a small country which in the field of sports could match the greatest. The disaffected were either expelled or bought by the West Germans, using well established criteria of aptitudes. In a nutshell the DDR would not admit dissent. It is then not surprising that in March at the commission for human rights in Geneva, the plan for the rationalisation of the territory (the technical description used by the Romanian government for the forcible regrouping of eight thousand villages) was condemned by a UN resolution which Hungary supported, while the DDR and Bulgaria abstained.

THE ROAD TO DEMOCRACY RUNS VIA
THE SOVIET UNION, POLAND, AND HUNGARY

By spring the changes in those countries already on the road to democratization confirmed their "liberal" nature although this was not without some opposition. In the USSR the Soviet electorate showed great political maturity, even though previously they had almost never been able to vote in free elections: through an incredibly complex electoral system, that virtually guaranteed the election of traditional party managers, the Soviet people removed corrupt or lazy apparatchiks from the Congress by using the tactic of voluntarily abstaining over individuals; a limited choice of candidates ended with a real contest; the symbol of the political and moral renewal of the country, Academician Andrei Sakharov, was finally elected to the supreme Soviet despite the various obstacles placed in his way by the nomenklatura, who considered him a nuisance. The interest with which the ordinary citizen followed debates in the supreme Soviet, which were fully televised (on a channel broadcasting the deliberations fully), bears witness to the depths of desire for democracy in a country where politics seemed forever to have been banished from the people's minds.

In June in the elections in Poland Solidarity won a resounding victory. The circumstances of this victory deserve closer attention for here again the ballot bears witness to the political acuity of the electors. The election campaign was dominated by the union party of Lech Walesa: "Stamped out by force about eight years ago, lacking political experience, Mr. Lech Walesa's movement dominated this electoral campaign throughout, imposing on it its own rhythm, themes, arguments and vitality."[28] Even so the agreement reached between Solidarity and the Polish PC (POUP), at round table discussions, guaranteed the latter 65% of the seats in the lower chamber of the Diet, whatever the overall result; unless the party's "unopposed candidates" failed to get a minimum of 50% of the votes in the first round. The results speak for

---

[28]Sylvie Kaufman, *Le Monde*, 3 June 1989.

themselves: even in the first round Solidarity won 160 out of the 161 "free" seats, while only five unopposed candidates, out of a total of 299 seats, managed to reach the 50% mark. The high rate of abstention of 37% was seen as further evidence of the failure of elections that are manipulated. After the second round things were even clearer: POUP on its own could no longer govern without the support of its former satellite partners (the peasant and social democrat parties) who were naturally tempted to redefine their own particular role, and inclined to reach agreement with the seemingly irresistible Solidarity movement.

So the electoral ruse and balancing act that had been thrashed out at the round table discussions blew up in the participants' faces. This illustrates the powerlessness of a fragile regime to overturn the verdict of free elections when people demand profound change. A month after the legislative elections the Polish parliament, by a tiny majority, made General Jaruzelski President of the Republic. Two months after the election General Kiszczak was unable to form a government headed by POUP. The incredible became possible. Tadeusz Mazowiecki, one of the leaders of Solidarity, was elected President of the council with the combined votes of Solidarity and the ex-satellite peasant and social democrat representatives (24 August). POUP was to retain five portfolios out of 28 ministries in the coalition government formed by Mazowiecki in mid-September. Even the minister for foreign affairs was a Solidarity member! The new tone was voiced by the president of the council: "We want to live in a sovereign, democratic and law-abiding country, a state which everybody, whatever their political views, can feel is theirs."

In Hungary, the process was slightly different, but the results were similar. In November 1988 the general secretary of the Hungarian communist party, Karoly Grosz, who in May 1988 had been elected to replace Janos Kadar, could still declare, in a statement to le Monde, that they would have to wait several years before a true multiparty system might be allowed and that neither in the short term nor in the long term was the rehabilitation of Imre Nagy foreseeable. Even reformers in the CP were keen to avoid rocking the boat. Seven months later a huge popular demonstration gave Imre Nagy a state funeral without representatives of the CP being present. Within the party itself diametrically opposite tendencies made it necessary to create a collegiate leadership, the first step to the demise of the Party, which would happen in October. By-elections marked by the rout of the communist candidates confirmed the need to widen the representation. At the start of October the president of the Hungarian Parliament declared: "We want to establish a true democracy; this will occur through a pluralistic party system.... Our goal is democratic socialism or real popular democracy. Judicially this means a democratic parliament. We want to rejoin Europe once more; we recognize certain bourgeois democratic values that are similar to our own." The democratic ideal had gained remarkable ground.

In 1987, Kurt Hager, the head of ideological questions of the DDR, when asked by a west German newspaper about the interdependence of the process of Soviet perestroika and possible reforms in his own country, replied: "If your neighbor changes the wallpaper in his apartment, would you feel obliged to change your own?" At the beginning of autumn 1989 the DDR's determination seemed unchanged, similarly its neighbor Czechoslovakia. At the end of August demonstrators had tried to celebrate the 21st anniversary of the Warsaw Pact's intervention against the Prague Spring but had been violently dispersed by police. Alexander Dubcek was still considered a heretic who had refused to admit his "doctrinal errors." The secretary general of the Czechoslovak CP, Milos Jakes, at the end of September continues to: "vigorously rebuff attempts by forces seeking to meddle in the internal affairs of socialist states and who have not renounced the objective of change in the post-war organization of Europe." A veritable alliance of the forces of rejection brought together the leaders of East Germany, Bulgaria ("in Bulgaria there will not be any other party in power than us; it is history that determines this," Tudor Jivkov asserted), Romania and Czechoslovakia. When Mikhail Gorbachev went to Berlin on the 6 October 1989 to participate in the celebration of the 40th anniversary of the founding of the DDR, the great winds of change did not seem to be on the verge of stirring these staunchly communist countries.

Three months later, none of these country's leaders were to remain in power, the Berlin wall would tumble down and all over the place the powerful winds of democracy would blow, in Poland and Hungary (the "precursor" states) as well as those more conservative and resistant to change. This profound upheaval was to shake the whole of Europe in the same way as 1848, the people's spring, which had overthrown the monarchies of the Holy alliance and the order established by the Vienna treaties. This further "people's spring" marked the brutal end of the popular democracies, and thus of communist power in eastern Europe. Eastern Europe was a thing of the past.

A QUESTION OF GENERATIONS

The events of autumn 1989 are still fresh in our mind. However, it seems pertinent to consider two fundamentally linked areas before attempting a global analysis of the hidden forces that would assure the success of democracy in eastern Europe.

The role of individuals becomes important when considering institutional change. 1989 in many ways marks the forced retirement of a generation. This was the generation who after the second world war had managed, and were permitted to first of all ascend in the Party machines of their own countries and then were held to be the successors of the founding leaders of the communist states (without their rabid Stalinism, but this did not in fact of itself mean that they were anti-Stalinists). It is no coincidence that the leaders who were removed or killed were over seventy; Kadar removed in 1988 was born in 1912, as were Honecker and Jivkov who fell in October 1989; Husak who relinquished his position as president of the Czechoslovak Republic in December and Ceauşescu who was tried and executed in December, were also well past it. They all belonged to the generation of young nationalist cadres, convinced that they were building a new world, Party militants who were devoted body and soul to the cause and absolutely sure that capitalism would never overthrow communism since the latter was the destiny of history. Having risen to the leading positions in their respective countries during the period of "supervised de-Stalinization" (in other words when it was imperative to ditch Stalinism but avoiding real democracy) in the 50s, but trying by various means to develop their country's economy, believing that in this way they might satisfy the masses without actually having to adopt political pluralism or parliamentary democracy. To contravene these principles was unthinkable. The long length of time at the helm of power reinforced their belief that they were justified and that if the people wanted democratic change it was the people who were wrong. It must be difficult for an old man who had given his whole life to "the Cause" to admit that he is mistaken. In several cases it was the next generation who would attempt, sometimes unsuccessfully, the transition, for instance Egon Krenz who was to follow Honecker. These 50 year olds were seen to be more open to suggestions of change, perhaps with the hope of reaching power themselves but also maybe in the belief that they might successfully restructure in the same way as the hero and inspiration of Perestroika, Mikhail Gorbachev, was doing.

The personality of the Soviet president was of course a major factor in the changes which took place during the autumn of the people. However one might look on the transformations that were taking place at the time in the Soviet Union, everyone would agree that "Gorby" played an essential and positive role in perestroika. He personified change; his popularity in Eastern Europe was a measure of his symbolism. He seemed at the time to have the means radically to transform the political structures, and the will to express ideas even if they were contrary to communism. The East German, Czechoslovak and Romanian demonstrators cheered the master of the Kremlin, in itself a complete reversal of past practices of open hostility to all who came from the "Big Brother." His popularity could also be explained by the tolerant attitude of Moscow with regard to everything that was taking place in eastern Europe. The reaction of the Kremlin at the formation of the Mazowieki government was a case in point. Moscow limited itself to suggesting that communist ministers be present in the ministerial coalition, satisfied at the moderation of the Polish Prime Minister who did not foresee leaving the Warsaw Pact. A Polish national government could not afford to forget that they preside over a state that is trapped between its German and Russian neighbors. By May

1989, during his trip to west Germany, Mikhail Gorbachev made it clear that the Berlin wall could come down, since it divided two parts of the same people. How could King Ceauşescu's subjects remain unmoved by Gorbachev's message in May 1987 during his journey to Bucharest: "Our objective is to make people aware of democracy and to create the conditions in which each individual is empowered to express the creative force of their personality." He also added: "Even if you tell me that in your country or your family all is well, I would not believe it since there are always problems." In conclusion, it was clear that Moscow, racked by its own internal problems, above all frightful nationalist disturbances, not only was prepared to allow change to take place among its allies, but furthermore the head of the Empire would repeatedly advocate greater democracy.

A second determining factor in the actions of the protesters was including the idea of human rights. In 1989 this link was easy because of the celebration of the bicentenary of the French revolution. Of course those involved in these upheavals were not uniquely guided by the thoughts of this revolution yet it would again be wrong to underestimate the psychological force of the ideas of 1789, especially among the intellectuals; how many writers, scientists and journalists drew on the major ideas of the *bourgeois* revolution as opposed to the *proletarian revolution* associated with the rise to power of the CP in the countries of Eastern Europe... as a consequence political change would not occur so that the communist system could be improved in keeping with the Czechoslovak slogan of "Socialism with a human face" coined during the Prague Spring of 1968, but in the name of human rights, freedom and democratic pluralism which are the legacy of the French Revolution. The people's of eastern Europe no longer wished to improve the existing order; they wanted to enter a different world, that blossoming in western Europe. The return to European civilization signified a return to democracy.

The word *return* is used on purpose. It was traditionally supposed that in their modern history the peoples of eastern Europe had hardly ever experienced democracy. In reality a strong current of thought, a vibrant tradition of struggle and partial success at the start of this century had marked the minds of the people. Hence the social democrat movement in the former Austro-Hungarian Empire had made the demand for true universal suffrage a major plank of their struggle at the end of the 19th Century. Even though the electoral practices of the inter-war states of the region might be criticized in terms of morality and justice, they seemed preferable to the bogus elections of the 50's and 60's. A tendency to idealize the recent past, pre-World War II, became widespread among ordinary people; strangely enough the powers-that-be themselves had a hand in this phenomenon, in their attempts to find precedents for the "national blossoming" which in theory had come with the people's democracy. For example having purged Czechoslovak history of T.G. Mazaryk the founder of the Republic in 1918, he was once more allowed to exist; yet was he not a symbol of pluralistic and humanistic democracy? Marshal Pilsudski's Poland, although closer to a dictatorship than a democracy, ended up representing a point of reference for pluralism. Romania in the 20's and the 30's was much better than under the terror of Ceaușescu. There are many other example. Although the communist regimes believed they had relegated the *bourgeois past* to oblivion it resurfaced beatified as a sort of democratic myth.

The young people of these countries, disillusioned with the regimes in place, searched and found in their past cause for excitement, in the same way that they saw the imitation of western cultural forms as a way of breaking the yoke of an outdated ideology. Singing and dancing to rock music, wearing jeans, liking the Beatles and doing abstract painting were forms of protest. They contained the seed of revolt within them. In these circumstances the democratic movement often operated obliquely with meetings of young people such as in East Berlin listening to those from West Berlin. Freedom of speech was to become a necessity for a population who felt watchwords transmitted from above to be worthless precisely because they came from above. The Youth protest, initially cultural, was to become more radical and political in the full sense of the word. It was not fortuitous that young people would have such an essential role in the mass movements which shook Prague, East Berlin, Sofia and Bucharest. They were alienated from the old men in authority but also alienated from previous generations who were felt to be too resigned to their fate.

In fact their parents did understand their impatience, but ground down and disheartened by previous stalemates such as the Prague Spring, they were to a large extent approving spectators rather than energetic actors. Consequently the idols for the young became committed intellectuals such as Vaclav Havel, Jelia Jelev or Andrei Sakharov since they voiced an absolute rejection of compromise and a return to humanist values which were qualified as bourgeois but in reality are universal. In the universities the students, so often the spearhead of protest movements even though here they might consider themselves beneficiaries of the system in view of gaining entry to this highly selective system, wished above all to reestablish links with the West as well as with its values. Here again, no hope of transforming the existing order from within: "We can not agree to the idea of perestroika" explained a Prague student. "It is not a question of rebuilding what already exists but of starting again from scratch." "Open out to the rest of the world" added another in a survey, conducted by Le Monde-Campus on 7 March 1990. This search for the ideal is sometimes synonymous with disorder since who and what could be believed? A Hungarian student makes the comment that: "People need to believe in something. Many tried to believe in communism but it did not work. So all of a sudden everyone returned to religion. One can always have your head in the clouds but your feet stay on the ground." In fact almost everywhere young people were returning to the churches, including in the Soviet Union, returning to the old practice of religious weddings to the great surprise of the older generation. In these circumstances the rapprochement with western Europe sometimes proved surprising since in the West ideas were evolving in a different way, above all among the young. However similar hopes of pluralistic democracy exist as well as the desire to protect the environment, which very often has been sacrificed to brutal industrialization. Is the Europe of the young being built today?

It might be easier to build than the Europe of the *mature*. It is questionable whether the generations who lived through 40 years of communism really understand the West, even though they all declare their attachment to democracy. Several weeks and months after the earthquakes of autumn 1989 here and there, those new to power, especially in the cultural field, highlighted the survival of thought processes acquired during the preceding years. "One can not change the thinking of a man from one day to the next. One can not dispel the fear, agony and mistrust. People can not believe that all this has gone... Ceauşescu's communism has formed a human type who is opportunistic and servile, who is beyond political division." This is the judgement of the Romanian minister of Culture Andrei Pleşu (*Le Monde* 7 Feb 1990). Is this just an exception in keeping with the excesses of the king of the Carpathians? Too many similar indications can been detected elsewhere for this pessimistic description to be seen as unique. It takes time to change collective attitudes. The underlying reasons for this also have to disappear, in other words an end to the exhausting every-day existence, marked by the continuous search for food and the black market. Or at least noticeable improvements. Yet at present doubts about the future and disillusionment are setting in. Of course a return to what existed previously is not possible, however, the increase of abstentions in free elections could be cause for worry. Democracy is still weak in eastern Europe.

Finally, was it a general movement which flattened the communist regimes of eastern Europe — the *velvet revolution* (so sparing in terms of human lives apart from Romania), or was it only the shock-waves sent from on high, i.e. from Moscow, orchestrated by Mikhail Gorbachev who wanted to change the corrupt and inefficient managers? The Czechoslovak vice-Interior Minister partly believed this in 1990: "From 1988 Moscow hatched a plan to replace the leadership of the three countries — Czechoslovakia, Bulgaria and Romania — which the Soviet Union wanted to keep in its sphere of influence, with reform-minded communists." The maneuver failed because ordinary people intervened in great numbers: "because the unease in Czechoslovak society was so deep-seated that people would not be satisfied with cosmetic changes but demanded a change of regime" (from an interview with Jan Rumi, *Le Monde* 21 September 1990). Yet everywhere the former apparatchiks continued to adapt to circumstances and survive. We now can see the true extent of the social, economic and technological underdevelopment of these countries and the qualitative and quantitative weakness of their managers. It is often said in jest that democracy is a luxury for rich people. Poverty in eastern Europe is obvious. How long will they be able to sustain the democratic revolution which in 1989 turned it upside down? The older democracies want it and should come to its aid. If such European solidarity is now essential, it is because the stakes for all of us are high. Let us all live in a shared house of course, but one where each is free and equal before the law.

BRITAIN AS REFLECTED
BY THE REVOLUTION

Bernard Cottret

A STORM IN A TEACUP

On the 13 July 1989, two centuries, less a day, after the storming of the Bastille, Le Monde echoed the disenchanted words of Margaret Thatcher: "The rights of man did not begin with the French Revolution." The "Iron" Lady went on reminding us of the "Judeo-Christian tradition that proclaimed the importance of the individual and the sacred nature of human beings." Then on a more insular note, went on to mention that the Magna Charter of 1215 as well as "our quiet revolution in 1688 when parliament asserted its supremacy over the monarchy."

Christopher Hill, one of the best English historians of our time, in the Guardian of 15 July publicly apologized to the French people for what seemed to have been a slip of the tongue. The controversy was not solely one of diplomacy or etiquette but a question of the origins of modern democracy. Christopher Hill made it clear that to call 1688 a "triumph of democracy" was a nonsense. The *Glorious Revolution* "established the sovereignty of Parliament, which perhaps represented 10% of the male population." Furthermore it guaranteed the supremacy of a "Whig oligarchy which would govern Great Britain until the 19th Century

71

when democratic movements, influenced by the French Revolution, were to forever change the rules of the game."

Yet this storm in a teacup can not completely hide the existence of a real dilemma, highlighted by Christopher Hill: "I feel that Mrs. Thatcher is criticizing the bicentenary for the wrong reasons. It would have been better, from her point of view, to recall that ultimately the French had taken their ideas of revolution, of regicide and republic from the example of the English in the 17th Century."

So the impact of the French Revolution and the democratic ideal which it promotes, has its place in a relatively ancient continuity and it is right to be aware of this, through the centuries, whether it involves the English popular movements of the 17th Century or the political radicalism which went with the industrial fever of the Victorian era.

ENGLISH DEMOCRACY FROM THE FRENCH POINT OF VIEW: TOCQUEVILLE AND GUIZOT

How can one judge (or measure) the importance of the democratic factor in English History? What criteria would one apply, that of law, electoral practice or the participation of various social strata in the economic fortunes of the nation? I would like to underline straightaway a double peculiarity. The British "Constitution" is not based (unlike the French or American) on a single and prescriptive document to which everything else must refer. It takes the form of a glossary or commentary of a non-existent document or at least one that is buried amongst many laws, customs, conventions and precedents. It is true that public life tends more and more to regulate by law the practice of sovereignty. Since 1832, there occurred a gradual widening of the electoral franchise that resulted in 1918 in universal franchise for men over 21 and over 30 for women, the latter having to wait until 1928 before having the age of eligibility lowered to that of men. In the same way it was only in 1948 that the possibility of voting twice, for university teachers and a few others in their home town and where they worked, was abolished. Finally in 1969 the young in turn became electors at the age of 18 ...

A second paradox: as Tocqueville pointed out, it is not solely by looking at the people that one discovers the awakening of democratic ideas. A study of the elites, from Voltaire to Montesquieu, is one of the main factors for philosophical Anglomania. Consequently in these pages we will not find a condensed history of four centuries of English social history but on the contrary a commentary that concentrates on several exceptional individuals.

Firstly Tocqueville who's thoughts Raymond Aron summarized thus: "There is no doubt that for Tocqueville the same democratic movement, in other words the elimination of distinction of rank or state, swept through England as well as France and America."[29] Tocqueville went three times across the Channel, in 1833, 1835, and two years before his death in 1857. He returned in the 1830's with an amazing harvest of on-the-spot impressions, notes and observations. Several lessons emerge: the progress of democracy seems irreversible — "Democracy resembles the rising tide;"[30] even though in the long term they were more or less condemned, the English aristocracy, by paying scant attention to the dichotomy of birth and wealth, managed to adapt to the modern world. This major factor for English social mobility, strongly qualified by recent studies,[31] is linked in Tocqueville's mind to an interesting distinction: that the supremacy of the aristocracy also had to be cultural. This then leads to an perceptive analysis of the relative

---

[29]R. Aron, *Auguste Compte et Alexis de Tocqueville juges de l'Angleterre*, Clarendon Press, Oxford, 1965, pp. 20-21.

[30]A. De Tocqueville, *Voyages en Angleterre et en Irlande*, NRF, Paris, 1967, p. 109.

[31]L. Stone, Jeanne C. Fattier Stone, *An Open Elite? England 1540-1880*, Clarendon, Oxford, 1984. While according to W.D. Rubinstein, (*Wealth and Inequality in Britain*, Faber & Faber, London, 1986) there would be a reduction of inequality in England in the 20th century.

fate of the words *gentilhomme* and *gentleman* in France and in England:

"The difference between France and England on this point emerges from an examination of one single word in their language. *Gentilhomme* and gentleman obviously have the same origins; yet gentleman in England is used to mean every man who has been brought up well, whatever his birth, while in France gentilhomme is only used for a noble by birth. The meaning of these two words that have the same origins has become so different because of the social conditions of the two peoples, that they now can not be translated apart from by paraphrasing. This semantic observation has more force than weighty arguments."

Therefore the French nobility were the antonym of the English aristocracy. *L'ancien regime et la révolution* (1856) returns to this point: the English were able to preserve an aristocracy — government by ones betters — which did not degenerate into a nobility — which here is synonymous with *caste*. Consequently the history of the word *gentleman* "is that of democracy itself," for in America the term "is used uniformly of every citizen."[32]

Ireland however is an exception to the rule. On the 26 July 1835 during his second journey to the United Kingdom, the author observes that "aristocratic rule can be one of the best or worst forms of government in the world." Even though the Irish aristocracy has the "same origins, customs and almost the same laws" as their English counterparts, they are among the most "detestable" that could be imagined.[33] This he explains is due to their colonial nature because they are a conquering nobility. Yet Tocqueville continues his analysis. Aristocracy does not find its justification in itself but in the dialectic which links it to the people. In England, in contrast to Ireland, a middle class had grown that aspires to the aristocratic life. "Inequality" ultimately "is good for the general wealth" by stimulating the forces of economic

[32] A. De Tocqueville, *op.cit.*, p. 108.

[33] A. De Tocqueville, *op.cit.*, p. 274.

life.[34] Anticipating a distinction that now Louis Dumont, the anthropologist, applies between "holistic" and "individual,"[35] Tocqueville hence demonstrates that "associative and exclusive feelings" bind reciprocal relations.[36] Hence the *club*, a motif of English sociability, is put forward both as a society of equals but also as a closed society. Consequently one might ask what in fact was Tocqueville's attitude to England: was it really a fitting subject for the analysis of democracy, or could it be that the noble Norman showed a fascination for the longevity of the aristocratic element and its integration in the general social fabric?

Guizot, a protestant, had a different type of sympathy for England, drawing from religion.[37] Forced from power in 1848, Louis-Philippe's minister asked himself: *Why did the English revolution succeed? (1850)*. This nostalgic question implicitly begs another: "Why did the French revolution fail?" As a historian and a statesman Guizot lists the trumps in England's hand: protestantism and the marriage of the democratic spirit with the aristocratic element. England in effect became a constitutional monarchy and the struggle of the various classes for influence and power did not take a violent form.[38] The English experience (the American revolution according to Guizot, being a case which needs to be distinguished) has an exemplary place in European history. "In Germany in the 16th century, the revolution had been religious and not political. In the 17th Century, fortunately for England, religious

[34]*Ibid.*, p. 272.

[35]L. Dumont, *Homo aequalis*, NRF, Paris, 1977, p. 11.

[36]A. De Tocqueville, *op. cit.*, p. 144.

[37]*Actes du colloques Francois-Guizot*, Societe de l'histoire du protestantisme francais, Paris, 1976.

[38]F. Guizot, *Histoire de Charles Ier*, Didier, Paris, 1854, vol. I, p. 11.

faith and political freedom were uppermost and two revolutions took place at the same time."[39]

These twin elements, religion and politics, democracy and aristocracy, should be borne in mind and according to Guizot's assessment are essential for the English predicament. They greatly influenced the "Puritan" revolution of the 1640's and the Glorious Revolution of 1688, that were "for the people in principle and result" but "aristocratic in their execution."[40] Therefore it can be said: "England had the good fortune that strong and binding links had been forged between the various classes of society. The aristocracy and democracy managed to live and develop together, mutually supporting and restraining each other."

Guizot, in the same way as Tocqueville, identified the peculiarities of English history, succeeded in highlighting the autonomy of politics by demonstrating its cultural and religious framework, yet on the other hand their analyses lack an empirical evaluation of the British parliamentary system. In short, to complete this picture, it would be necessary to look from the political system to actual power politics. Two famous observers allow us to enhance our perceptions: John Stuart Mill and Walter Bagehot.

INSULAR CONSIDERATIONS: MILL AND BAGEHOT

J.S. Mill maintained a lively correspondence with Tocqueville, to whom he confided: "I love France, but I would admit that one France in Europe is enough."[41] Also it was from Tocqueville that Mill got the concept of tyranny of the majority.

How in fact would they bridge the gap between the political landscape — conceived as the vital forces of a nation — and

---

[39] *Ibid.*, p. 3.

[40] *Ibid.*, p. 107 for this quote and the next. Also B. Cottret, *La Glorieuse Revolution d'Angleterre, 1688*, Gallimard, Paris, p. 224.

[41] R. Aron, *op. cit.*, p. 5.

politics — in a political sense? This is what leads Mill to discuss the question of representation — *Considerations on Representative Government* (1861). The philosopher shows a liking for a "widening of the franchise" which would even include women. Furthermore the "representative democracy" that he calls for should not be based on wealth: a voting system based on a poll tax would only result in a period feature and not by any means an everlasting order. For J.S. Mill the only true criteria had to be culture, or better still education: they would have to be able to read, write and count. Democracy had to be deserved: apparently it is a question of culture rather than principle. Therefore Mill rejected implicitly the dichotomy, that was so common and widespread in France, of rights and privileges. He accepts on the contrary a reformist scale. Freedom, that once had been the privilege of a few would become the condition of the greatest numbers.[42] In an inductive way the spread of this privilege seems preferable to the abstract universality of law. Thus framed, is there not, at least in an etymological sense, an aristocratic element in his proposed definition of democracy? The people must better themselves, otherwise the utopia of democracy be usurped for bureaucratic or totalitarian purposes.

The whole *community* must one day exercise its *sovereignty* such is the "ideal form of government."[43] J.S. Mill also acknowledged the need to include the working classes. He even admits to the existence of a *communist society* yet underlines that in the short term this concerns the "elite of humanity."[44] A strange paradox!

In fact, the democratic society that he predicted is singularly unattractive: modern civilization leads inescapably to "collective

---

[42]J.S. Mill, *Utilitarianism, On Liberty, and Considerations on Representative Government*, Dent, London, 1972, p. 210. For J.S. Mill, I also consulted R. Lejosne, "John Stuart Mill," *Le Quatrieme Pouvoir en Grande-Bretagne*, Erasme, La garenne-Colombes, 1990, pp. 9-12.

[43]*Ibid.*, p. 211.

[44]*Ibid.*, p. 209.

mediocrity," even to "pedantocracy."[45] Democracy is permanently in danger of sliding into deception. Certainly, the author tried to think of solutions to these shortcomings: he agreed that representation should be full to avoid foundering under the pressure of sectional interests. Yet it is a bleak picture that emerges from his treatise. The exercise of democracy — the wishes of everybody — is based on a functional sham: the majority holds sway over unanimity. "Democracy how it is generally understood and exists in practice, is the government of the people by a mere majority of people who are represented in an exclusive way."[46] As such one is left to think that the question of the minority remains unanswered.

Walter Bagehot was outraged after reading Mill's work, not least because he found fault with his pessimism over democracy. Fundamentally, Bagehot could not tolerate such a degree of abstraction. *The English Constitution* (1867) defies "literary description." Is it correct to study a living and teeming reality through books, and even less in the "refinement of literary theory."

The unwritten nature of the British Constitution no doubt partly explains the two men's differing views. Mill reflected from the philosophical point of view, paying more attention to principles rather than practice, while Bagehot proceeded from the opposite direction. This was very important for example on the question of a royal veto. In theory, according to Mill, the crown could refuse to sign a new law even after it had been voted. Of course, this right was never used for reasons of "constitutional morality."[47] More down-to-earth, Bagehot adopts an ironic tone: "The Queen has no right of veto. She would have to sign her own death sentence if both chambers sent it to her."[48]

---

[45]*Ibid.*, p. 265 and p. 246.

[46]*Ibid.*, p. 256.

[47]W. Bagehot, *The English Constitution*, Collins, Glasgow, 1975, p. 229.

[48]*Ibid.*, p. 98.

Even so, under Bagehot's pen this fundamental realism leads to unforeseen and in the ultimately unexpected conclusions. Far from becoming bogged down by trivia, it led Bagehot to a spark of genius. The overriding importance of the British constitution on political theory plays on two contradictory ideas: *efficiency* and *dignity* ("the efficient and the dignified parts"[49]). In short this deference gives rein to uncertainty and contingency. Bagehot's functionalism paradoxically buttresses the non-functional side of things. He concentrated on the theatrical and perhaps even mystical or occult sides of royalty that have such influence on, and compels respect, from the majority.[50]

At the same time Bagehot did not hide his deep anxieties over the idea of universal suffrage: in rural parts the majority would assure the dominance of the landowners and the squires; in urban areas, on the contrary, the *lower classes* would want to impose their mixture of skepticism and coarseness.[51] So he feared that universal suffrage would result in extremism. It is not just a question of counting votes, more of *weighing*[52] them. The England that he describes remains steeped in *deference*.[53] Also, in the introduction to the second edition of his work that he wrote in 1872, Bagehot does not hold back from pouring scorn on the French cause: "Ever since 1789 France has given herself over to political experiments which provide lessons for everyone else but which never seem to be learned by France [...]. The French as a nation do not like parliamentary government [...]. Now that

---

[49] *Ibid.*, p. 61.

[50] *Ibid.*, p. 60-61.

[51] *Ibid.*, p. 162-163.

[52] *Ibid.*, p. 171.

[53] *Ibid.*, pp. 270-271. Also, D.C. Moore, *The Politics of Deference*, Barnes & Noble, New York, 1976.

suffrage is universal, the general intelligence and average cultural level of the constituent parts is extremely low."[54]

Yet the British constitution remains in many ways obscure. In fact, contrary to what is believed, it is not based on the separation of powers, but on the very opposite — the "quasi fusion of the executive and legislative," by way of the *Cabinet*.[55] Bagehot quickly dispelled two persistent delusions:

1) "That the legislative, executive, and judiciary were separate.";

2) "It is claimed that the mark of excellence of the British Constitution comes from the balance of the three institutions. In other words monarchic, aristocratic, and democratic elements share supreme sovereignty, and the agreement of all three is needed to exercise sovereignty. According to this theory, the King, the Lords and the Commons are not only the outward appearance but the actual essence, at the heart of the constitution."[56]

The first error that the Victorian constitutionalist picked up on is quite easily checked: it goes back to when Montesquieu confused the "separation of powers" and the "mixed monarchy." I myself would say that this blunder of my 18th Century compatriot was in a heuristic sense answerable to a Kantian paradox. Whereas the author of *l'Esprit des lois* (1748-1750) claims to base his argument on observation when he claims to find in the English constitution a separation of powers, he is in fact putting forward a theoretical model that does not exist and which would become a principal reference point in political theory.[57]

---

[54]W. Bagehot, *op.cit.*, pp. 296-298.

[55]*Ibid.*, pp. 65-66.

[56]*Ibid.*, pp. 59-60.

[57]B. Cottret, *Bolingbroke. Exile et écriture au siècle des Lumieres. Angleterre-France (vers 1715-vers 1750)*, still to be published.

The second model that Bagehot impugns — "polybian whiggism," a magnificent term coined by Michel Baridon,[58] it is very difficult to define exactly. One must recall that between the 16th and 18th centuries there took place a redefining of medieval trifunctionality which can be more easily understood by way of a graph:

Medieval Model	Insular Model	Classical Model
Oratores	King	Monarchy
Bellatores	Lords	Aristocracy
Laboratores	Commons	Democracy

Medieval trifunctionality has almost completely disappeared. The king, lord and commons replaced those who prayed, those that fought and those that worked. On the other hand the classical heritage put forward by Polybus, the 2nd century BC Greek historian, allows us to match the English constitution with the three pure forms of politics which were *monarchy, aristocracy and democracy*. So the English institutions are based on a careful balance of these three elements. Yet Bagehot impugns precisely this genetic fiction which, above all in the 18th century, was widely believed[59]. In fact, although loathe to make excessive systemization, Bagehot replaced this tertiary model with a binary design: "the efficient and the dignified parts." This narrative pair is expressed by the author at the end of *The English Constitution*: England has "two governments," which allows for the coexistence of the "royal prerogative" and of the "empirical power of the Prime Minister."[60]

---

[58]M. Baridon, *Edward Gibbon et le mythe de Rome*, Champion, Paris, 1977.

[59]B. Cottret, "Le roi, les lords et les Communes," *Annales*, ESC 41, 1986, pp. 126-150.

[60]Bagehot, *op.cit.*, p. 266.

A TEMPERED DEMOCRACY

While in Guizot's mind the English revolution had a religious meaning — the English Revolution was a "success" — republican tradition enthroned the 1789 Revolution for opposite reasons. Albert Soboul, a *Jacobin* historian outlined its legacy: "The English revolution was however much less radical than the French: to quote a phrase of Jaures used in his *Socialist History*, it was to remain `restrictively bourgeois and conservative' in the eyes of the French revolution which was `openly bourgeois and democratic.'"[61]

It is certainly difficult to use the term democratic in connection with the events in England in the 17th Century. In fact one might be opening oneself to the possible charge of anachronism? A contemporary historian however has taken up the challenge, in portraying the first English revolution, that of the 1640s, as the confrontation of "divine right" and "democracy."[62] Consequently the rights of the people, demanded by the levellers and other radicals above all within the army, could be seen as democratic demands. The term *democracy* nevertheless still belongs to scientific language. I have found several uses of the word in counter-revolutionary writings[63] without being exhaustive. Was this just coincidence? Or else can one conclude that democracy was understood, up until the end of the end of the 17th century, to mean an antique form of government, hence tarnished for modern latter day thinkers. It is clear that the French revolution helped fix democratic demands, often dubious, on known historical

---

[61]A. Soboul, *La Civilization et la Revolution française*, Arthaud, Paris, 1982, vol. II, p. 69.

[62]*ibid.*

[63]R. Anon, *Advis Chrestien et politique a Charles II. Roy de la Grande Bretagne*, Jean Remy, Paris, 1649; *Responce du nouveau roy d'Angleterre*, R. Feuge, Paris, 1649.

exemplums.[64] The term democrat in fact is now becoming increasingly popular: nobody would now think of denying the fact that the United Kingdom is a democracy — in the same way that France, Spain, Italy, Holland and the United States are democracies. Nevertheless from Tocqueville to Bagehot by way of Guizot and J.S. Mill I have underlined the enduring nature of other complementary or antagonistic political categories — the monarchy and the aristocracy. Hence, the democratic element existed for a long time within a whole constellation, which catered for the contiguous existence of other forms of authority, cloaking them in allegorical values: the aristocratic or monarchic spirit.

Even in 1910, Charles Bastide could comment: "The government of England can be seen as a limited democracy because of the survival of monarchic and oligarchic institutions. Sovereignty belongs to the people who up till now have agreed to keep the monarchy at the head and to delegate most of its power to an oligarchy who is only partially subject to electoral control. The elected representatives are generally chosen from the ruling classes."[65]

In 1929 the same author continues: "England for 200 years has been a democracy which has preserved the appearance of a constitutional monarchy [...]. The principle of the sovereignty of the people, on which it is said that democracies are based, is not recognized by traditional English theoreticians. Sovereignty belongs, they say, to the legislative power. In England consequently, sovereignty is jointly held by the crown, the House of Lords and the House of Commons since no law is complete without having been voted by the two houses and sanctioned by the King."[66]

---

[64]L. Jaume, *Le Discours Jacobin et la democracie*, Fayard, Paris, 1989.

[65]C. Bastide, *Les Institutions de l'Angleterre sous Edouard VII*, H. Paulin, Paris, 1910, p. 7.

[66]ID., *L'Angleterre nouvelle*, F. Alcan, Paris, 1929, p. 16 and p. 30.

So, Charles Bastide shows, whatever one might think of what he wrote, a constant uneasiness in relation to Great Britain at the time: he found in the English constitution more than just a wet (*diluted*) form of democracy — excuse the joke. His analysis in fact stems from a system of allegorical identification that shows the democratic element as permanently isolated, which in any case is indistinguishable from the aristocratic element — in his own words oligarchic — or even from the monarchic. Hence for the continental, democracy, in its purest form, does not permit other traditional political forms or legacies from the past.

Coming to the end of this study, let us set out a program, that is perhaps too ambitious, and define a few hypotheses. There still remains the need to write a history of the use of the word *democracy* in latter day English political culture. The historian J.C.D. Clark has this to say of his experience as a teacher in the United States: "The English have always failed to see, what is believed widely all over the world, that their political system is a *democracy* and that it had its foundations on democratic values."[67] He continues by showing that English freedom relies more on the *Rule of Law* than on democracy. Emmanuel Todd appears to share this point of view when he describes the relative "indifference to the principle of equality" in England at "the end of its democratic development."[68] Even so the meaning of the term democracy has to all appearances changed across the Channel in the last 40 or 50 years. It has been extended, above all in the ideology of the labor movement, for instance in the workers' participation in the running of factories ("*industrial democracy*").[69] But above all concentrating on its political meaning, democracy has ceased to be the antonym of monarchy. It discovered, in the light of the struggle against

---

[67] J.C.D. Clark, *Revolution and Rebellion*, Cambridge University Press, 1987, p. 168.

[68] E. Todd, *L'Invention de l'Europe*, Le Seuil, Paris, 1990, p. 369.

[69] W.E.J. McCarthy, *Trade Unions*, Penguin, Harmondsworth, 1985, pp. 73-123.

Naziism, then the exposure of Stalinism, that it has other enemies: totalitarian dictatorships.[70] From then on democracy was to correct its aim: not so much against past tradition but bolstering human rights and the multiparty system. In conclusion, in Great Britain today the desire for freedom has in many ways made the desire for equality less acute.

---

[70]K. Popper, *La Societé Ouverte et ses ennemis*, which first was published in English in 1945, no doubt contributed to this development.

CHRONOLOGY

1642-1660	The *Puritan* Revolution.
1648	The execution of Charles Ist and declaration of the Commonwealth.
1660	Restoration.
1688-1689	The Glorious Revolution. Bill of Rights.
1714	Ascension of the Hanovarians.
1776	Declaration of American Independence.
1790	Burke/Paine controversy over the French Revolution.
1817-1819	Widespread radical agitation.
1825	Voting of a law dealing with associations.
1828	Emancipation of non-conformists.
1829	Emancipation of Catholics.
1832	First electoral reform: widening of parliamentary representation with the *Great Reform Act.*
1833	Founding of the first National Union federation.
1835	Law concerning local government.
1837	Drawing up of the six demands of the future people's Charter.
1838-1848	Growth of the Chartist movement: demand for universal suffrage.
1860	First implementation of the principle of testing when recruiting civil servants, finally adopted in 1870.
1864	Founding in London of the Ist International.
1867	Second electoral reform. Publication of the first edition of *The English Constitution* by Walter Bagehot. Birth of the National Conservative Union.
1868	First session of the Trade Union Congress.
1870	The *Education Act* stipulates the provision of compulsory primary education.

1872	Adoption of secret ballots.
1877	Birth of the National Liberal Federation.
1881	H.M. Hyndman outlines Marxism to the British.
1883	The Social Democratic Federation founded in 1881 becomes the most important English Socialist party.
1884-1885	Third electoral reform. Randolph Churchill develops his ideas on democratic Toryism.
1888	Creation of elected county councils.
1889	The *Fabian Essays* defines socialist democracy according to the Fabian Society.
1894	Organization of elected district and parish councils.
1900	Founding of the Labor Representation Committee, first beginnings of the Labor movement.
1906	Birth of the Labor Party.
1911	The *Parliament Act* confirms the preeminence of the House of Commons.
1911-1913	Period of revolutionary strikes: the *Great Unrest.*
1913	Failure of a draft bill on votes for women. Feminist disturbances by the Suffragettes.
1918	Electoral reform gives the right to vote to all males and establishes limited suffrage to women (over 30 years old).
1928	Universal suffrage extended to women ages 21 to 30.
1968	Age for voting lowered to 18 years old.

THE THEATER OF FRENCH DEMOCRACY

Steven Englund[1]

A history of democracy in France since 1789... In fact the subject should be: *The History of France since 1789*. Under the Old Regime the philosophers defined democracy as one of three or four possible forms of government. Yet since the era of "democratic revolutions" at the end of the 18th Century, it was clear that democracy acquired an even wider meaning, until, in the case of France for example, completely dominating the sphere of political ideas. With its various meanings — and this is the purpose of this piece — democracy in France would become, for better or for worse, as Tocqueville far-sightedly noted, the ideal of modern political thought, a touchstone to measure political systems.

From this point of view, the French case is seemingly not very different from that of other western countries — the democratic system influencing all social, economic and cultural factors in the nation. Yet the term *nation* itself is revealing, chosen over *country* or *state*, it is felt to have a strong meaning for French democracy. The French reader, brought up in the republican school system, seemingly at ease in a political culture which is still very centered on France, might not even be aware of this. Democracy has almost become second nature, together with some other key

---

[1]The author would like to thank Robert Palmer, Robert Tombs and Ezra Suleiman for their valuable help.

concepts such as *republic* or *revolution*. Research seems to become bogged down with the obvious and diluted by common sense banalities. Having said this, if every French person acknowledges the values of democracy, each seems to have her or his own differing definition. For in France, the idea of democracy has spawned almost as many attempts to define it, as arguments over it.

Democracy in fact in terms of the form the French state has taken over the last 200 years has been reduced into a number of regimes unparalleled by any other western country. With two basic assets — the judicial status which Augustin Thierry was to call the "equality of rights," as well as the font of legitimacy — the sovereignty of the nation or the people. French democracy had an influence on all the political systems of the 19th and 20th Century. From the Jacobin concept of terror, to the Romanticism of the two Empires, the aristocratic "dukes republic," to the new classes of the "teachers republic" ending up with the strange compromise under the same regime and constitution, of Gaullist, liberal Giscardians and socio-liberal democrats. The continuity of the French state, even though turbulent as has been seen, allowed the citizens and politicians to experiment with various possible combinations. Not to mention — no doubt a mistake — the many democratic forums (sectional, union or associations) that were formed to counterbalance the power of the state.

ACT 1: WHERE SEVERAL DEMOCRATIC OPTIONS FLOW FROM THE REVOLUTION

Let us look at the first act of this democratic play. The revolution of 1789 of course was not the first democratic revolution. The British and the Americans in any case continually argue over which movement — 1649-1659, 1688 or 1776 — should have this distinction. Yet 1789 was really the first time that a state, embodying the entity called "the nation," issuing from a clean political break with the past, produced a *novus ordo seculorum*: democracy or the government of the people. The radical consequences of the new order consequently was based less on political and judicial reform, in vogue at the end of the 18th Century, but would create a sort of rhetoric and ideology that drew on numerous hidden political and cultural sources: writing, speeches, dress, ideas of the family, time, political groups, art, music etc...The primary strength of revolutionary democracy was that it captured the imaginations of very many.

The second was in keeping, even after the fall of the monarchy, the ability to give birth to various forces opposed to the regime of the day or even the state itself. This is one of the essential characteristics of French democracy, its *aura*, its strength, but also in a certain way its weakness. For democracy, according to the way it is interpreted, legitimizes both the powers that be (an Assembly) as well as the opposition (a club, a faction etc.). Thus democracy, a legitimizing principle, could "make despots quake" "overthrow tyrants" but also give impetus to clubs, sectional interests and the press, who claimed to represent more closely than the National Assembly the people's will and even the spirit of the revolutionary crowds at the height of the revolution. Yet this also produced a degree of political idiosyncrasy...hence the revolutionaries, in the face of unforeseen circumstances or grave danger had to gambled their very existence, sometimes even denying the democratic rights that they had given birth to, for example between 1793 and 1794, joining *dictatorship* with *freedom* in the name of the defence of the motherland.

It is clear that notwithstanding the great efforts made in the name of democracy, the result was corruption of the spirit of democratic selflessness; confused, crushed and buried by their many subterfuges. Now this fact seems relatively obvious and is no longer an issue to be rejected by the national conscience or through the skilful stratagem of linkage which tries to portray 1789 and 1793 as one and the same. Democracy, for a time and perhaps under the pressure of external events, clearly at the wish of the revolutionaries, betrayed itself. Francois Furet and Mona Ozouf have become authorities on this subject. Without forgetting the context of the birth of French democracy — the bad will of its royal parents, the internal and external opposition which the budding democratic revolutionaries encountered, the unsavory reputation that the concept itself had at the time, associated with anarchy rather than classical antiquity or the Anglo-Saxon model, and finally the strong continuity of the state under the monarchy and then the republic. One concludes that if the Revolution put forward an example of heroic selflessness for democracy, it also is an example of a elemental idea: the unintentional transformation of one idea into its opposite. In a word the *Irony* of democracy.

Let us look at an example, not the Terror because that would be too easy but a long and important debate on *la volonte generale* (the general will) and the problem of representation in theory (and practice) is at the heart of the democratic system. In the autumn of 1789, three months after the break with the past, after the 17-20-23 June when the Assembly proclaimed itself sovereign and national as opposed to the notion of a divine monarchy, after the emancipation in early July when the deputies freed themselves from their binding mandate to represent the people in the way that Sieyes and Talleyrand meant, and after the declaration of rights adopted on the 26 August. The question was no longer about when a representative system would emerge, nor above all how to give it full institutional guarantees, but of redistributing power between the king and the assembly, structuring the relationship of representative and represented and then distinguishing active citizens from passive ones. In other words: the most heated argument was over how to limit the sovereignty of the people, whereas in principle it should have been the opposite; all power to the people...

The coming of the vote,[2] a practice which should have fulfilled many democratic desires, in itself was to lead to several dubious results. On the one hand making equality hostage to a fixed economic and cultural level (a poll-tax), leading on the other to majorities ultimately hostile to democracy, and in a more general sense isolating the individual from their class, making them go without transition from direct active democracy (the network of

---

[2]Patrice Gueniffey, article "Suffrage" in the *Dictionnaire critique de la Revolution française*, directed by Francois Furet and Mona Ozouf, Flammarion, Paris, 1988.

clubs and sections) to representative democracy (national assemblies). The conflict between these two models, up to the riots of Year III (prairial), left the revolutionaries with a rather narrow and delicate path to follow, between the two types of democracy. In some ways the uncertainties and tragedies of this period can be found in this rivalry.

This is not a question of denouncing the revolution, but solely illustrating the dialectical and indefinable nature of the strength of revolutionary democracy. The Revolution, in a similar way to the struggle between an old power and a new legitimacy, is the product of an fierce rivalry between modern systems of representation (parliamentary monarchy, suffrage based on wealth, universal suffrage, direct democracy, parliamentary dictatorship, Roman type democracy), which explains why the revolutionary matrix is so diverse. Mona Ozouf gracefully highlights this process when she writes:[3] "Formal equality without a doubt camouflages true equality, yet it does not protect them for long. On the contrary it emphasizes the huge lie of society in terms of the principle on which it is based. It introduces into ordinary life, what Tocqueville so fully understood, the germ of endless upheaval." Democracy on the French Revolutionary model therefore is important above all for its "guiding principles": once established in their name there has to be fresh demands, on a political timescale that leads, in France as with the rest of the world, right up to the present day. The revolutionaries were clearly aware of this, speaking generally in terms of a universal and eternal idea, fundamental to the democracy they were forging. So what remains of this period, is not so much the blindness of the actors but the heart-rending clearsightedness with which they saw their own actions. The way they were able to weigh up every decisions, continually comparing their political acts with those intangible principles, measure the reason of State in the light of the Declaration of rights: each one, one of a thousand and one cuts to the taut fabric of the original dream of democracy. This was clearly present in their speeches, would be debated, examined closely and reconsidered. The

---

[3]Article "Equality" in the *Dictionnaire critique...*

revolutionaries, the first, tried to align their political behavior with the founding democratic texts, even when they most wanted to subvert them. Yet this subversion would only be possible if there existed a corpus of democracy that was an unsullied inspiration...

ACT II: MEETING DEMOCRATIC CAESARS

French thought during the III republic tried to fuse the two notions of *democracy* and *republic* together in the public mind. The success of this attempt can be gauged by the frequency with which even today one comes across sentences such as: "The French Republic was the starting point — the only starting point — for modern democracy."[4] Yet what the collective memory now reinterprets does not necessarily portray most accurately historical reality. So, whatever one might think of Alphonse Aulard, who in 1866 was the first holder of the post of the Revolution at the Sorbonne, and his scheme to begin the mammoth task of a "History of Democracy between 1789 and 1804"[5] it is no coincidence that this work quickly skates over the Napoleonic hold on French political tradition. In 1901, when Aulard's book was published, the Napoleonic legend was really unfashionable. Yet, Bonapartism, explicitly, as a political mythology together with later regimes (Consuls, Empire and Liberal Empire), provided a stimulus for the democracy that was inaugurated in 1789.

France as a nation under Bonapart, was democratic in the way it relied on the support of the ordinary man who was given greater protection from strife and disorder than could be guaranteed during either of the first two republics. The price that was paid, above all in terms of liberty, mostly angered the intelligentsia, without in itself destroying the revolutionary nature of the Imperial regime. Quite the opposite, the *republican* discourse of the Empire was

---

[4]Pierre Nora, article "République" in the *Dictionnaire critique...*

[5]Alphonse Aulard, *Histoire politique de la Revolution française. Origine et developpment de la démocratie et de la république (1789-1804)*, Colin, Paris, 1901.

vigorous, copying in its way the rhetoric of Augustus Caesar. The praise of *popular sovereignty* and of *equality* was reinforced by the principle of popular consultation as well as by the final destruction of the old order of society.

The fact that posterity has for a long time concurred with Gambetta's negative opinion over the "counterfeit democratic nature" of the Imperial system, should not stop historians from asking the real question: could this Imperial "counterfeit" have been transformed into "democratic gold" if during this period the additional Act of 1815, the achievement of Benjamin Constant and Emile Ollivier and the Liberal Empire, which would occur 50 years later, had then become firmly entrenched. Ever since Chateaubriand, the most astute historians — however much they might scorn Imperial culture — have readily agreed that the French, in the words of Francois Furet, were "prisoniers de la gloire de Napoleon plus encore que de sa police"[6] (more prisoners of Napoleon's glory than his police service). It would be wrong to explain this fascination in terms of straightforward national vanity, as a simple cult of the savior. It also needs to be seen, right up to De Gaulle's republic, in terms of a strong emphasis on democracy: a direct "appeal to the people" to choose their destiny, incarnated in one increasingly powerful man.[7]

SEVERAL BRANCHES OF THE DEMOCRATIC TREE OF 1789: SECULARITY AND THE SOCIAL QUESTION

Apart from Bonapartism, there were other political ideas that were put into motion by revolutionary democracy. The first would

---

[6]Article "Napoleon Bonaparte," in *Dictionnaire critique...*

[7]For the relation between democracy and Bonapartism, refer to T.A.B. Corley, *Democratic Despot*, London, 1961; S. Horvath-Peterson, *Victor Duruy and French Education. Liberal Reform in the Second Empire*, LSU Press, 1984; Bernard Menager, *Les Napoleon du peuple*, Aubier, Paris, 1988; S. Englund, "Les idees napoleoniennes," from the *Dictionnaire des oeuvres politiques* (s.d., Catelet, Duhamel, Pisier), PUF, Paris, 1982. The seminal book refuting "authoritarian democracy" remains Prevost-Paradol: *La France nouvelle*, Paris, 1869.

be the much publicized ambivalence, if not open hostility, between the policies of the state and the Catholic church. It is not just a question of militant anti-clericalism which might emerge during short outbreaks of violence, but something with deeper political roots: was the secular current that flowed through French democracy anti-clerical in an sporadic, contingent way, or was it by its very nature anti-clerical? I think, without fear of being mistaken, that one can say that throughout the Revolution as well the subsequent century, one of the main trends of democratic thought was to identify Catholicism not only as an implacable enemy as a result of circumstances, but as the number one rival to the Revolution.[8]

From a cultural point of view, the Revolution no doubt should be seen as a movement of renewal in direct competition with the religious model. With brazen courage the revolutionaries tried to transfer the system of belief from the spiritual to the political sphere: the Republic, embodied in the character of "Marianne" was the mother of this change of portrayal: democracy the fictive lover, providing the woof for a new sacred narrative. Popular sovereignty, for example, is often portrayed as being resurrected again and again from the ashes, establishing a continuity of principle with the figure of Christ and resurrecting the Catholic concept of *plenitudo potestas*. In order to manage this transfer the revolutionaries, and their successors of the 19th Century, had to destroy the beliefs of twelve centuries of catholic ideological domination, had to get to the roots of traditional political and world views. What was the "beatification of the nation" — the "religion of France" from 1789 to 1914, proclaimed by its most eloquent disciple, Jules Michelet, if not a challenge made to the universal philosophy of Catholicism by the (paradoxically) universal dream of the national ideal. The French Revolution tackles this problem to a much greater extent than its Anglo-Saxon sister democracies.

---

[8]E. Poulat, *Liberté et laicité. La guerre des deux France et le principe de la modernité*, Le Cerf, Paris, 1987; Claude Nicolet, *L'idée républicaine en France*, Gallimard, Paris, 1982; Steven Englund, "Rome et Cesar en France", *Communio*, XIV, mai-âout 1989.

I referred to the revolutionary period as part of the a "first act" of the French democratic play. But I could have seen it also as a one act play, because as has been often from Marx to Furet said since, the first scenes of this drama which took place between 1789 and 1815 would become the model for the whole of the 18th Century. Consequently it is both unfair to the revolutionaries and an extreme simplification to claim, as is sometimes done, that the stumbling block for the politicians that emerged from the turning point of 1789 was "social question." The Babouvist affair alone should prove this. I am mainly thinking of the *Manifeste des egaux*, which remains a seminal text, informs and allows us to understand most written treaties and demands that the question of "social democracy" threw up and would give rise to so many hopes and conflicts during the 19th and 20th Centuries. Hence all the declarations of principle of the Revolution, proclaimed *urbi et orbi*, and immediately received as such in many parts of the world, retained a strong class element as Habermas points out.[9] The majority of movements that have their inspiration in the Revolution, over the 150 subsequent years, emphasize the social consequences of upheaval that at the time was centered mainly on politics in relation to all the social problems. The inheritance of the Revolution in this sense reaches every aspect of democracy, to the minutest detail.

ACT III: THE DEMOCRATIC APOTHEOSIS

In one sense at least our history since 1830 has been straightforward: democracy increased. It was expanding together with the social dimension, its ideal reaching maturity and with a form of government... Following different tacks, either through revolutionary upheavals or clothed in the shrewd actions of novel respectability, the democratic ideal consolidated its hold on more and more parts of the world and differing social classes. From its two initial nuclei — the urban masses and the enlightened elites —

---

[9] J. Habermas, *The New Conservatism. Cultural Criticism and the Historians' Debate*, MIT Press, 1989.

it extended its influence among the upper middle classes and the liberal aristocracy. Yet clearly, as the founders of the III Republic would ceaselessly recall, the triumph of democracy was built on the gradual taming of rural populations, the peasants as well as the humbler worthies (doctors, teachers, chemists, low public servants..) who Gambetta described with the term "new social strata." A whole series of studies by Maurice Agulhon, Philippe Vigier, Raymond Huard and Eugen Weber have shown brilliantly how, slowly but surely, democracy was to become established in the countryside. Relatively quickly in the "Village republics" of the south east and center of the country, already contaminated by the first revolutionary seed, but more slowly in various isolated regions of the South West, the Alps, the Massif Central or in places in the west where the clerical counter culture was strong and where, as Eugen Weber points out, it took some time for the peasants to become *Frenchmen*, in other words democrats.

Yet the progress of democracy in the habitus or through the vote does not answer the fundamental question posed here: what type of democracy was gaining ground? In the first part of the century it is possible to define the democratic movement in terms of its combative militancy; the democratic forces (an alliance of republicans and bonapartists) against the royalists and supporters of elitist political power. At the core of the debate, somewhat uncomfortably but always passionately, the Liberals who were mainly Orleanists. For although they agreed with the practice of balance of power and believed in a parliament, tolerating even a modest freedom of the press — two of the fundamental pillars of the democratic system — they were less happy with another underpinning fundamental element: universal representation of the nation. Indeed the main question at the time was universal suffrage. This above all differentiated Guizot, a modern thinking Liberal who was opposed to every attempt by the democrats to extend the right to vote.

In 1848 however, this cause appears to have won the day; the principle of universal suffrage was adopted and henceforth was unassailable. [10] The Liberals spent their time, unfortunately for them unsuccessfully, trying to stop the progress of democracy. From then on decisively and dramatically, with the introduction of universal suffrage, French politics became *modern* while it would to take the other countries of Europe almost fifty years to adopt the principle of universal suffrage (apart from women which is another issue...). So after 1848 the democratic debate went down another track, pitting republicans against bonapartists. This quarrel over linking national sovereignty to freedom (the "five essentials" according to Thiers), ended with the victory of the former over the latter who at the same time as proclaiming the belief in popular sovereignty preferred authoritarianism and military glory rather than liberalism. The evolution of the Second Empire clearly illustrates this process. The republic would ultimately take over at the running of the Empire, forcing Napoleon III's regime away from military prestige and the populist appeal of riches, to become a Liberal Empire, tolerant of the opposition press and which would revive the role of parliament. The government of Emile Olliver, during the first 7 months of 1870, reformulated that recurring question over Napoleon; after the 100 days in 1815 what might moderate Bonapartism have given? We will never know... Whatever the case might be, it is undeniable that the Empire enjoyed resounding popularity, that it had a firm hold on the *demos*, hence it was almost a democratic regime in the liberal sense of the term. Notwithstanding the negative aura that the Empire had after its demise, in 1881 a perceptive republican journalist still lamented: "French Caesarism was a form of democracy..."[11]

Classical democracy in its republican or bonapartist forms was sometimes following 1848 wrong-footed by another form: socialism. Whatever this might be, and in France there were very many forms, French socialism during the 19th Century always tried

---

[10]Raymond Huard, *Le Suffrage universel en France (1848-1946)*, Aubier, Paris, 1990.

[11]R. Frary, *Le Peril national*, Didier, Paris, 1881.

to base its system on the mechanism of self-government and on demands for greater equality in various areas of life, above all the social conditions of the workers. These two areas, self-government and the wish for social equality, might have modified or transformed the very nature of French democracy as much as 1789 had done, but this was not to be the case.

Indeed, after 1870, the fight against socialism, which was ultimately victorious (since even the 1981 socialists are more willing to trace their roots back to the republican left of the last century rather than Guesdist, Broussist, Proudhonist or anarcho-sindicalist tendencies) was a watch-word for democratic republicanism. Following the Commune the founding fathers of the III Republic made efforts to distinguish themselves: democracy should be a non-violent means of gaining power through the ballot box, to then govern, and not a prelude to the "grand soir." For Gambetta, Ferry and their "opportunist" friends, rejection of socialism was absolute. The consequences of this deep distrust would soon to be felt. Republican France was, at one and the same time, in the avantgarde of political democracy in Europe and in the vanguard for social progress; left far behind monarchial Great Britain or Imperial Germany in terms of social reform.[12]

So the republic of Leon Gambetta and Jules Ferry was to prove to be the apotheosis of political democracy in France. It was successful, even more so than its revolutionary ancestor, in forging an intimate union of democracy and nation; rallying numerous social classes to its cause and placing the forces of tradition onto the defensive. The republic in fact succeeded in becoming what up until then had seemed impossible: democracy. Democracy as a form of government, perhaps even the most effective and stable form, avoiding the shortcomings of other systems of government: the rigidity of reaction, as well as socialist turmoil or Napoleonic epic adventures. In short, even avoiding the social question and taking refuge in the field of politics, embodied by the overriding vision of the *nation*, French democracy was to find ample ground

---

[12]Judith Stone, *The Search for Social Peace: Legislation in France (1890-1914)*, State University of New York Press, 1985.

for action. An example that best illustrates the advantages as well as the short-comings of the republic was its policy of secularization. In as far as the extensive and coherent policy of education produced better educated and self-reliant citizens (hence better democrats) the policy fits into the framework of the democratic ideal of the Revolution. On the other hand, the emergence of a "Republican catechism" — in many ways as hollow and partisan as its Catholic counterpart — and extremely violent attacks, at times unwarranted, on the Church did not do anything to cast the democratic cause in a favorable light. On the contrary it succeeded more in trapping opposition forces in an outdated political folklore, of for instance the mayor against the priest, rather than attempting a cautious compromise that would have reinforced a democracy of national unity, the explicit goal of the founding fathers of the 3rd Republic.

ACT IV: GAULLIST DEMOCRACY

Looking at contemporary history without too much false modesty, the Gaullist republic appears to have a happy political mix. The General seems to have manage to integrate a sizeable portion of the French democratic tradition. The Orleanist elements and classical republicans were not excluded from this synthesis, nor were Bonapartist ingredients (even though these have on the whole been exaggerated). David Thomson[13] in fact states that de Gaulle purposely chose the time and place for outlining his new constitution in 1958: Place de la Republique on the 4 September. This was explicit Gambetta-like symbolism and did away with Bonapartist rituals. Rather than an authoritarian system, de Gaulle thus established a *monarchic expression of republican democracy*.[14] The speech which he delivered at Bayeux in June 1946, gives its

---

[13]David Thomson, *Democracy in France since 1870*, Oxford.

[14]M. Duverger, *La cinquième république*, Paris, 1959; R. Remond, *Les Droites en France*, reed. Aubier, Paris, 1984; F. Choisel, *Bonapartisme et gaullisme*, Albatros, Paris 1987; F. Mitterand, *Le coup d'état permanent*, Paris, 1965.

essential elements: "The time has come to build, in order to preserve the prestige and authority of the state, new institutions that channel our perpetual political vitality." This man, who saw himself "above party politics," wanted to build democracy as a model of stability. Classical democracy is present in the Bayeux proposals: bicameralism, respect for the Senate, separation of powers and ministerial responsibility. The new factor lay in the devolved role of the president of the Republic who was entrusted with the task of, in the words of the General: "establishing national arbitration which stresses continuity rather than political scheming." Placed outside the sphere of partisan democracy, the president needed to rely on a different sort of legitimacy. In 1946 de Gaulle did not mention universal suffrage, which in a way had a dual role, influencing on the one hand partisan party politics associated with the legislative process and on the other ensuring the head of state's own legitimacy. This, as we know well, would only come about later during the 5th Republic. In the meantime democratic party politics was to have, for better or for worse, a free hand.

Yet what at the same time the 4th and 5th Republics succeeded in doing, apart from, in their own different ways, governing and managing political democracy, was to make a framework for social democracy. These regimes managed to a limited extent to fill the vacuum of socio-economic reform left by the 3rd Republic. Relying on favorable circumstances (the "trente glorieuses") French politics increasingly was concerned with economic questions, thus no doubt marking the end of a type of political blindness which only existed in democratic France at the end of the 19th Century. Yet the strong duality between on the one hand the opposition's social demands — up until the Socialist and Communist Parties' joint Program — and on the other a response that was strictly financial and political, continued to be the case in France. The country therefore still has a social stratification which is very unjust,[15] with 20% of the population having greater wealth

---

[15]E. Suleiman, *Elites in French Society. The Politics of Survival*, Princeton, 1978; and by the same author, "The politics of Corruption and the Corruption of Politics," *French Politics and Society*, vol. 9, Winter, 1991.

than the remaining 80%. Also here more than anywhere else, the elite, above all the administrative elite, have to a remarkable degree managed to avoid "social democratization."

ACT V: WHERE DEMOCRACY UNDERMINES THE QUESTION OF NATION

This situation was however further complicated by a problem that in France has been more acute for a long time than in other western democracies: the problem of integrating a large immigrant population.[16] Not only did the socio-political demands (citizenship, similar social cover etc.) of the immigrants pose a real challenge to the republic, ever increasing verbal and even violent clashes occurred which tarnished the reputation of French democracy. Yet, I believe sincerely, the immigrant question does not truly damage the democratic tradition of the republic, at least not as much as the negative effects of the social hierarchical divisions mentioned in the previous paragraph. On the contrary, as a foreign observer, I am impressed by the lack of any real appeal of French National populist ideas and above all by the lack of power of the National Front despite the oratorical prowess of their leader. While the reaction of the French to immigrants does not seem to me to pose an internal threat to the exercise of democracy, the newcomers pose a challenge to one of the key concepts of the democratic tradition in France: the idea of the nation. It is not a question, whatever one might feel, of assimilation since secular France as well as "tala" France have, over the last two centuries, established the cultural, intellectual and economic means of absorbing two million arabs into society. The trouble is political: the nation. Most newcomers in fact, including those who were already citizens (the Beurs) do not seem to care about, or are even hostile to traditional national political integration.

Jean-Marie Le Pen undoubtedly does have a unique role to play in present-day French politics. He characterizes a choice

---

[16]Gerard Noiriel, *Le creuset français. Histoire de l'immigration aux XIX et XX siècles*, Seuil, Paris, 1988.

which, without his unpleasant presence, might have escaped general scrutiny. By unashamedly advocating a "national preference" rather than the development of democracy (in other words according to the Scandinavian model, the integration of foreigners in the electorate, initially local and then national). Le Pen in a theatrical way illustrates the conflicting fate of ideas of nation and democracy in France.[17] What in 1789 had been asked for and incorporated into the idea of "national sovereignty," then kept alive until 1880, was quite brutally snuffed out at the end of the 19th Century and then during the 1st World War. Two branches of the same tree would henceforth vie for importance in two different fields: human rights, a recently rediscovered legacy — the Declaration was rarely referred to during the 19th Century apart from in a negative way — and nationalism, the degenerate bastard of the idea of nation. The nation seems to have adopted as its sole ritual function, the role of calming the storms caused by political and social divisions. In this (impossible) role, grandiloquently deployed before the fight, or as a way of mobilizing "good French" against the socialist opposition. The national flag has become a banal way of identifying people, depriving it of its soul as well as its body, and its significance is now greatly weakened for many French people, especially the young, for whom in many ways it is even a hinderance to a real achievement of democracy. In short the "crisis of national identity," brought into such disrepute by contemporary political discourse, does not strike me as a serious or new illness. It is a simple consequence of the rapid ageing of an ideal, that of the nation. In itself this crisis does not really pose a threat to French democracy. For the national ideal might even end up dying a death, taken out of the political field by democratic ideas and European cooperation (integration), its twin sister two centuries ago. At the risk of being

---

[17]Jean-Yves Guiomar, *La nation entre l'histoire et la raison, la découverte*, Paris, 1989; Suzanne Citron, *Le mythe national. L'histoire de France en question*, Ed. Ouvrieres, Paris, 1987; Steven Englund, "The Ghost of Nation Past," in *Journal of Modern History*; J. Breuilly, *Nationalism and the State*, St. Martin's, 1987.

controversial I would say the same thing about secularization which also has been gradually overtaken by its democratic rival — the huge demonstrations of 1984 demonstrated this — whereas these two concepts, as we have seen, became amalgamated during the 3rd Republic.

So, French democracy which gave birth to ideas that are intimately linked, ends up seeing them diametrically opposed and the development of a multiplicity of possibilities. The staging of the French "democratic theater," that we have tried to describe, is so varied and startlingly complicated, accommodating both the "official" interpretation as well as those of minorities that sometimes are very well organized — we would at this stage like to talk about the French democratic counter-societies which often flourished (Jules Ferry for example used to lament: "How beautiful the Republic was under the Empire." The French democratic experience is doubtless, if we take into account all the circumstances, the greatest political laboratory in the world. In the end, despite the existence of a consensus over the vocabulary of democracy, an idiom that by and large has been accepted ever since the July Monarchy, and subsequently gradually reinforced, the attraction (rather it might be seen as a fascination) in France has been for the forces of opposition that have sprung from expressions that *a priori* everyone agrees on. In this sense democracy in France remains a constant source of conflict, which seems to me to be a sign of vitality rather than tiredness. Indeed a brilliant intellectual remarked that "the French Revolution was over" and that France had peacefully rejoined the ranks of the other western democracies. Declaring the struggle over, in the complex French Republic, is still the best way of reviving it... One might comment with the dying words of Messala to his enemy brother Ben-Hur: "The struggle goes on, Juda, the struggle goes on."

CHRONOLOGY

1788   The Estates General are summoned in August by
Louis XVI for 1 May 1789 (they would
meet on the 5th). In December the royal
council decided on a doubling of the
representation of the Third Estate.

1789   *January*: Sieyes publishes *Qu'est-ce que le tiers-
état?*

March-April: Elections for the Estates General
and drawing up the grievance books.

17 June: The oath at the Jeu de Paume.

23 June: Royal meeting; the third estate refuses to
obey the King's orders.

27 June: The King gives way and enjoins the
clergy and nobility to support the third
estate.

July-August: Popular movements of revolt (taking
of the Bastille; "great fright" in the
countryside) which results in the
dismantling of the "Ancien Regime." The
destruction of the feudal regime is
confirmed on 4 August.

26 August: Declaration of the rights of man and the
citizen.

11 September: The King is allowed by the
Assembly the right of veto and suspension.

29 October: decree of the "silver mark": a rather
high census is needed to be eligible.

1790   Civil constitution for the clergy (12 July).

1791   *Le Chapelier Law* banning coalitions. September:
revision of the Constitution (suppression of
the "silver mark," yet the electoral census

	continues), to which the King swears an oath.
1792	Decree on the arrest of priests who refuse to take an oath. Storming of the Tuileries and the abolition of the monarchy.
	10 August: Election of a National Convention by universal suffrage (low participation).
1793	The Convention votes for the death of the King who was executed on the 21 January.
	10 March: Creation of a Revolutionary Tribunal.
	6 April: First Committee for Public Welfare.
	31 May-2 June: Paris sections rise up against the convention which results in the fall of the Girondins.
	24 June: Constitution and declaration of rights.
	23 August: The Convention decrees an uprising of the masses (popular army).
	5 September: The Terror becomes widespread.
	17 September: Voting in of the law of suspects.
	November-December: Period of frenetic de-Christianization.
1794	The Great Terror (19 June-27 July), then fall of Robespierre (9 Thermidor-27 July).
1795	Freedom of belief. Final riots of the sans-culottes who invade the Convention before being disarmed 91-5 Prairial- 20-24 May). New Constitution, and declaration of rights and duties (22 August).
1797	Death penalty for Babeuf (conjuration of equals) on 26 May.
1798	Adoption of the Jourdan law implementing compulsory military service.
1799	Coup d'état that brought Napoleon Bonaparte to power (18 Brumaire- 9 November). New Constitution: the Council of State and the Senate are adopted.

1800	Closing of the list of emigres. Promulgation of the Civil Code.
1805	Setting up of a Press Office to oversee publications.
1806	Creation of industrial tribunals.
1814	Abdication of Napoleon (6 April). Proclamation of the Charter (4 June).
1815	The "Hundred Days" of Napoleon (20 March-18 June): B. Constant participates in drafting the additional Act, and injects a liberal tone. The return of Louis XVIII is marked by the election of a conservative house (August).
1816	Chateaubriand: *De la monarchie selon la Charte.*
1818	Madame de Stael: *Considerations sur la Revolution francaise.*
1820	A. Thierry: *Lettres sur l'histoire de France.*
1823	Guizot: *Essais sur l'histoire de la France*; Thiers: *Histoire de la Revolution.*
1824	Mignet: *Histoire de la Revolution francaise.*
1830	Revolution: the Glorious Three Days (27-29 July) force Charles X to withdraw his anti-Liberal edicts, then to abdicate. Louis-Philippe, the French king, bases his rule on a more liberal revised Charter.
1831	Doubling of the electoral roll following a reduction of the poll rating.
1835	Toqueville: first part of his *De la democratie en Amerique* (*Democracy in America*).
1847	Michelet: *Histoire de la Revolution francaise*; L.Blanc: *Histoire de la Revolution*; Lamartine: *Histoire des Girondins.*
1848	*February*: Abdication of Louis-Philippe and proclamation of the II Republic. Abolition of the politically motivated death penalty.
	March: length of the working day limited to ten hours. Freedom of the press, assembly and

universal suffrage (elections to the
Constituent Assembly on 23 April).

June: Popular riots and repression in the east of
Paris.

December: Election of Louis-Napoleon Bonaparte
by universal suffrage as president of the
Republic.

1850   Law limiting the right of vote. (31 May).

1851   Louis-Napoleon Bonaparte's Coup d'état, that
restores universal suffrage (2 December).
Plebiscite confirming his position (21
December).

1852   Restoration of the Empire. Plebiscite ratifying the
new constitution.

1856   Tocqueville: *l'Ancien Regime et la Revolution.*

1858   Proudhon: *La Justice dans la Revolution et l'Eglise.*

1860   The Houses are granted the right of enquiry and
ministers have to defend their policies to
the Assembly.

1864   Law concerning coalitions: the right to strike is
granted.

1869   The legislature shares with the emperor the drafting
of laws.

1870   Liberal government of Emile Ollivier. A
referendum-plebiscite approves the policies
of the Liberal Empire. Defeat against the
Prussians and declaration of the III
Republic (4 September).

1871   Elections: Royalist majority; however count de
Chambord, the king in waiting, refuses to
give up the white flag. Failure of the
royalist restoration.

Thiers is president of a "Conservative Republic"
that crushes the Paris Commune.

1873   Thiers resigns after having a minority in the
house. Mac-Mahon (royalist) replaces him
as president.

1875	Law organizing political power: the president of the Republic is elected by the two chambers whose powers are restricted. Republican victory in the by-elections.
1877	*16 May*: ministerial crisis — Mac-Mahon sacks Jules Simon, a republican. Dissolution of the houses. The elections however confirms the republican majority and confirms the regime.
1879	Republican electoral victory: J.Grevy is elected president. Freycinet government. Return of the houses to Paris.
1880	Amnesty of the communards. First celebration of 14 July as a national holiday. Ferry government.
1881	Law on free primary education. L. Gambetta government.
1882	Law on compulsory education and lay teaching.
1884	Laws allowing unions, divorce and municipal elections.
1889	Boulangist agitation: election, victory and then flight of general Boulanger.
1891	*Rerum Novarum* encyclical.
1890-1897	Steady rallying of Catholics to the republic.
1894	Sentencing of Dreyfus.
1895	Founding congress of the CGT at Limoges.
1898	E. Zola: *J'accuse*. Founding of the League of Human Rights.
1899	Anti-parliamentary agitation (Deroulede) and Republican counter-demonstrations over the Dreyfus affair.
1900	J. Jaures: *Histoire socialistes de la Revolution francaise*.
1901	Founding of the radical socialist party (the first organized party).
1905	Founding of the SFIO. Law on the separation of church and state.

1906	Congress of the CGT at Amiens: the anarcho-syndicalist influence was on the increase.
1914	Assassination of Jaures (11 July). German declaration of war (3 August): The house votes unanimously full powers to the government (Sacred Union). Guesde and Sembat both socialists join the Viviani government.
1917	Mutinies in the army; workers strikes in Paris.
1919	Law over an eight hour day.
1920	Split of the socialist party at Tours.
1934	Anti-parliamentary riots in Paris (6 February). The Socialists and Communists reach agreement over an "anti-fascist union."
1935	Huge Republican demonstrations on the 14 July.
1936	Electoral Program (January) followed by electoral victory of the Front Populaire (5 May). The Blum government concludes the Matignon agreement following an extensive strike movement, then agrees to the extension of schooling up to 14 years old, paid holidays and a 40 hour working week (June).
1939	France declares war on the Reich (3 September). Censorship imposed and the French Communist Party dissolved (August-Sept).
1940	Resignation of Paul Reynaud. P. Petain in power (16 June). Call for resistance by General de Gaulle from London (18 June). Constitutional acts founding the French state. In Vichy the council of ministers issued a law governing Jews (3 October). Petain asks the French to begin collaborating (30 October).
1943	Founding of the National Council of the Resistance (CNR) on the 27 May.

1944	Program of the CNR for France following the Liberation (15 March). C. De Gaulle goes down the Champs-Elysees in liberated Paris (26 August). Government of national unanimity under the control of De Gaulle. Right to vote for women (5 October).
1945	End of censorship (12 June). Instructions over social security (5 October).
1946	Resignation of De Gaulle (20 January). The constitutional Assembly agrees constitutional proposals (29 September).
1947	Removal of communist ministers (4 May).
1954	Start of the Algerian uprising (1 November).
1956	Three weeks paid holidays (28 February).
1958	Investiture of De Gaulle by the Assembly (1 June); then referendum on the new constitution, legislative elections in support of De Gaulle who was elected President of the Republic and also of the community (21 December).
1962	Referendum over the election of the president of the republic by universal suffrage (28 October).
1965	First presidential elections using universal suffrage.
1967	Orders concerning the interest of employees in company profits (17 August).
1968	Student movement, followed by barricades in Paris (3-11 May). Demonstrations and social strikes (13-27 May) leading to the Grenelles agreement. Gaullist demonstrations (30 May) and legislative elections in favor of the general (23-30 June).
1969	Resignation of De Gaulle (28 April). Election of G. Pompidou to the presidency of the Republic with 58% of the vote (15 June).

1974   Election of V. Giscard d'Estaing to the presidency
with 50.8% of the vote (19 May). Law
concerning the legal age of 18 and divorce
through mutual agreement (July).
Expansion of the right to submission of the
Constituent council to 60 deputies or
senators (October); Veil's Law granting
IVG (November).

1975   Initial dinner by V. Giscard d'Estaing with a typical
French family (22 January).

1976   The FCP abandons the notion of a dictatorship of
the proletariat.

1981   Election of F. Mitterand to the presidency with
51.7% of the vote (10 May). End of
expulsion of foreigners and social measures
(the SMIG raised by 10%) in June.
Dissolution of the Court of State Security
(July). Authorization for 300,000 illegal
immigrants to legalize their situation. End
of the death penalty (30 September).

1982   Lowering of the legal limit of time at work to 39
hours.

1984   Demonstration of more than 1 million people
supporting private schools (24 June). The
National Front gets 11% of the vote in the
European elections, whereas the FCP goes
down to 11.2% The FCP announces that it
will not take part in the new L. Fabius
government (17 July).

1986   Success of the right in the legislative elections (16
March). Jacques Chirac, the Prime
Minister, inaugurates the period of
"Cohabitation" (20 March).

1988   Re-election of F. Mitterand to the presidency with
54.1% of the votes cast, who then makes
M. Rocard Prime Minister.

THE UPS AND DOWNS
OF THE GERMAN ROAD TO DEMOCRACY

Michael Werner

The history of the last two centuries is there to bear witness to the slightly problematic relationship that Germany has with democracy. Therefore in trying to outline the major events of the democratic movement in Germany one attempts to grasp, in a comparative way, the famous question of Germany's "lonely road" *Sonderweg* in European history. Was the evolution of Germany towards National Socialist dictatorship written in the general lines of its past? Or was it only a diversion or loss of control that can be explained by the political conditions of the 1930's?

Furthermore, the restoration of unity in 1990, with an enlarged Federal Republic, might tempt one to describe the German road to democracy in the light of this conclusion, within the logic of *a posteriori* legitimization, after many tribulations to a sort of *happy ending*. This viewpoint we would agree carries the obvious dangers of all teleological history: exclusivity of a single logical explanation, refusal to accept alternatives and absence of critical perspective in relation to the hypothesis that will be defended. If it clear that this is not our intention, nevertheless both phenomena, the rise and fall of Naziism and the setting up of stable democratic institutions after 1945, are undeniably linked. Yet rather than stating the facts, it seems to us at present more interesting, from a

113

European viewpoint, to illustrate the complicated nature of these links and to highlight the increasing interdependence of national development. In so doing we will review a number of theories put forward by specialists to explain the singularity of German history in terms of democracy. Also at the same time we will try to examine the cultural and social dimensions of these phenomena, rather than solely the national political and judicial elements that are often used in relation to this question.

THE TWO TYPES OF *SONDERWEG*

The theory of German *Sonderweg* breaks down into two very distinct phases. Prior to the First World War and up until the 1920's, its supporters were from amongst the conservatives. Such people as Treitschke, Sybel and Marcks felt that the unique road that Germany had taken to modernize was a sign of success: absence of revolutionary upheavals, modernization through successive reforms coming from above, authoritarian Monarchic power, progressive social legislation, existence of an effective, efficient and powerful bureaucracy, all these factors seemed to give Germany the edge over the western democracies, threatened by "decadence" and destructive individualism — a legacy of 1789. The glorification of the civilizing role of Germany in the history of the world concluded with the "ideas of 1914" and the German armies being given the task of spreading the "German model" (considered superior to English and French parliamentarism) across the whole of Europe. Highlighting *Sonderweg* was not only a way of distinguishing Germany but also of giving it a strongly antidemocratic orientation. So the conservative idea of the uniqueness of Germany was taken up by the opponents of the Weimar Republic after the First World War. According to the ideologues of the "conservative revolution," the Republic did not in any way answer to the political or cultural traditions of the real Germany. To try and subject it to the model of western parliamentary democracy was doomed to failure. Sooner or later, they maintained, Germany, showing its unique ability to reorganize and make modern society more efficient, would have its revenge.

The rise and fall of the 3rd Reich gives body to the second version of Sonderweg, as a type of negative reversal of the former. To explain the disaster of National Socialism, one has to link it with the main themes of recent German history: the initial antidemocratic nature of German nationalism that emerged from the Napoleonic wars, the failure of the Bourgeois Revolution of 1848, the creation "by force" of Bismark's Reich, the authoritarian spirit of its institutions and its political practices, the role of the military in a state dominated by the values and traditions of Prussia, the expansionist and messianic streak of "German ideology" — many factors which concurrently worked towards the historical tragedy of the German nation. This train of argument espoused above all by left-wing historians in the 1960's and 70's attempts to provide an answer to the disturbing question: how could the horrors, committed in the name of the German nation, have been possible? To account for the uniqueness of the Nazi crimes, the "distinct road" seemed to provide a framework for a plausible answer. However, let us take note of the duality of this framework: on the one hand in emphasizing its singular character, incommensurable with the Nazi crimes, it implies a moral judgement which is in keeping with the ethical role of the historian. The disputes in 1987 during the "historians' quarrel" illustrates this dimension of the question. The revisionist banalizing of the Nazi period, together with its out and out relativization, has been rejected by the overwhelming majority. On the other hand, by tracing the coherence of the evolution to the "German catastrophe" (Friedreich Meinecke), by unravelling the structural impediments of society that blocked the road to liberal democracy, historians of the Federal Republic appeared to be saying that this catastrophe was a consequence of the continuity of German history. What is put forward as an "irreducible particularity" springs from, at the same time, a structural analysis over a long period and a moral judgement.

Another element needs to be borne in mind when using the outline explanation of *Sonderweg*: the dialectics of continuity and change. When historians and sociologists, from Hans-Ulrich Wehler, Jurgen Habermas to Jurgen Kocka, emphasize the logic of pre-1945, they do so to give greater weight to the break with the past that subsequently occurred. To add credence to this "new beginning" of 1945 it was necessary to show that the particular road that Germany travelled had reached its fatal destination. The historical end of *Sonderweg* opens the way to the introduction of western democratic traditions that had formerly been opposed.

SOME GERMAN CHARACTERISTICS

Apart from the general interpretation of *Sonderweg*, German history has several characteristics that are useful to remember. An observation is often overlooked when speaking from a French point of view: the great variety of situations in Germany. Each region has its own differences. For example right up to the end of the 19th Century the difference between Bade and Pomeranian lands was much more pronounced than that which distinguish the Palatinate from Luxembourg. Differences of religion, social stratification, judicial system, tax system and even cultural differences. To such the extent that one could speak of actual cultural frontiers crossing the country from north to south and east to west. Under such circumstances it is not surprising that the process of national union should have taken so long and been so difficult. Nevertheless it was to adopt a unique solution, from among many options, in this instance under the leadership of Prussia. In any case, the enormous contrasts between one place and another make generalizations much of the time suspect, especially in the context of a study of democratic traditions and practices.

The second characteristic is as obvious as the first: the link between the problem of national unity and the democratization of states. In France as well as in Great Britain, the establishment of a national state was achieved at the very latest by the 18th Century. Political and social modernization was to take place on a more or less stable nationwide basis. German democrats on the other hand had to contend with the dual task of social change and the creation of a national state. History has shown that when faced by the need to choose, on the whole, they preferred national unity. Hence what at first sight seems to have been a break in the process and consequently lost its linear character.

Finally the third set of problems that further complicates the perspective is represented by the many differences between various levels of democratic practice. The absence of a central state and the variety of local and regional traditions tended towards the development of various practices, even before attempting the more general problem of a constitution, be it democratic or no, of a national state as in 1871.

Let us begin on this first point. Recent research on the forming of communes (rural and urban) from the 13th Century have led to the suggestion of the principle of "communalism" Tocqueville already observed that "the institution of communes introduced democratic freedom into the heart of monarchic feudalism." In contrast to the hierarchical˙logic of feudalism, communalism was a levelling principle, based on the active participation of citizens and villagers within municipal assemblies, local laws, the free use of labor and finally values of "common utility" and common wealth. It was above all in the west and southern German territories that this form of local democracy became established and continued to survive until the end of the Ancien Regime. In these regions the relative weakness of the nobility and the possibility that the (mostly quite small) towns of the Empire had to appeal to the Imperial court to settle differences, fostered this form of rule. In the east on the other hand where there were far less communes, the authority of the masters of the estates, underpinned by the economic argument of large landowners, managed to hold in check the aspirations of rural communes for autonomy.

Wherever it was allowed to develop, in favorable conditions, communalism generated, like Switzerland, urban republics and rural cantons that managed to keep their independence. In all the areas where this phenomenon took place, in the Baden lands, Wurttemberg, Alsace, the Palatinate, Francony and Bavaria, as well as the Tyrol (this list is not exhaustive) there emerged a form of political culture, in the countryside as in the towns, that has left many vestiges. Especially since in some towns it was adopted and even extended to areas greater than their initial territorial limits with municipal statutes given similar interpretations (what Mack Walker calls the *German Home Towns*). Of course this was an unequal democracy which prevented many inhabitants from exercising civic rights, yet in other ways, both mentally and formally, the principles of democratic control were established: parliamentary representation, political and judicial elections, control of the executive by assemblies, the process of political decision-making through free discussion of all points of view, etc. The relative strength of the liberal and democratic movement in the south west and south of Germany in the 19th Century, the resistance of these territories in the face of the Prussian model no doubt bears some relation to these very same traditions. There is of course also the fact that these regions were far more touched, because of their geographic and cultural proximity, by the influence of the French revolution.

Another set of initial factors that needs to be taken into consideration concerns religious differences. Often it has been asserted that Protestantism, as a doctrine that questioned the authority of the Church, and as a form of organization that relies on presbyterian councils and synods, prepared the ground for the implementation of democratic practices. At the same time it is no doubt also right to add further differences: Lutheranism and its theory of two kingdoms often lived side by side with politically authoritarian regimes; piety can lead to two conclusions: individual and interior freedom or mystical irrationality carrying the seeds of political aspirations. Also within the Catholic creed, during the 19th Century, there had developed tendencies that were in favor of democratic ideas which later were reinforced due to the effects of Bismark's *Kulturkampf.* Finally one has to allow for the effect of the position of minority groups, geographically fixed, in many regions where Protestants or Catholics could be in the majority and which often resulted in different political forms of expression. Hence for example the strength of the liberal movement in certain regions of the south west, sometimes linked with there being Protestant enclaves. Nevertheless, even though the influence of the religious factor is undeniable, the variety of situations and constellations were such that it is difficult to draw any general conclusions.

There remains the overriding problem of a German space that was geographically changing. The *Aufklarung*, the main ideological factor in the birth of German democracy, stretched over a huge swathe of Central Europe and encompassed a large part of Austria. Also the 1848 Revolution which was the other major political event of this period. After 1871 the view was concentrated within the frontiers of the 2nd Reich, then in 1918 to those of the Weimar Republic prior to its division in 1949 in the face of the reality of the BDR and the DDR. It is not just a question of the instability of frontiers, but it does again beg the question of the complex interaction of social, political and cultural factors within the German sphere.

CHRONOLOGICAL LANDMARKS: FROM THE FRENCH REVOLUTION TO THE PARLIAMENT OF FRANKFURT (1848)

Recent studies have emphasized the similarities between both French and German society on the eve of the Revolution. However in both countries the passage to the modern age occurred by two different processes: revolution in France and reform in Germany. Even so this casting of roles needs to be tempered. Both models of social change are in reality interdependent, complementary and dovetail into each other. The French Revolution set in motion in Germany a tidal wave that was felt at every level of society. It generated political movements which spread the ideas of 1789. Finally, and above all, through the agency of Napoleon's policy in the Rhineland, it led to far-reaching and profound reforms of the political system as well as society. Only in Prussia did the reform movement, following the defeat of Iena and the need to modernize the country, take on an anti-French character. This would become the famous "revolution from above" or defensive modernization which was meant to narrow the gap with the French. The influence of the French model, even in Prussia, is evident in this reform process.

Again, notwithstanding the war waged against Napoleon to liberate Germany, the campaigns were not waged against the principles of the Revolution. On the contrary, in order to mobilize public opinion and the middle classes, the conservative dynasties were forced to allow, in the form of liberal constitutions, the participation of the bourgeoisie in state affairs. Yet once rid of the French, Austria and Prussia, under the pretence of an enemy within, refused to grant the previously promised political changes. Caught up by the logic of the restoration, Chancellor Metternich set his sights on slowing down the constitutional movements in the other German states. To such effect that, faced with the coalition of conservative powers, national aspirations and liberal ideas in many ways became intertwined during the German *Vormarz*.

The difficulties were much more complex by the time of the 1848 Revolution. Faced by the twin task of building national unity and accomplishing a political revolution, the German liberals would fail on both counts. The constitution, drawn up by the Frankfurt Parliament following a year of strenuous deliberations, would never be put into practice. The Prussian king turned down the Imperial crown offered by the people's will. The federal government desperately lacked the means of implementing its policies in practice. Parliamentary discussions in Frankfurt were completely divorced from the reality. In the meantime the Prussian and Austrian armies, having put down the revolutionary movements in Berlin and Vienna, stamped out the last uprisings in the Rhineland, the Palatinate, Baden and Hungary. This was the triumph of the reaction.

However, the failed revolution of 1848 was far from being a total disaster for the liberal movement. In Prussia a constitution was granted, of course from above, within the kingdom, taking up the main points worked out by Frankfurt at a national level. Within the Berlin Assembly the Liberals would play, for several decades, a decisive role. Apart from Austria, all the German states henceforth were under the influence of the constitutional ideal, stated with bravado by the Frankfurt Parliament. The socialists were also able for the first time to measure their strength and at least for a brief time influence events. Political parties in general crystallized, organized themselves and drew up programs. Tendencies emerged, above all between the liberals and the democrats, and then within the liberal movement between the right wing and the left. Its failure, rather than simply being due to the weakness and incoherence of the revolutionaries of 1848, was because of the tenacious power of the counter-revolution, of the conservative elites who kept control of the two most powerful hegemonic powers — Prussia and Austria — states which meanwhile were not yet ready to give up their sovereignty and become part of a national body. Against these conservative powers, but also faced by many immediate problems (political, social and economic modernization at every level) the revolutionaries' position was desperate, above all from the moment their political base started to splinter into factions (which occurred after May 1848). Furthermore the Liberals themselves, in other words the majority of deputies in the *Paulskirche*, much preferred reform measures rather than revolutionary demands but basically had been as much surprised as the conservatives by the power of events in the first few weeks. Thus the failure of the "Bourgeois revolution" was to a large extent symbolic rather than in terms of political and social change. It was a setback to the wish to give themselves political structures freely drawn up by representatives of the German people. Coming out of this was a feeling of humiliation because Germany seemed unable in historical terms to take responsibility for its own destiny, or if you prefer, to raise itself to the level of the great powers of western Europe. From this point of view the repercussions of 1848 would continue to be felt for a long time.

Finally the discrediting of parliamentarianism and democracy itself belongs to this same episode. Both the left and the right laughed at the inefficiency of the Frankfurt debates. Bismark, at the time leader of the Prussian ultras, declared in 1850: "In my opinion, Prussian honor does not lie in Prussia having to play the role of Don Quixote all over Germany for the benefit of famous ruffled parliamentarians [...] I myself believe that Prussian honor lies above all in refusing to enter into dishonorable alliance with democracy." Did this mean that the evolution towards a more democratic society was therefore blocked? What is sure is that the two objectives, of national unity and the democratization of society, became progressively divorced to the extent that it has been said that a national state was created *to counter* democracy. On this subject it is only right to avoid taking tenuous short-cuts. Bourgeois liberalism in the middle of the 19th Century had little to do with ideas of democracy in the 20th Century. It involved the exclusion of large parts of ordinary society, defined by class, sex or political view-point. In this sense bourgeois liberalism in the 19th Century was antidemocratic. Consequently, introducing the concept of a "failed bourgeois revolution" to explain the political defeat of the 1884-1849 movement might result in glaringly anachronistic postulates. In fact, despite the clear polarization, 1849 to 1876 marks the high-point of the liberalization of society.

FROM BISMARK TO WEIMAR

The creation of the second Reich in 1871 occurred as a result of a compromise between the conservative elites, especially Prussian, and a large section of the liberal bourgeoisie. Concessions were made by both sides. Bismark and the *Junkers* understood that, in order to channel the liberal movement in the long-term, they had to agree to their national aspirations. Since their Austrian opponents were militarily out of the game, there was nothing in the way of a "lesser German" solution. The great majority of liberals also agreed to the method to be used for this which was hardly in keeping with the liberal spirit: unification "by the sword and by blood" and the isolation of democrats and left wing liberals. Once more the "revolution from above" undermined demands of popular movements "from below." On the other hand Bismark gave the liberals not just national unity but also a constitution that included some very important concessions, amongst them the creation of a *Reichstag* elected by universal suffrage, not to speak of an economic policy to stimulate trade and industry.

The effects of the 1871 dual compromise were felt in contradictory ways right through Bismark's Reich. On the one hand authoritarian structures, a legacy of Prussia: the preeminent role of the Emperor who appointed the Chancellor and called and dissolved the Reichstag; Prussia represented almost two thirds of the Reich, had a hegemonic role on the Bundesrat, the council that brought together all the states of the federation; the power of the military and the *Junkers* who, by means of the Prussian parliament elected by restricted poll-tax suffrage, continued to have a weighty voice in political decisions; finally a powerful modern bureaucracy, invested with prerogatives directly linked to monarchic power and to whom it alone felt responsible. Bismark scorned the parliamentary institutions. In 1878 he contemplated a coup d'état if the Reichstag refused to vote special laws against the socialists. For him the will of the emperor rode roughshod over the will of the people. During the 1880's he continued to erect "barriers against the advance of democracy and anarchy," within Germany and abroad. After his departure in 1890 William II, surrounded by a camarilla loath to follow the practices of democracy, wielded full monarchic power.

Yet, in other ways, a series of developments can be distinguished that pointed to a gradual liberalization of society: the establishment of the principle of individual private property rights; the disappearance of orders and corporations to the benefit of a citizens' society; the massive increase in associations; progress and diversity in the cultural field (theater, literature, museums etc.) especially post 1890; a more active participation of the parties in the political process; growth of the press; development of youth and women's movements — all these changes were not exactly proof of a deep-rooted democratization yet are indicators of a modernization of society, similar to those taking place around the same time in England and France. The difference with the German situation was that the two movements, towards authoritarianism and a more liberal society, were taking place in parallel and at one and the same time.

In view of this the situation of the social democrats is very informative. The only party, apart from the left wing liberals, including a commitment to democracy in their program, they were victimized by Bismark who instituted a systematic policy of isolation: laws of exception in 1878, banning and judicial pursuit etc. Even so in national elections the party constantly improved its score. From 3.1% in 1871 it rose to 9.1% in 1877, crossed the 20% barrier in 1893 and ended up at 34.8% in 1912 making it the largest party in the Reichstag. It had control of many satellite organizations, from sporting associations to newspapers and publishing houses that developed into a sort of counter-culture in the Reich. Even though it was to become, together with the union movement, an central social force, its integration into the Reich's

Democracy in Europe

political system would remain restricted. Despite several half-hearted attempts, an alliance with the liberal democrats would prove impossible. The social democrats resisted the temptation of reform, nor did the left-wing liberals dare to demystify the idea of a "red specter."

In general, on the eve of the war, tensions within the social structure were increasing. This has been explained above all by the lack of correspondence between extremely fast economic development and an archaic political system. What is certain is that the system proved incapable of bringing about essential structural changes.

FROM WEIMAR TO POTSDAM

The system drawn up by the constituent assembly at Weimar in 1919, was the first democratic constitution in Germany in the modern sense of the term. Conceived notably by Hugo Preuss, with the advice of Max Weber, the Weimar constitution was a compromise between liberal theories and the political aspirations of the social democrats who were in the majority. Drawing on the British model, the draughtsmen of Weimar hoped for a balance between parliament and the executive, conferring on the president, elected by universal suffrage, the role of arbiter with powers of appeal, similar to those of a constitutional monarch. They distrusted the political parties and public opinion, which are both essential ingredients for a healthy parliamentary system. This resulted in a structural imbalance between the government and the parliament, and within the Reichstag itself which was elected on a proportional basis and was split up into a multitude of parties. Weaknesses that the president, whose role remained rather vague, could not hope to counterbalance.

Notwithstanding external pressure (Treaty of Versailles, reparations, problem of borders) the Weimar Republic was above all prey to strong internal tensions that historical studies have highlighted: in political terms, after the 1920 elections, a republican coalition of three parties: the SPD, DDP (left-wing liberals) and Zentrum (Catholic Party), found themselves in a minority position. (In 1924 and 1928 they would have small majorities before a landslide defeat in 1932.) From the first confidence in the new republic was low and a growing extremism of both the left and the right occurred. Too busy dealing with the aftermath of the war, the social democrats were unable to introduce significant social reforms apart from the 8 hour working day in 1919.

More generally, the old conservative elites, the state bureaucracy, as well as many middle class intellectuals especially university professors, continued to be hostile to the republic. The army formed a state within a state and remained aloof. The leading industrialists, retaining a paternalistic mentality and disciplinary structures inherited from the Empire, were not about to agree to class compromise. Lastly and above all, the middle classes, already in 1923 impoverished by inflation, took the full force of the great crash and the economic crisis. Admittedly this was a global phenomena and other countries affected by the crisis were also open to the specter of fascism, yet unlike Great Britain and France, democratic traditions were not firmly entrenched. The traditional right wing also failed to integrate and channel the extremists. The labor movement, socially isolated and deeply divided, did not even temporarily succeed in attracting those social classes that had been impoverished by the economic crisis. Finally, despite the National Socialist's anticapitalist stance, some industrialists were willing to ally themselves with Hitler to defend themselves against the rise of communism.

Therefore it was a combination of the effects of economic crisis and political traditions that belonged to a previous era more than anything else, and only slightly exacerbated by what has been called the "conservative revolution," that were to characterize the drift towards National Socialism. In the June 1932 elections the NSDAP only got 37.4% of the votes. When in the same year, in November this dropped to 33%, its leaders put pressure on old president Hindenburg to accept the nomination of Hitler as Chancellor. This came about with the support of von Papen's ultra conservatives on the 30 January 1933. The rising tide of the NSDAP which in the space of 4 years, between 1928 and 1932, increased the number of votes twelvefold, from 3% to 37%, illustrates the political weakness of the Weimar system. In the last free elections in November 1932, the democratic "constitutional" parties would represent barely 39% of the electorate, while the communists would score 16.9%, their best ever result. The bankruptcy of the bourgeois parties was more or less obvious. In fact, only the organized worker's movement and the catholic electorate were to resist the fascist epidemic. One should add that by that time the struggle was no longer being fought by democratic means. Once legally in power, Hitler quickly imposed a state of emergency and suspended constitutional guarantees. What was left of Weimar democracy was brutally destroyed.

1945: ALIEN GRAFT OR RETURN
TO HIDDEN TRADITIONS?

The fall of the Nazi regime in 1945 provided the opportunity for a profound reorganization of political structures. Outside conditions were established at the allied conference of Potsdam. However, the cold war and the consolidation of the political division of Germany that followed, gave a singular dimension to the development of democratic ideas. Two phases are discernable. In 1949 the constitutional establishment of a German Federal Republic and a People's Democratic Republic of Germany attest to the negative experience of history. The "Fundamental Laws," drawn up by Bonn, tried to avoid the short-comings of Weimar by strengthening the executive (constructive vote of no confidence, in other words an obligatory link between a vote of censure and electing a new government), modifying the rule of proportionality and introducing a 5% threshold to avoid splintering into tiny parties. The federal structure was reinforced. A constitutional court would guarantee that the political process would operate within the bounds of the fundamental laws. During the first period of economic and political reconstruction, the national question remained important, both in political terms and in terms of international law with a final settlement postponed to some future peace treaty. In the People's Democratic Republic an authoritarian socialist system was installed, based on the principle of "democratic centralism." All the parties gathered round the SED into a "National Front," the SED in the 1968 constitution being guaranteed the "leading role."

The second phase, in the Federal Republic can be seen as a gradual democratization of civil society, especially towards the end of the 1960's. This was not only a question of the important repercussions of Federal power alternating with the first social democrat government, but above all the development of new forms of social interaction, initiatives by ordinary citizens (*Burgerinitiativer*) and "local democracy" especially at district level. Social and ideological tolerance increased notwithstanding the terrorist activities of a few militant left-wing extremists whose repercussions were briefly felt but failed to check the process of improved social relations. On a backdrop of economic prosperity there developed what Jurgen Habermas has called *Verfassungspatriotismus* a "constitutional patriotism." With widespread affection for the democratic constitution, the old ghosts of the nation's past were exorcised. Anchoring Federal Germany to the bosom of western democracies seems to have worked.

This development was in part only possible because of the cataclysm of 1945 which eliminated from the political scene the strength of the Prussian *Junkers*, put an end to the power of the military, shattered the links and reproduction of traditional political elites and overall loosened former social constraints. Finally it put into parenthesis the question of a national state, its accomplishment seemingly a politic stalemate, to such an extent that the new West German identity was formed by a systematic distancing from the old discourse on nationhood. The second set of factors concerns the westernization of German culture, due to the ever present American model especially the media but also because of greater European integration and the increase of contact with other peoples. It is true that apart from these external influences there have been attempts to revive past traditions that were characteristically German, such as those of the liberal revolution of 1848. But it is just as significant that the measure of these developments — and this is where we return to the problem of *Sonderweg* — is provided by the more or less idealized image or representation of western democracy. As if Germany, while at the same time recognizing its own differences, were obliged to compare itself with its western neighbors.

The problem of course was not viewed in the same light in the People's Republic of Germany where they tried, more systematically that in the Federal German Republic, to reactivate the democratic inheritance of Germany: from peasant wars to the workers movement, through the protagonists of the *Aufklarung*, the classical humanists and the German Jacobites. Yet here also, apart from the official historians, eyes were turned towards the west, similar to all the other countries of central Europe. For many, French history and in particular the ideas of 1789, were the reference by which political and social processes were judged. To the extent that one might say that the apprenticeship for the autumn 1989 occurred as echoes of the bicentenary of the French Revolution. Which explains why Franco-German relations (and to a lesser degree Germano-British) reflect the *moral and institutional* health of democratic ideas.

In many ways the interaction of these two democratic areas raises questions that even now underpin the democratic process. The relative stability and smooth functioning of the democratic institutions of Federal Germany should not obscure the fact that a true sign of the democratic organization of society is that its citizens actively participate in resolving problems. Also the ability to integrate the forces of contention and the aptitude to generate ways of containing government that adapt to continual structural changes. From this point of view, this is an endless process especially since yesterday's enemy no longer serves as an external threat. Self-satisfaction at having finally established democratic legitimacy should not still the imperative for continually renewing the process of legitimization, nor the periodic assessment of what has been achieved.

The new German state will not be able to found its democratic culture solely as a reaction to the pre-1945 era. Democracy needs to be established as the contemporary German "norm," while at the same time maintaining the twin dynamism of continuity and a break with history.

CHRONOLOGY

1786	Death of Frederick II, King of Prussia and an enlightened despot.
1789	The events in France were greeted with hope and even enthusiasm by the intellectual elites of the German *Aufklarung*.
1790	Death of Joseph II, emperor and an enlightened despot.
1792	Revolutionary France declares war on the Hapsburgs. Prussia joins the anti-French coalition (April).
1796-1806	The French armies, as a result of victories and reversals occupy most of Rhenania.
1806	Napoleon forms the Confederation of the Rhine. End of the German Holy Roman Empire: François II releases the Germans from the oath of allegiance to the emperor.
1806-1825	Romantic political thinking (Schelling, Fichte, Schlegel, Muller, Gorres, Savigny, Kleist) reacting to the Aufklarung, tried to elucidate a doctrine specific to the Germans against the principles of 1789.
1818-1825	Birth of the "National Liberal" movement (Wecker, Bassermann, Hecker, Struve, Dahlmann), drawing on the English and French examples in their demands for institutions which involved elected representative assemblies.
1848-1849	Revolution breaks out in Vienna (13 March) then in Berlin (18-19 March). Under pressure, in many German states the overpowered sovereigns were forced to agree to reforms or liberal constitutions. In Frankfurt, a

Parliament elected by all the Germans proclaims their "fundamental rights" and attempts to set up a Liberal Empire under the Prussian king Frederick William IV. The latter refuses (1849): failure of the attempts at reform and limiting of freedom.

1848-1870   At home or in exile (Paris and London): spread of German socialist thought (Moses Hess, B. Bauer, A. Ruge. K. Marx, F. Engels, Rodbertus, Duncker, F. Lassalle, Schulze-Delitzsch), underpinned by several key dates. The *Communist Manifesto* 1848; the forming of the General Union of German Workers by Lassalle in 1863; the first volume of *Das Capital* in 1867; founding of the *Arbeiterbildungsverein* in 1868.

1859   Founding in Frankfurt of a *Nationalverein* (National Union) that suggests it takes on the task of the 1848 Parliament.

1862   Bismark heads the Prussian government.

1866   Prussian victory at Sadowa: Prussia defeats Austria and becomes the major German power. The National liberals, until then hostile to Bismark's authoritarianism, strongly rally round, in both the Prussian Landtag and the Reichstag of the new North German Confederation.

1869   Congress of Eisenach: founding of the Social Democratic Workers Party with at its head W. Liebnecht and A. Bebel; Marx's influence is strong.

1870-1871   Prussian victory over France. Treaty of Frankfurt (May 1871): The Empire (II Reich) is formed around William I (1871-1888) and his chancellor Bismark (1871-1890).

1872-1875   Bismark's policy of *Kulturkampf*.

1875	Congress of Gotha: founding of the *Sozialdemokratie* with the amalgamation of Marxist and Lassallian groups.
1891	The Erfurt program was adopted by the *Sozialdemokratie*.
1899	Mayence Congress: the Christian movement is formed around a political party Zentrum (the largest party in the Reichstag from 1901 onwards) and an association of Christian worker's unions.
1914	Rallying to war, including the *Sozialdemokratie*.
1916	Forming in March of *Spartakusbund*, for an end to the fighting.
1918	Large Spatakist disturbances. Founding of the KPD (Communist). The government includes Social Democrats (Max and Bade).
1919	Treaty of Versailles (28 June). Democratic Constitution of Weimar preceded by a declaration of the fundamental rights and duties of Germans.
1923	Re-launch of the NSDAP in Munich.
1932	Victory of the NSDAP in the elections (July: 37.4%; November: 33%).
1933	Hitler in power (30 January). Disappearance of the Weimar Republic (burning of the Reichstag 27-28 February). % March elections: NSDAP: 43.9%. Vote giving Hitler complete power (23 March). From November on, all union, socialist, Christian and liberal structures were dissolved or dissolved themselves.
1945	Unconditional surrender (8 May). Quadripartite occupation system set up by the allies (30 July). Potsdam conference which established the terms of quadripartite

	occupation. The Soviets, in their sector, entrust much responsibilities to the nascent German political parties : KPD, SPD and CDU. Agrarian reform and desire to build an "anti-fascist democratic order."
1946	In the Soviet sector the amalgamation of the KPD and SPD (April) to become the SED. This party wins the elections (September) with 47% of the vote against the Liberals (25%) and the CDU (24%).
1948	Break-down of the quadripartite agreement (June-July). Need for an American aerial bridge to supply the western sectors of Berlin which were isolated by the Soviet blockade.
1949	The constituent Parliamentary council adopts the "fundamental laws" of the future Federal Republic (8 May). The Congress of People's in the Soviet zone in Berlin adopts the constitution of the Democratic Republic (30 May). Konrad Adenauer (CDU 1949-1963) was elected Chancellor (15 September) of the Federal Republic. Creation of the German Confederation of Unions (DGB).
1950	Multiparty elections are ended in the DDR (May). Henceforth they would be based on single lists.
1953	Revolt in east Berlin (16-17 June). Social (against increases in work loads) and political demands (free elections). The Red Army occupies the town. Purge of the SED under the leadership of Walter Ulbricht.
1956	The Franco-German rapprochement is enshrined in the Luxembourg agreement signed by Adenauer and Mollet.

1959   *Sozialdemokratie* agrees on the Godesberg program for "democratic socialism."

1961   To stop the influx of east Germans to the west the Berlin wall is built (August).

1963   The DGB adopts its "fundamental" program rejecting the collective appropriation of capital and reaffirming its belief in fundamental democratic rights.

1969   The Social Democrats (Willy Brandt) come to power. They will stay until 1982 (Helmut Schmidt 1974-1982).

1971   At the VIII Congress of the SED, Erich Honecker is Ulbricht's successor.

1972   Fundamental treaty between BDR and the DDR: mutual recognition of the frontiers of the two states, prelude to the policy of "peaceful coexistence" (November).

1982   Rise to power of Helmut Kohl (CDU-CSU) after a vote of "constructive no-confidence" that made the SPD fall following a change of alliance by the FPD liberals (Genscher).

1989   *22-23 June*: SED condemns the "anti-socialist forces" in Eastern Europe and reaffirms its support for the Chinese regime.

29 July-10 September: Breach and then dismantling of the Iron curtain in Hungary; almost 25,000 east Germans cross to the BDR.

24-25 September: The New Forum movement unites groups in opposition to the communist regime. 8,000 people demonstrate in Leipzig demanding the legalization of NF.

2 October: 20,000 demonstrators in the Ring of Leipzig following the religious service in the church of Saint Nicholas.

7 October: 40th anniversary of the DDR. Gorbachev is there. Demonstrations in Berlin and Leipzig are put down by force.

9 October: 70,000 demonstrators in Leipzig.

18 October: Start of the "end" (Die Wende): E. Honecker relinquishes all his powers and is replaced by Egon Krenz.

26 October: First meeting between the SED and New Forum. Public debates are held in every town.

4 November: 1 million demonstrators in East Berlin (the largest protest gathering ever to take place in the DDR).

6-8 November: Proposal granting East Germans freedom of travel. New electoral law with the introduction of pluralism.

9 November: Opening of the Berlin wall. 4 million East Germans visit West Berlin and the BDR over the following two weekends.

17 November: Modrow coalition government in the DDR.

28 November: In front of the Bundestag, H. Kohl presents a plan for swift reunification.

8 December: Gregor Gysi is elected president of the SED instead of E. Krenz and chooses the new direction of "radical democracy."

1990

18 March: Elections in the DDR. Christian Democrats: 48%; SPD: 22%; Communists: 14%. Lothar de Maizieres becomes Prime Minister.

1 July: Economic and monetary union of both Germanys: one DM for 1 eastern mark.

12 September: Signature in Moscow of the treaty giving the final blessing to the reunification of Germany. The BDR would spend 12 billion DM for the departure of Soviet troops from the DDR.

3 October: German reunification.

2 December: General elections: Helmut Kohl's CDU wins.

ITALIAN DEMOCRACY

Eric Vial

There are several specific problems that have to be considered when looking at the history of democracy in Italy. For although there existed a long tradition of ideologues and theoreticians, starting with Giuseppe Mazzini and Carla Cattaneo in the 19th Century, they were marginalized by a history that was enacted without or against them. Reality had primacy over ideas. Later, and above all now, it would be much more acceptable for an Italian to write about Italian democracy; of its vitality and its failings. But coming from a Frenchman such a discourse could seem unjust or aggressive, even when it might appear more flattering than what is said in Italy itself. Notwithstanding, the history of Italian democracy is first and foremost that of universal suffrage; which for men was achieved in 1919 and for women in 1946 (and by 18-21 year olds in 1975). It is also a running commentary on the role of the ordinary citizen in the rule of the city and the spread of power within society; where at times dramatic problems become linked with remarkable successes.

THE FRENCH LEGACY:
THE NATION AND LIBERALISM.

The democratic ideal in Italy in the first part of the 19th Century appears to have been brought over by the armies of the French Revolution and to be intimately linked with the idea of union. In fact Italian democratic traditions joined together with unity, democracy and French intervention; one must bear in mind the existence of a vigorous Italian Jacobin tradition, of sister republics founded by the Directory and of the three states under Napoleon, the abolition of frontiers which stimulated trade, the creation of an Italian army, the new part to be played by merchants, lawyers and men of letters who henceforth were aware that they could run the country just as well as the clerics and the nobility. Everything was mixed together, but 1789 seems to have been the source of it all.

As for opponents of democracy, they insist that there was a national feeling that was expressed in literature before the French Revolution, on the small number of people who supported France, and on the fact that the only truly popular movement had been the *sanfedist* uprising: clerical, nationalist, anti-French and very anti-democratic. In their minds, the anxiety of revolution and the subsequent reaction to the invasion arrested the trend to unity that they felt was being traced at the end of the 18th Century.

Whatever the case, after 1815, when the wish to forget the revolution was nowhere greater than in Italy — split up into ten states, as everywhere else in Europe, it was easy, with nostalgia, to confuse the relative unity of the Napoleonic era with the principles of 1789: nationalism, democracy and liberalism made common cause.

Initially, liberalism had the upper hand over nationalism. The secret societies (*Carboneria*) demanded freedom of the press, assembly, religion and constitutional guarantees. But in 1830 their uprisings were to fail, without the desired French help and above all due to lack of coordination on a national level. Mazzini affirmed, in the light of this failure, the need for a popular uprising and a united republic: nation, liberalism and democracy would henceforth be joined together in people's minds. Yet the many attempts: in 1843, 1844 and 1845, were to result in total failure in the face of popular apathy or hostility.

From 1846 to 1848, popular uprisings and revolutions swept through Europe. All over constitutions and laws were agreed. Austria was forced out of the Lombardo-Venetian areas. Tensions increased. While revolution waned in Europe, Italy exploded. A republic was declared by Mazzini and Giuseppe Garibaldi in Rome and in Florence; democratic representatives defied the king of Naples. Rebel Messina was mercilessly bombarded. Austria crushed Piedmont and then "restored order," in Rome, in conjunction with the French of the Second Republic that had become conservative and clerical.

The liberals and republicans had failed. Victor Emmanuel II, the new king of Piedmont, was the only one to support the ideas of 1848. With this minimal guarantee of liberalism, unity around his person became the only priority. With the help of Napoleon III, the war against Austria resulted in the conquest of Lombardy, which was exchanged for Nice and Savoy. Then there was Garibaldi's expedition to Sicily; the democratic movement served as a pretext for the conquest of almost the whole of the peninsula. Europe favored unification around a king, rather than more contagious movements. In 1864 and 1870 the Austrian and French defeats by Bismark resulted in the annexation of Venice and Rome. Unification had been achieved. It had not been democratic, nor revolutionary, but dynastic.

A UNITED ITALY:
THE MONARCHY, TRANSFORMISM
AND DRIFT TO FASCISM

Every one of the annexations had been approved by male universal suffrage, yet this was far removed from democracy. The regime was defined by statute but the king had considerable power (ministers beholden solely to him, decrees having force of law...). However, the ministers who framed it resigned immediately it came into force, holding themselves responsible to the elected chamber. The letter of the text was given to parliamentary scrutiny. So as can be seen there existed liberal as well as potential authoritarian practices.

Elsewhere people were impressed by Garibaldi's expedition. Garibaldi, who was a democrat, created Italy through action and not in the name of an experiment in government. "The country was therefore open, when times were hard, to the lure of dramatic events." This went hand in hand with rejecting, apart for people such as Cattaneo the federalist, the idea of the rights of man that in the minds of many was associated with the 18th Century and French hegemony, in favor of the notion of duty, a favorite idea of Mazzini. Even among the republicans (monarchic) unity was to became more important than democracy. Francesco Crispi, Mazzini's right-hand man, rallied to the king in 1864: "Monarchy unites us, the republic would divide us."

Finally, and most importantly, the people were excluded from the nation by a voting system based on a poll-tax (although variable) and above all by a unity that operated against the Church and the south of the country. Pius IX, rejecting the liberalism of his youth, condemned the "usurping" state, and his text *Non Expedit* forbade Catholics from becoming "electors or representatives." The south of the country experienced military occupation under the guise of a policing operation against "brigands" that left festering wounds and allowed *mafia* type criminal organizations to appear as defenders of the people against the state, guaranteeing a basic form of "justice" while at the same time reinforcing the domination of the most powerful. These are rather glaring failures. Paradoxically they explain the evolution of Italy towards democracy — yet also its initial fragility.

The counter-attack of the Bourbons in the south, and by the clergy elsewhere, was a threat to the state which defended itself by widening its support among the middle classes. Hence the rise to power of Mazzini's democrats rallying round the king, the advent of the *historical left*. By stages it extended the legal nation until universal suffrage for all men was adopted. For Giovanni Giolitti, the leader of the government from 1901 to 1914, it was a question of integrating the masses, getting them used to the "parliamentary

system," avoiding revolution and involving all the Italians in the
running of the nation.

Transformism logically arose from this. The historical left
hoped to transcend parliamentary cleavages and so compensate for
the restricted nature of the electoral system. Consequently there
emerged large coalition governments based on compromise and
corruption; this was the price for widening the political spectrum
and progressively attracting opposition representatives. Giolitti in
any case was not just content to bring a few opposition members
into the moderate coalition, but swung whole groups onto the side
of government, offering the socialists its neutrality in social
conflict and in turn using them as bogeymen to force the Vatican
to abandon its *Non Expedit* in order to save society.

The political and social consequences of transformism were
quite considerable. But was this democracy? It has been viewed as
such in order to condemn more strongly, by contrast, the fascist
dictatorship. Or else it was rejected to avoid a straightforward
restoration following the war. In fact, it did lead to universal
suffrage; yet it failed to consolidate it and finally collapsed. It
might have become a democracy but did not know how to defend
itself in the face of reactionary tendencies and ultimately fascism.
Consensus and parliamentary alliances precluded the forming of
large popular parties that might have produced a truly adversarial
system. Furthermore the democratic opposition, powerful among
the working class, who in 1879 had created the *Democratic League*
together with the socialists (but they feared the effects of universal
suffrage because of their distrust of the catholic peasantry), were
thoroughly beaten in the 1890 elections as a consequence of their
limited social aims. Marginalized by the liberal block and the rise
of the socialists, it never became a viable alternative. Above all
criticism increased over the general mediocrity of the individuals
involved, their lack of interest in the common welfare, southern
client politicians, the absence of idealism or vision and corruption.
Transformism could not manage to cope with democratic change
through traditional means nor the rise of alien subversive forces.

Italy illustrates the idea of Arno Meyer concerning the
aggressive return of the Ancien Regime around the 1900s.
Intellectuals were "antipositivist" and anti-democratic; apart from

a few exceptions such as Luigi Einaudi or Gaetano Salvemini. The Catholic Church was far too strident in its condemnation of even liberalism to understand political democracy, and traditional liberals such as Gaetano Mosca rejected universal suffrage in the name of *reason*.

From Germany came the idea of an *ethnic state*, divorced from the *will* of its citizens, superior to the nation and individual rights and akin to government. Francesco Crispi in power between 1887 and 1896, wanted to save the executive from the vicissitudes of elected representatives, whereas Sidney Sonnino, leader of the right, demanded a return to the statutes (his reading rather than that of parliament). Giolitti himself was chosen by the king without parliamentary support. The winds of change (restoration) were in the air.

More seriously subversive ideas were gaining credence. On the left Giolitti's reappointment caused opposition. The socialist party veered away from reform to the extremism of its rising star: Benito Mussolini. Revolutionary syndicalism, too literally, drew support from the writings of George Sorel. Above all on the right nationalism mixed Nietzsche and Annunzio, a desire for action with violence, hatred of democracy and of France (characterized by Pigalle), of the Enlightenment and the principles of 1789. All came to a head during the *glorious May*, when ordinary people in the streets forced Parliament (and the majority of Italians), in support of the king, into war; the First World War, still heralded by some nationalists as the end of *parliamentary dictatorship*. (sic)

A few democrats also wanted to fight the "right's" war, jumping at the chance to help republican France and the destruction of the "peoples' prisons".... However war would destroy social cohesion, aggravate the tendency to violence and undermine democracy just when universal suffrage was instituted and would serve as a matrix for fascism. Fascism, by totally different means, would for its own purposes espouse the plan of integrating the masses, gathering about itself all anti-democratic factions, both underground and literary, for as long as the political system continued to survive.

PARLIAMENTARISM AND DEMOCRACY

Following the fall of Mussolini, democracy was not a high priority. The first government of Badoglio (July 1943 to April 1944) was said to be apolitical and established an ultra conservative regime. Part of the Catholic Church wanted to put people from Catholic Action at the head of structural fascist organizations to create a Salazar-type regime. The strikes of 1943 decided otherwise; as well as the Resistance, the national liberation committees, the fact that Italy was henceforth on the side of the democracies and the need for outside models following fascist self-sufficiency (autarchy).... Palmiro Togliatti, head of the Italian Communist Party, was in the second Bodoglio government as were the leaders of all the anti-fascist parties returned from exile in subsequent governments under Ivanoe Bonomi .

The birth of democracy was dominated by two mass movements: the Communist Party (CP) and the Christian Democrats (CD), representing the people and the Church. Both were absent from the first Italian democratic experiment of the 19th Century. Both confused characteristics of state and party and had democratic credentials that were not above reproach. Traditional democratic parties remained marginalized and the rapid disappearance of the Action Party, spawned by the resistance, was an indication of their failure. Nevertheless, the Italian Communist Party had been formed in opposition to Mussolini (unlike the French Communist Party who had been against Poincare and Herriot), its leaders acutely aware that geographically Italy was in the west. As for the Christian Democrats, Alcide De Gasperi, originally a liberal, was unsuccessful in convincing the whole Catholic hierarchy of the wisdom of his policies of integration.

In 1946, following a referendum using universal suffrage of males and females, Italy became a republic and formed a constituent Assembly dominated by the CD (35.2% of the vote) the Socialist Party (20.7%) and the ICP (19%). They drew up a constitution which was agreed by almost a full majority at the end of 1947 and remains in force today. Some were opposed to this text because it was felt to be too bourgeois, anti-democratic and although it paid due regard to freedom it did not encourage involvement in public life... Nevertheless the constitution was a turning point; with its emphasis on universal suffrage and the rights of man, a novelty in itself. It went further than just notional freedom, considering how each person might fulfil their role, anticipated the role of the parties and above all the regions which were given extended powers, hence bringing decision-making closer to the citizen. It also involved elements of direct democracy: the right to petition, introduction of laws and referenda on popular demand.

In fact the Constitution was not enforced for a long time, or rather was restricted to what would establish a simple parliamentary system. The laws on referenda were passed in 1970, also when the first regional elections took place (apart from in Sicily, Sardinia, Trentin-Upper-Adiga, Frioul-Venetia, Julia and Val d'Aoste where decentralization had already been operating). The supreme council of the judiciary, guarantor of the independence of justice, was set up in 1958. The constitutional court was set up in 1956 to reformulate laws deemed incompatible with the constitution. Another example: the fascist law prohibiting ordinary citizens from moving from villages inside Italy — that in fact forced people to move secretly to the big cities where they might remain anonymous, to the detriment of medium sized towns — was only repealed in 1961.

This can be understood as a consequence of the violent conflict between the DC government and the left wing ICP and ISP. During constitutional discussions the left favored Jacobin centralization, while the Catholics advocated decentralization in the name of the principle of subsidiarity. When the legislative elections of 1948 resulted in the victory of the CD with 48.5% of the vote and an overall majority of seats, yet with the left dominating certain regions, their positions changed. The CD refused to water down their central powers while the left wanted counter-powers. These tensions emerged during the cold war, whipping the pro-Soviet CP and SP into a frenzy. Furthermore the attempted assassination of P. Togliatti in July 1948, together with mass demonstrations and the occupation of strategic points, alarmed the government. The reaction of the government was transparent:

Mario Scelba's policy, as minister of the interior from 1947 to 1958, encouraged discrimination, dismissals, court actions against former resistants and bloody repression...

Even so democracy was not really under threat. The ICP did not have any intention of staging an uprising. And as a buffer to the influence of the Catholic church, despite its CD majority in parliament, De Gasperi made alliances with the small center parties who were the guardians of the liberal and democratic tradition. Apart from transformism and outside influences on the internal struggle within the Christian Democrat movement, a fundamentalist swing would have been impossible. For example, in 1952 the Vatican supported a CD-MSI (fascist party) list in the municipal elections in Rome but the maneuver failed.

The wish of the Christian Democrats to develop better political relations, as well as the decrease in tension of the cold war, by and large explains why from about the mid-fifties they adhered more closely to the constitution. Following the victory of Aldo Moro's "Democratic Initiative" movement at the Christian Democrat congress in 1954, and the election with the support of the left of Giovanni Gronchi as president of the republic, a few initial moves were made from 1956 to 1958. Despite strong tensions following the formation of a largely CD government with the ISM support, provoking numerous demonstrations between 1959 and 1962, this development led to a broadening of the political base of democracy by involving the ISP, which had distanced itself from the ICP, in political power. The center left, approved of by Kennedy contrary to the advice of the State Department and by John XXIII against his Curia and by the big bosses against the others, did very little to enforce the democratic potential of the constitution, although they did open up state employment to women.

Yet the general trend of society made government less willing to act in an authoritarian way, in Italy as elsewhere. Social tensions, less marked by the reverberations of 1968 than by the "hot autumn" of the unions in 1969 and the electoral rise of the ICP, meant that the government in the end threw out ballast; hence the laws allowing divorce, organizing the popular initiative referendum and the first regional elections. These last measures also created a separate avenue for mediation, thus avoiding every conflict going to central government.

The reverse side of the coin was that there were plans for coup d'états, for instance in 1970 with prince Borghese, the right wing terrorist attacks in Milan's Piazza Fontana in December 1969 which aimed to destroy democracy by forcing it to defend itself "in the name of order"; as well as the blunders of the secret services which are being investigated at this moment. A further "other" side of the coin has supporters of the far left and Catholics becoming more radical, leading to the bloody terrorism of the Red Brigade (96 dead among whom Aldo Moro, between 1976 and 1980). These were the years of "lead," where for some people, hatred of the state and the ICP which supported it, a wish to show that democracy is a bait to ensnare us and a straightforward fascination for violence, became all mixed up.

Even so terrorism was defeated without undermining democracy and ... without any inexplicable suicides of the terrorists. Since 1970 most of the institutions outlined in 1947 have been set up: the Italians live institutionally in a system which should allow local autonomy and the spread of political power throughout the strata of society.

ON DEMOCRACY TODAY

There are many ways of proving that Italian democracy remains vibrant and vital. For example, participation in elections: every citizen is on the electoral list, ballots are frequently staged yet 80-90% will vote. Also the ability to take to the street to voice concerns without causing a breach of the peace which was a frequent occurrence. Hence at the end of 1984, over a few days, two huge demonstrations organized against fascist terrorism which had resulted in the death of twenty people in the Florence-Bologna train and in support of aid — subsequently given — to the third world. One might add the real, widespread interest in politics, or the stability of the IMS at 5% of the votes; or again the fact that the ICP (which since the congress of Rimini in Feb 1991 has become the Democratic Left), as its new name suggests, is a perfectly "democratic" party. Indeed all this should be emphasized.

Yet there are still many grey areas. The CD has been in power since 1945, even though in 1981 they lost their monopoly of the presidency of the council. There is no changeover/alternating of political power. It is sometimes said to be an "imperfect bipartisan system."[18] Furthermore the people's vote has less importance than the negotiations of the leaders of the parties. Hence, during the 1960's, change occurred because of the drawing in of the ISP into mainstream politics. In 1973, by suggesting, through a "historic compromise," joint government with the CD the ICP followed the same practice. During the "years of lead" the party joined in with the majority parties, and still works extensively in parliamentary commissions. With an "eternal majority" negotiating with an "eternal opposition" the idea of neo-transformism raises its head: "good government" is linked more to negotiated unanimity than a clearly defined majority and minority representing the electorate. This of course is the *Italian* idea of democracy. However, this lack of possibility of a changeover of political power for example might explain at least partially the advent of terrorism.

Furthermore, the "eternal majority" tend to feel that they own the state itself. The state in turn, ever since fascism, has controlled an extensive share of the economy, hence a distribution of posts and fiefdoms, the *lotizzazione*, which results not only in patronage of the bosses but also those who control the actions of government. Political patronage in some ways seems to be a way of rewarding the negligence or arrogance of some administrations.... On another level the idea that the political class have ownership of the state is reflected in the fact that parliamentary votes are secret which means that the electorate has no way of controlling its representatives. As for the permanent nature of the majority, this is reinforced by hidden structures which are meant to, by all means fair or foul, combat an alternative left-wing majority, as well as a corresponding "hidden state." For indeed, while the problem of

---

[18]G. Galli, *Il bipartitismo imperfetto*, Il Mulino, Bologna, 1966.

left-wing terrorism was very satisfactorily dealt with, many of the massacres which were claimed by the extreme right remain unpunished.

Finally, and this is a problem increasingly getting worse, patronage is being joined, from Palma to Naples, by the economic and political rule of organized crime, the *mafia* and others, so corrupting regional and even national politicians. How can one speak of democracy when local elections in Calabria result in dozens of "politico-economic" murders? Real power is no longer in the ballot box. This at least tempers our optimism over the vitality of Italian democracy and explains why there are some movements of rejection: the growth of the northern regional leagues for example, relying on "racism" against southerners, or else the election to Parliament of a porn star....

CHRONOLOGY

1791-1795	Repression of the Jacobins.
1796-1799	French conquest, sister-Republics.
1799	Collapse of the latter, Sanfedist uprising.
1800	French reconquest, reorganization of the country into the Italian kingdom, the Church states and the Kingdom of Naples.
1815	Splintering of the country under Austrian control.
1818-1821	Liberal revolutionary plots foiled in Romagne as well as Milan, Naples and Modena.
1830-1831	Further revolutionary outburst and failure.
1846-1848	Every Italian states give itself a constitution.
1848-1849	National republican uprising in Tuscany, Rome and Venice, put down by Austria and France; Liberalism survives only in Piedmont.
1859-1861	Piedmont conquers Lombardy with French help, then the whole of Italy apart from Rome and Venice during Garibaldi's expedition of "a thousand" to Sicily.
1864	Taking of Venice.
1870-1871	Capture of Rome which is proclaimed the country's capital.
1876	Rise to power of the "historic" left.
1882, 1888, 1913	Extension of the electoral body.
1915	Participation in World War I.
1919	First elections with universal suffrage for men.
1922-1926	Conquest of the state by fascism with fascistic laws abolishing pluralism.
1943	Fall of Mussolini, government of Marshal Badoglio.
1946	Women vote, referendum establishing the republic by 12 million to 10 votes.

1947	Exclusion of the ICP and ISP from government, start of several Christian Democrat De Gasperi governments with Liberal, Republican, and Social Democrat participation; approval of the constitution.
1956	Creation of the constitutional court.
1958	Creation of the Upper Council for Justice.
1960	Resignation of the Tambroni government, who came to power thanks to the neo-fascists; large demonstrations against the latter.
1963	Aldo Moro government with the support of the socialists: start of the "center left."
1964	Attempt at a coup d'état using the carabinieri.
1969	Start of a series of fascist inspired acts of terrorism.
1970	Law on divorce, law organizing referenda; first regional elections.
1973	The ICP proposed the "historic compromise."
1976	Giulio Andreotti government invested thanks to the abstention of all the "constitutional spectrum" including the ICP.
1978	Assassination of Aldo Moro by the Red Brigade, the pinnacle of extreme left-wing criminal actions.
1981	Giovanni Spandolini, a republican, the first leader of a non-Christian Democrat government since 1945.
1987	Ilona Staller, "Cicciolina," porn star, elected deputy.
1990	Local elections, rise of the regional leagues in the north (19% of votes in Lombardy); consolidation of mafia type power in the south.
1991	At the congress of Rimini the communists change their name: the Democratic Left.

SPAIN:
A LATECOMER TO
THE LAURELS OF DEMOCRACY

Guy Hermet

Like Germany, Italy and Portugal, Spain belonged to the branch of "late-developers" in the European family of democracies. Yet it was to do so for its own specific reasons. From the 19th Century up until the 1920's, Liberalism which everywhere else in western Europe had become accepted, was confronted by two ideologically different enemies, that in reality were joined: the anarchists and Catholic traditionalist. Later, the intolerance of the political classes would destroy the republican regime, born in 1931, well before its final destruction in the civil war of 1936-39. This ultimate "war of religion" was the price that Spain had to pay to liberate itself from the final vestiges of its ancien regime, leading to the inauguration, after 1975, of its own brand of democratic monarchy, and so in the end a less different destiny from that of the rest of Europe.

THE REJECTION OF LIBERALISM

It is rather surprising that Spanish Liberals were the first to give liberalism its political meaning when from 1820-23 they had a brief progressive episode. Yet they were soon defeated by the "hundred thousand sons of Saint Louis," sent by France in accordance with the Holy Alliance of anti-revolutionary monarchies. Above all Spanish liberalism found itself divorced from its roots which were then in France and Great Britain.

In terms of ideals, Spain would turn its back on the spirit of the Enlightenment after the Napoleonic invasion. Up until the 1850's the most influential thinkers were rather the theoreticians of the counter-revolution: Burke, De Maistre, Bonald et al. among these Balmes and Donoso Cortes. Their renown was international among reactionary circles, whereas their liberal homologues, by comparison, were far less famous. Nor were things to change much afterwards. During the first half of this century, of course, the majority of writers and artists were on the side of liberalism and progress. On the other hand the only noteworthy thinker of world renown, the philosopher Jose Ortega y Gasset, was a skeptic who viewed democracy as the dangerous eruption of the uneducated masses.

On the level of political events, the shortcomings of the secular liberal classes were also plain to see. The French occupation of 1808-13 heaped opprobrium upon them. Henceforth Liberals were deemed to be collaborators — los afrancesados — or else extremist resistants — the Cadix Council members — tainted with revolutionary impiety. In the absence of a modern ruling elite, power was therefore fought over by the ultras and the military; the latter wreathed in glory because of their fight against the French. Spain would begin an era of "pronunciamientos," from the constant intervention of the military in political life over the period 1814-74. Over the next 70 years the reigns of monarchs, as well as governments, would begin and end because of them, together with the first liberal reforms which were equally the product of a military initiative. Civilian politicians were only a front for the officers, on whom they depended to get to power and maintain themselves in power. In any event the military caste with greater wealth became more bourgeois, and could see that their interests coincided with those of the upper middle classes and modern aristocrats, with whom they progressively formed a new ruling class.

The progressive officers, of whom the figurehead was General Espartero, governed the destiny of the country until 1843. They were then followed by moderate colleagues. Anxious to avert social revolution, they strove in vain between 1870 and 1873 to buttress the constitutional monarchy of King Amedee of Savoy, before being overcome by the ephemeral Ist Republic of 1873. Then the legitimate Bourbon dynasty was restored through a coup d'état on the 3 January 1875. Yet even though this restoration marked the end of the era of "pronunciamentos," and augured in formal political liberalism in Spain, it did not lead in itself to the birth of a parliamentary regime similar to that of neighboring countries.

Indeed this regime found itself burdened by the impossibility of creating a constitutional party to serve as a political axis for a society that would remain profoundly Catholic. This inability would form the legacy for a protracted armed conflict between the Carlists and successive liberal governments. The Carlists represented the spearhead of traditional Catholicism. In contrast to the French Chouans, their advantage lay in the protracted nature of the struggle, their military strength and their doctrinal coherence. From 1829 to 1876 they represented, depending on the period, a virtual or real counter-government in Spain, and would lead three civil wars in 1833-40, 1846-49 and 1872-76 against the Madrid government which was considered to be atheist. During these periods of open conflict the Carlists held sway over the territories of the north of the country. They recognized successive monarchs from what they considered to be the legitimate line, had a regular army, a fledgling administration, issued currency and maintained quasi-diplomatic relations with the Holy See. More damaging was the fact that Carlism would survive its military defeat in 1876 and subsequent desertion by the Vatican. On the one hand it was transformed into a party deeply hostile to the parliamentary monarchy of 1875-1923, thus blocking the way for the development of a broad Catholic political formation that might have consolidated the regime. On the other hand Carlist elements firmly implanted in Catalonia and the Basque country, gave birth to the autonomist movements of today. One way or another the Carlist legacy explains why a large section of the middle classes would reject the national parties, either to become actively opposed or else to rally solely round the Catalan or Basque parties. Either way they deprived the first parliamentary and electoral experiments in Spain, of moderate support which was sorely needed.

At the other extreme of the political spectrum, the spread of anarchism led to similar shortcomings among the common people. Introduced in 1868 in Barcelona, it quickly gained hold of the agricultural proletariat of Andalusia. The libertarian current would hold sway over a large part of the Spanish working class right up until 1936. Although its ideology has much in common with democracy, its impact on the democratic process would be most harmful. Anarchism paralysed the Spanish labor movement and transformed it into an archaic exception within a Europe generally at grips with unions and parties of marxist or social democrat persuasion. Furthermore, by advocating systematic abstention in elections they turned the masses away from "bourgeois democracy." They made the constitutional monarchy illegitimate in the eyes of the proletariat without proposing any viable alternative to replace it.

Of course it has to be said that the leaders of the parliamentary regime did nothing to woo the reticent or openly hostile populace. Convinced that the country was not ready for universal suffrage, which would be proclaimed in 1890, they preferred to stage-manage the regular transfer of power from conservatives to liberals and vica-versa, with electoral fraud and intimidation. The *Caciques* imposed their own laws in each electoral area. Patronage and the buying of votes were commonplace, while major decisions would not be made in parliament but elsewhere in secret negotiations between the few political leading lights. In 1907 a new electoral law made the situation worse with the decision that unopposed candidates in an electoral area should be declared elected without holding a ballot. By assassinating rival candidates if need be, a seventh to a third of the electorate, depending on the year, were deprived of their effective right to vote. At the same time the number of deputies "elected" in this way increased from 119 out of 404 in 1910, to 146 out of 409 in 1923. Even though this procedure helped to maintain the hegemony of the two dominant parties at a time when their hold was crumbling, obviously it did little to diminish the lack of credibility of the electoral system in the eyes of the Spanish. So on top of voluntary abstentions was added henceforth those deprived of the vote. Those who really took part in the electoral process, who in 1899 were only 35%, dropped from 46% in 1910 to 44.6% in 1919, and 29.4% in 1923.

In the years following the Russian Revolution, barely nascent Spanish democracy in effect succeeded in losing its legitimacy. It appeared to some on the one hand to be the mask behind which destructive popular forces hid, and to others as the subterfuge of the counter-revolution. As in Italy the ground was ready for a providential dictator. From 1923 to 1930 this took the largely benign form of Miguel Primo de Rivera. Relatively liberal, he would turn out to be far preferable to Mussolini or General Franco. Yet through him the fatal current of authoritarianism would for the first time this Century overtake the Spanish.

THE FAILED REPUBLIC

The Republic which was declared on the 14 April 1931 was the second of its kind in Spain, following after a lapse of more than half a century the Ist Republic which had been born in 1873 and died 10 months later. This Republic meanwhile came out of very different circumstances, with an ease that would surprise the republican leaders themselves. Of course the heteroclite character of the coalition that was formed was cause for worry. Yet this assembly of die-hard republicans, representatives of left and center parties, of Catalan autonomists and penitent monarchists, was also a measure of the inevitable need for compromise and moderation. Nobody could foresee the chain of events which would lead this initial experiment in true democracy to the catastrophe of July 1936.

This in part was a result of the anarchist rivalry vis-a-vis the republican authorities, reviled almost as much by the libertarians as the monarchy. Also up until 1935 the communists perceived those socialists who from 1931-33 had joined the government as "class traitors." In turn the extreme religious right hatched plots which led to the failed putsch of General Sanjurjo. Yet the most serious threat derived from the gulf that developed between, on the one hand the republicans and the socialists, and on the other Catholics who were prepared to rally to the new regime.

Problems began in the autumn of 1931 and the drafting of a constitution. The left dominated the assembly elected on the 28 June. Its leader, Manuel Azana wanted to hurry things along to weaken the reactionary forces in society and to satisfy the maximalists. Consequently he came into conflict with the Church over the abolition of the religious budget, the banning of the Jesuits and the suppression, in reality impossible, of Catholic schools. After the promulgation of the constitution he continued his punitive design as president of the council. Azana turned his attention to the army which he proposed to modernize by reducing the numbers of officers. He challenged the landowners by instituting agrarian reform, which although ineffective, was felt to be revolutionary measures. In short the new republican regime seemed intent on uniting, at one and the same time, all their enemies rather than dealing with them one at a time, splitting them when the opportunity might arise.

The victory of the right in the elections of 19 November 1933 confirmed these blunders. It also added to the conflict in another way. The main winner of the election was the CEDA, a legalist, if not republican, Catholic party under the leadership of Jose-Maria Gil-Robles. Yet the defeated left refused to allow it to form a government, labelling it fascist. In these circumstances Lerroux, a radical, became president of the council. Even so much worse was to happen only the following year. On the 4 October 1934 CEDA forced the fall of the cabinet in order to end their isolation. In order to get the investiture of a new government, the president of the Republic Alcala Zamra, was forced to agree to giving them three ministries. The reaction came immediately. In Madrid the socialist union UGT launched a general strike and tried to seize power with the support of the communists. In Catalonia the president of the Generalitat Luis Companys, declared full autonomy. In the coal rich zone of Oviedo in Asturias, the miners succeeded in uniting all the tendencies of the workers: socialists, communists and anarchists.

Everywhere else the uprising failed, while in Asturias the miners alone continued to resist. Well disciplined, with explosives and arms seized from local arsenals, they occupied quite a large area including Gijon, Mieres and Sama de Langreo. The revolt in the Asturias had begun. It would last for a month until it was stamped out by colonial units sent from Morocco under the command of Generals Franco and Goded. Then the ever-ready to compromise republic crumbled. From then on the condemnation and amnesty of insurgents would occur in relation to each sides' ideological beliefs. Spain had already become divided into two irredeemably hostile camps.

A year and a half later, by a swing of the pendulum, the Popular Front just won the elections of February 1936 with only 48.3% of the total votes cast. Once more president of the Republic, Azana strove to temper the desire of the left for revenge without truly succeeding. The left/right cleavage deepened in line with the exactions that were being meted out all over the place. Above all, the Catholic masses and the middle classes, robbed of their electoral victory in 1933, withdrew their support from a regime that they perceived was partisan. The party armed militias marched through the streets, strikes followed on one after another, the Phalangists made important headway, the *pistoleros* fought and meanwhile the military hatched their plots. The "tragic spring" of 1936 began to resemble an armed wake in anticipation of a putsch. The right wanted it because they could not foresee any other alternative to revolution that they feared was approaching. The left was also waiting expectantly; convinced that they would crush it with a massive popular reaction, from which would arise the new revolutionary Spain.

The coup d'état took place on the 18 July 1936. It failed in military terms since the government kept nominal control of Madrid, Barcelona and most of the country. Yet they would lose real power when the civil war began. Two states were formed. In the republican zone, slowly but surely eroded by the "national" army, the powers seized by the unions and workers parties were only partially restored to the legal government by the end of 1937. There took place well before the term was coined a popular democracy, under the often strict control of the communists who controlled the police and the armed forces, reorganized with material assistance from the Soviet Union. In the nationalist zone, where General Franco seized power on the 1 October 1936, a part fascist part clerical dictatorship was consolidated and was spreading out territorially. He carried the day on the 1 April 1939 when he occupied Madrid, in which the republicans had just finished tearing themselves apart with the last internecine civil war of communists, socialists and anarchists. The first Spanish attempt at democracy had ended, even though it would remain in the hearts of hundreds of thousands of exiles.

THE DEMOCRATIC MONARCHY

Over a period of 39 years, the seemingly endless Francist parenthesis was synonymous with repression and absence of legal democratic expression. Yet it encompassed at least two distinct periods: the first was total oppression and material stagnation, the second — from 1960 onwards — of gradual liberalization of everyday life and economic and social upheaval. This second phase saw Spain join the group of industrialized societies. It did away with the agrarian problem which the republic had stumbled against. It also coincided with a fundamental change in outlook, involved at the same time changes in mores and social interaction as well as the disappearance of anarchism and Catholic "aggiornamento." Francism, furthermore bequeathed a future monarchy to Spain, when in 1969 the old *Caudillo* designated Prince Juan Carlos as his heir. In many ways the Spanish were already emerging reconciled from the Francist era, even though this was not the overt intention of its authoritarian builders.

Nevertheless on the death of General Franco, on the 20 November 1975, political forces had to be developed so that the building of a future democracy could claim legitimacy. It was no easy task. The authoritarian structures remained in place. The army was keen on continuity. The population itself were anxious. Attracted by ideas of freedom and wishing to have a similar political system to their neighbors, they were nevertheless afraid; afraid of fresh conflict, afraid of losing recently acquired material benefits, seen as a product of the order imposed by the dictatorship. As for the king, everyone, equally within Spain as well as abroad, saw him as a young man of poor calibre; a product of Franco under the tutelage of his supposedly anti-liberal entourage. Furthermore the problem of constructing a democratic framework was not solely limited to the two basic problems of drawing up an acceptable constitution and the emergence of a party system. It was also important to work out the relationship between the center of Spain and the outer limits, something which had not happened previously; in other words between the Spanish state and the autonomist provinces. All this without forgetting the most urgent task of maintaining government stability without falling under the sway of the Francist diehards and beginning, despite the reticence of the latter, a constitutional phase. Finally to convince the political parties as well as the Spaniards themselves of the democratic nature of the elections which were about to take place. After all Juan Carlos' promised democracy was initially nothing more than democracy granted by the presumed heirs of Francism, without a clear break with dictatorship.

It was however precisely because of this that the king was able to overcome these obstacles; more precisely due to the trust that the army placed in him as the guarantor of political change without any dramatic break. Though Francist at heart, its commander, General Castanon de Mena obeyed him because of his charisma as king. A charisma that gave the sovereign the right to demand of the military what would have been refused to an elected president. Thus an immediate anti-democratic putsch was averted, above all following the first decisive act of transition which came about on the 1 July 1976. That day the king forced the Prime Minister Carlos Arias Navarro, who had remained in place after the death of Franco, to step down. His appointed successor was Adolfo Suarez who had the dual advantage of being both a product of the Francist (and even Phalangist) system yet belonging at the same time to the same generation as Juan Carlos and conscious of the fact that a slight adjustment of the system would not be enough.

The second decisive phase took place from September 1976 to June 1977. With the backing of the president of the Francist Cortes, Torcuato Fernandez Miranda, the king managed to agree to dissolve itself. Then, on December 15,1976, a referendum on a law of putative political reform heralded a period of constitutional rule without the word being mentioned. In March 1977 Suarez further continued the process. Against all expectations he legalized the Communist party. This move symbolically cut the Gordian knot left by the civil war. With the support of the Communist leader Santiago Carillo, it forced the whole of the left-wing opposition — above all the Socialists — to back the process of change within the framework of a monarchy by agreeing to take part in the elections held on the 15 June 1977. This led to the victory of the party formed with odds and ends by Suarez, the Democratic Center Union (UCD). The way was clear in political terms. Furthermore the winds of compromise took hold equally of the communist unions — the Workers Commissions — and the socialists — General Workers Union — which signed an agreement known as La Moncloa. This was to guarantee social peace during the transition.

Adopted following a referendum on the 6 December 1978, the new constitution was not only worthy of praise because it restored representative government but also responded to demands for autonomy. Already accepted by the national parties and unions, the democratic monarchy could also be acknowledged by the Catalan and Basque leaders. It also was in favor of developing further regional movements, giving every province the power to benefit from self-government by degrees depending on their specific characteristics within the framework of a structure halfway between Italian regionalism and federalism. Even though the intentions of the government might have seemed ambiguous, and Basque terrorist outrages disturbed this picture, every province — including Madrid — took advantage of this possibility to transform Spain into a unique model within the democratic sphere.

The victory of the socialist party — the PSOE — in the 28 October 1982 general elections put the final gloss on the success of transition. Accomplished without the support of the communists who fared badly in the election, this triumph was one of moderate and pragmatic socialism. It shows that the Spanish have got over their fear of each other and that the divisions which still exist are only those of democratic pluralism. Confirmed in the autumn elections of 1988, this consolidation of power does not mean that, apart from the tragedy of the Basque country, there are no more difficulties for democratic Spain. These are characterized by the party system and the possibility of having a changeover of power.

The elections of 1982 and 1988 not only showed the victory of the socialist and the personal charisma of its leader Felipe Gonzalez, but from 1982 reflected the irreversible decline of the center party the UCD. In 1988 it showed that the right — *Alianza Popular* then PAP — were unable to become a plausible alternative majority to take over from the socialists. The latter have become transformed into the dominant party, naturally worn down by being in power, yet less so than the opposition was by the remoteness of all hope of being in power. Of course there are other European democracies where there is no, or hardly any, changeover of power, above all in Sweden and Denmark, but it is not clear if this lack of change corresponds to the expectations of the Spanish people. This is the present political challenge. The democratic transition in Spain was conducted by a few extremely gifted leaders with remarkable strategic vision, especially the king, Adolfo Suarez, Torcuato Fernandez Miranda, Santiago Carrillo and Felipe Gonzalez. There still remains to be found a person capable enough to rally a convincing opposition to make the changeover of political power possible.

CHRONOLOGY

1808-1813	French occupation.
1812	First Liberal constitution, known as the Cadix Constitution.
1814	Restoration of absolutism.
1820-1823	"Liberal Triannate" with the support of the military.
1833-1840	First Carlist war.
1839-1843	"Progressive"governments under the scrutiny of the military.
1843-1854	The moderate military rule the country.
1856-1868	Governments of Liberal Union. Growing involvement of civilians in public life.
1868	Overthrow of Queen Isabella II. The Ist Internationale is established in Spain. Start of the spread of anarchism.
1869	Constitution establishing a parliamentary monarchy.
1870	Amedee of Savoy, King of Spain.
1872-1876	Renewal of the Carlist war.
1873	Abdication of Amedee of Savoy. Ist Republic.
1874	Restoration of the Bourbons with a military coup d'état.
1876	Promulgation of the constitution that would last until 1923. Parliamentary monarchy based on electoral fraud and the artificial alternating of the liberal and conservative parties.
1890	Universal male suffrage. Increase in electoral corruption.
1909	Uprising in Barcelona against the sending of troops to Morocco. The *tragic week.*
1917	Appearance of the military junta for security. Wave of violent strikes.

1919-1923	Permanent climate of worker unrest and political assassinations perpetrated by the anarchists. Scandal over the colonial war in Morocco.
1923-1930	Soft dictatorship of General Primo de Rivera.
1931	Fall of King Alphonso XIII. Republican constitution. Forming of an autonomous Catalan Generalitat.
1932	Agrarian reform. Conflict with the Church and communist and anarchist agitation. Failed putsch by General Sanjurjo.
1933	The Catholic right carry the elections. They are refused power.
1934	Uprising in Asturias.
1936	The Popular Front wins the elections.
1936-1937	Civil War.
1939-1975	Dictatorship of General Franco.
1975	*20 November*: Death of General Franco. Juan Carlos becomes King of Spain two days later.
1976	*3 July*: Adolfo Suarez, Prime Minister.
	18 November: The Francist Cortes dissolves itself by agreeing to the proposal for political reform.
1977	*1 April*: Official disbanding of the former sole Phalangist Party.
	9 April: Legalization of the Communist Party.
	15 June: Election in fact of a constituent assembly even though it is not termed such. Victory of the UCD.
	29 September: Reestablishment of the Catalan Generalitat.
	25 October: Moncloa pact.
1978	*17 June*: Restoration of autonomy in the Basque Country.
	6 December: Approval by referendum of the constitution.

1979   *1 March*: Legislative elections. The UCD remains in power.

1981   *10 February*: Resignation of Adolfo Suarez. UCD government with Leopoldo Calvo Sotelo.

23 February: Failed putsch by Lieutenant Colonel Tejero.

1982   *30 March*: Socialist victory in the legislative elections. Filipe Gonzalez heads the government.

1982-1983   All the territories gain the status of autonomy.

1986   *1 January*: Entry of Spain into the EC.

22 June: A further victory of the Socialists in the legislative elections.

1989   *29 October*: Legislative elections. The Socialists just manage to stay in power.

SWITZERLAND: A DEMOCRATIC MODEL?

Andre Reszler

"Switzerland a democratic model": from the title of a classic work by Andre Siegfried. Switzerland is not only the oldest democracy in the world but during the period of Hitler's rule of Europe it was the guardian of a much threatened democratic ideal. Although this view, which dates back to the post war period, has in fact been somewhat diminished by the return of the rest of Western Europe to democracy, the Swiss example is now a focus of attention for the Eastern European countries who are impatient to "rejoin Europe." In his book on "rebuilding" Russia, Solzhenitsyn himself devoted several paragraphs to the deep impression that direct democracy, as expressed in Appenzell, had made on him.

A rather disturbing dual paradox immediately needs to be outlined. On the one hand, if in spite of the change of perspective already mentioned above, Switzerland's prestige as a distinctive model of democracy generally remains untrammelled, yet within Switzerland itself a broad swathe of the intelligentsia have for many years denounced Swiss democracy as an illusion, or rather a farce; on the other hand, although the institutions of direct or semi-direct democracy might be universally admired, they have not survived nor did they provide a basis for drawing up new democratic mechanisms in other countries. It would seem that

Switzerland is portrayed both as an archetypal modern democratic system and at the same time as an unique historical experiment. Whatever the case Swiss politicians have been wary of promoting Swiss democracy as an universally applicable value. As for foreign observers they have tended to see it as a case in point, springing from the psychology of a small nation eager to go against the flow of history in general, and as a consequence avoiding the lure of nationalism and state centralism, which in the rest of Europe were felt politically to be major factors for modernization.

A Swiss democratic model therefore does exist, even though it has not taken root outside the territory of the Swiss Confederation. Yet there also exists a broader phenomenon which might be called the Swiss model. Only to a relatively small extent does the latter rely on its democratic element. Where does the uniqueness of the Swiss model come from? Clearly from the mechanisms for popular initiative and referendum; from the way that the Swiss, even now in the 20th Century, continue to implement the still vigorous ideals of the *Landgemeinde*, based on the much narrower framework of the Swiss cantons of medieval times. Where does the originality of the Swiss model come from? From the institutions mentioned above, but also from a certain number of characteristics born out of this very same particularly strong political culture, which alone give this democratic experiment its value as an exemplum: federalism with the permanent renegotiation of the distribution of power between communes, cantons and the confederation; the exercise of local autonomy; the formative role of the army in terms of molding civic awareness and the richness of community life.

It is strange however that in 1991 when Switzerland celebrated the 700 years of its foundation — celebrations that took place, as mentioned previously, on a backcloth of skepticism and even sullenness —, it was not democracy but *utopia* that was chosen by the authorities as the central theme of the celebrations.

DEMOCRACY OR ....UTOPIA?

Switzerland as an ideal and example of utopia! This is a joke, for if the term is interpreted in its original sense, no country is so far from utopian as the Swiss Confederation. Not only do they show, throughout history, an untempered distrust of great men — while king Utopos was the all powerful master of Thomas More's *Utopia* —, they disdain sweeping generalizations and confront the most wonderful theories with the most uncompromising pragmatism; as opposed to the theoreticians of utopia who glibly standardize ways of life, of thought, of feelings. The Swiss confederation however cultivates an innate respect for differences and owes its success to the reconciliation of ethnic, religious, cultural and linguistic differences within both such a united and at the same time diverse community. If historians are right in considering Soviet society and popular democracies as the implementation of utopias then Switzerland at first glance would appear *anti-utopia...*

Nevertheless ... When one looks closely, Switzerland has a certain number of features that resemble the imaginary utopia and are perhaps as important in understanding the Swiss reality as semi-direct democracy. Let us take for example two utopian characteristics par excellence: *insular sensitivity* and the need for understanding, *harmony*.

In general terms an utopia has the natural framework of an island. Since its inhabitants hold security and the stability of their social order as the highest ideals they retreat from the international community. Also perfection has this strange particularity; it has problems resisting bad outside influences, hence its preoccupation with closely controlling all trade: of peoples, ideas and goods. As for its geographical position, Switzerland seems to be an ancient nation: situated in a mountainous area of the continent; a crossroads joining the south of Europe to the north. Its very existence is inalienably linked to control of the Alps. Its inhabitants have also developed over the centuries, reaching perfection this century, an extremely strong insular ideology. Switzerland is both a country by and large open to the world (hence headquarters for several international organizations) and a community which owes its happiness to the fact that it keeps to the sidelines of world affairs. The symbols of this wholly accepted *otherness*: its ideology developed against the tide of events and the status of neutrality. Its uniqueness, over and above its responsibility in relation to the whole world, such is its destiny. "Switzerland is an island," wrote Paul Valery in 1948, "a model state which patiently and thankfully managed to resolve almost all the problems that over the centuries have beset the rest of Europe and now shake the whole world." For Valery perfection was to be measured in social terms. This is where the need for harmony comes in: a golden age recreated due to the vigorous search for life-enhancing consensus.

Switzerland, because of its very need for internal peace, is an example of consensus. (*Konkordanzdemokratie*). As well as its neutrality in international relations, there in fact exists in so many and diverse ways a corresponding inter-ethnic and religious *entente cordiale*. Whereas this should be the field of battle for all the different groups within, the long history of tolerance shows that harmony has become second nature: harmony being the source of "good," then all conflict has by definition an element of "bad" in it.

The quest for harmony, the *Konkordanzdemokratie*, resulted on a social and political level, in the creation of two relatively recent institutions; quite in keeping with the oldest traditions of the country: "peace in work" and the "magic formula." "Peace in work" is what the agreement reached between metal workers and employers organizations in 1937 is known by, and by extension all similar agreements in other parts of the economy where subsequently it was used as a model. According to this formula, which even now has not really been challenged, employers and workers commit themselves to resolving any dispute which might arise by arbitration and conciliation. The class struggle was henceforth a phenomena alien to the Swiss mind. The "magic formula" extends, in practice, "social peace." Established in 1959 it guarantees the major national parties representation corresponding to their electoral strength. In the same way as the three "so called bourgeois" political formations, the socialist party is part of a government of national security elected in peacetime... for continued peace. The make-up of the canton governments is modelled on the distribution of portfolios within the federal government, while at the same time respecting any local balance of power.

Is public life in Switzerland exempt from the type of conflict that gives political life in neighboring countries its particular flavor? Does the world of work tend naturally towards the collaboration of classes? It is impossible within the confines of this study to answer such questions. We ought however, to point out that there exists a Swiss method of resolving conflicts and, in terms of political culture, a mental predisposition that encourages attempts at compromise, and above all imbues this notion (often disliked in other countries) with connotations that are fundamentally positive.

SWISS POLITICAL CULTURE

This compromise is based on several basic worries. The search for negotiated solutions at all costs presupposes firstly, more than just a muted anti-intellectual approach, faith in common sense, an unconditional attachment to plain facts, also to "first impressions," to ways and means of testing things out, to the human condition and from this the inevitable limits that confront all human activity and obstacles that need to be overcome... As voters the Swiss put their trust in people who have proved themselves in the world of business and who bring to politics managerial skills. Then, even before being Swiss, every person in Switzerland is a "bourgeois" of a commune and a citizen of a canton. This triple belonging is based on a pluralistic view of society and promotes affection for communities on a human scale, fosters idiosyncrasies and social development from the bottom to the top... "The principle of this form of democracy is in fact communal before becoming cantonal and cantonal before federal" as Andre Siegfried wrote. Finally the wish for national independence, embodied by William Tell, has as its corollary, in terms of internal politics, a visceral *republican* instinct. The opposition of the Swiss to a personalized state, government of one or a dynasty, might mistakenly be taken as a innate penchant to democracy. As will be shown later it also dovetails with all sorts of oligarchies who are entrusted with running things. Consequently why it is easy to feel that people do not count and that government relies more on the excellence of the system.

Distrust of famous people, of laudable but abstract political theories, of the concentration of too much power in the same hands (or to the same agencies): it is clear from these few characteristics how the political class reacts to events (and also why these virtues might, through a dialectical inversion of roles, become vices for their intellectual opponents).

To the catalogue of suspicions we have just established, Machiavelli added another of the kind aroused by gentlemen and aristocrats: "...the Swiss not only hate princes, as the German communes do, but also hate gentlemen. Their country does not support either of these types, and they themselves all benefit from the most widespread freedom: not the least distinction between them, apart from when they sit as judges." Has Switzerland as seen by the author of *The Prince* remained faithful to this situation? This does not seem to have been the case. Indeed, quite quickly, even in the cantons that retained the institutions of the *Landgemeinde*, the people would entrust the job of dealing with routine matters to those best able to deal with them. Even where a patriarchy of privilege did not exist, some families held actual power thanks to a network of generally accepted traditions. So in parallel to the democratic cantons there existed, up until the end of the Ancien Regime, oligarchic states (Zurich, Bale...), aristocratic (Berne, Lucerne, Fribourg...) federal (le Valais...) and even monarchic states (the principality of Neuchatel). Until the French Revolution — and perhaps even well after, — Swiss history corresponded to a great extent to the history of a few families of aristocratic/oligarchic tradition, well versed in the exercise of power and imbued with a sense of their own responsibility. Former and modern Switzerland was and still remains a country of nobility; people ennobled through the posts of magistrate, posts acquired and bequeathed from generation to generation in the same way as property or wealth. Even after the creation in 1848 of the Federal state, the cantonal governments were to retain a patrician feel to them. According to a particularly apposite formula coined by William Martin, Switzerland has always been "a democracy marching towards oligarchy."

So, in the same way as Venice, Switzerland gives an example of a very long period of stability. As with the Serenissime's republic, it would work out a social formula based on the relative proximity of the classes. Also both represent, in terms of their institutions, a sort of mixed government. In *De magistratibus et Republica venetorum* (1543) the Venetian patrician Gasparo Contarini put his city forward as a sort of Platonic republic or, even more, as a utopia in action in which "life is particularly happy." Its harmonious existence and the longevity that it established arose from the perfect balance of its constitution. A veritable *mixed state*, it responded to the popular will within the great council; the Senate, and the Council of Ten reflected the aristocratic way; the Doge embodied the monarchic element.

As with Venice, and like all democratic states, Switzerland is made up of "popular" and "oligarchic" elements. In contrast to the Venetian Republic however, it completely ignores the monarchic element. The Federal council operates (and the same principle prevails within the canton governments) according to rules of collegiality which precludes the preeminence of what-so-ever of its members. Its authority is strictly collective. Its decisions are taken collegially. The operation of each department is subject to the control of all the heads of department. Because of this political culture, Switzerland is a mixed state but truncated towards the top...

I have already briefly mentioned the Swiss people's need for order and stability. In terms of government this need is insured by the perennial nature of the Federal Council. Even though the members of the council are elected individually, apart from in a few cases, they are reelected almost automatically at the end of their mandate (on condition that they end their career as supreme magistrate of their own accord). The Assembly is completely powerless to remove them from office: in Switzerland there is no vote of no-confidence nor an *impeachment* procedure. The continuation of a federal councillor in power does not depend on the success of their program, nor would the failure of one of their projects lead to their resignation. The people place their confidence in a general way. Under these circumstances the average length of a councilor's mandate is greater than ten years. (One federal councillor stayed in power for 32 consecutive years.)

A survey made by a French speaking weekly casts light on the level of confidence that members of the government might enjoy. On the question of whether the federal council hold sway over the most important problems of today, such as the environment, drugs..., only 6.1% of those asked replied "yes." According to 52.1% "they have difficulty with them." Finally, in the opinion of 36.5% they are totally "overpowered" by them. Notwithstanding this evaluation of the work of the federal government, the same representative cross-section of the population gave a overwhelmingly favorable opinion of the personal qualities of the federal councilors in power, and the mark they gave on a register of 0-6 varied between 4.86 (close to "very good") and 3.86 (almost "good"). The Swiss people would never contemplate rejecting a team that they clearly feel are unequal to the task...

In conclusion then: the Swiss people elect their representatives in the most democratic way. Thanks to the referendum they still retain the final say on legislative matters. "Popular initiatives" give them the right to initiate new laws. Then, between elections, they also entrust their governments with a form of discretionary power who then act as members of an oligarchy secure in their privilege. This paradoxically puts into question the ideal of "direct democracy" or "democracy of small places," that from Rousseau to Solzhenitsyn, intellectuals of a slightly nostalgic nature have found in Switzerland. In most countries, the state and governments tend to create around themselves a preserve of autonomy; in Switzerland this area is no doubt larger than in other European countries.

THE END OF FOLKLORE

"The end of folklore": it was in these terms that a French speaking daily paper declared on the 16 November 1990, the end of a tradition — the persistent refusal of "able-bodied men" of inner

Appenzell Rhodes to grant their wives and daughters over 18 the right to vote in cantonal matters. Following the decision of the federal tribunal, released the previous day, the last bastion of anti-democratic opposition in Switzerland surrendered. Long after every other European countries, Switzerland was finally to become truly democratic. Had the country acquired its democratic credentials in the past by mistake or out of ignorance? Some of the most prestigious intellectuals of the country such as Freidrich Durrenmatt, Max Frisch and Adolf Muschg think so. Are they right? Or are their positions nothing more than sanctimonious posturing?

A few weeks prior to his death Durrenmatt declared that although it portrayed itself as the mother of democracy, urban Switzerland — above all Bern — shamefully exploited its bailiwicks. Was the state itself, whose police have secret files on more than 700,000 citizens the majority absolutely loyal to the country, truly democratic? The author of the *Visite de la vielle dame* compares Switzerland to a huge prison where the citizens are above all their own guards, constantly keeping an eye on each other, their compatriots curiously feel free, "freer than everyone else, free as prisoners in the prison of their own neutrality."

At the same time political scientists, sociologists and economists question whether semi-direct democracy will mean that Switzerland becomes increasingly isolated in a Europe which is under construction. In their opinion not only have people's initiatives and referendums lost their effectiveness due to their manipulation by organized sectional interests, but they have also lost their raison d'être in the sense that they are clearly out of step with the European "scene." "Closer ties and participation in Europe dictates a reorganization of our political institutions" Raimund Germann, director of the *Institute des hautes etudes en administration publique*, stated.

Is Switzerland sick of Europe? Added to the existential (Kierkegardian) unease that for a number of years it has been feeling, there is the fear of loss of identity within a European community which is not bothered with Swiss particularities. "Switzerland as a special case — *Sonderfall Schweiz* — has had its day," so Flavio Cotti the president of the Confederation was to say. Is it also the end of Switzerland as a unique variant within the larger European democratic model?

Do these problems lead up to think that there is an actual crisis of democracy or do they just reflect an underlying unease that some portray as an unprecedented crisis of identity? Almost everywhere in Switzerland, in the most far-ranging areas of life, under a veneer of unity and unanimity which still remains de rigueur, violent conflicts (even though the stakes might appear laughable) continue to rally militants and volunteers. "Authoritarian" tendencies try and impose their own ideas and are at pains to portray them as the "general will." Furthermore politics, a factor which traditionally divides people, has become a factor for unity. If and above all on the cantonal level, the "magic formula" has undeniably had the virtue of bringing people and parties together, it also has had the result of wiping away any difference of ideas. Within the cantons — whose size has tended to diminish — a form of permanent majority has been built: a coalition of sectional interests that by and large are satisfied by things and loath to make changes. This is Tocqueville's prophetic fear of the attitude of democratic societies as reality — "I fear that men finally allow themselves to be possessed by the craven love of present delight, that their own future interests and that of their descendants are forgotten, and that they might prefer weakly to follow the tide of destiny rather than make, when need arises, a sudden and vigorous effort to change it."

CHRONOLOGY

1798	Collapse of the Ancien Regime. Declaration, under French influence, of the Swiss Republic "one and indivisible": emancipation of subject lands, religious equality, freedom of trade and industry....
1803	Act of mediation. Return to cantonal sovereignty. Bonaparte chooses federalism since it would be a source of weakness. Nomination of a federal *Landammann*.
1815	The Pact replaces the act of mediation. The Confederation remains an alliance of sovereign states. A *Vorort* made up of three cantons replaces the *Landammann*.
1830-1833	The cantons revise their constitutions.
1845	The *Sonderbund*.
1848	Adoption of the Constitution. Switzerland will henceforth be a Federal country. The right of personal initiative and the possibilities of referenda extends democracy to the entire country.
1849	The cantons of Zoug and Schwytz give up their *landsgemeinde*.
1874	Revision of the constitution. This extends the right of referendum to laws voted by the Parliament.
1937	Establishment of "industrial peace."
1938	Romanchian becomes, together with French, German and Italian, the fourth national language.
1959	The Federal Council was elected for the first time according to the formula known as the "magic formula" (*Zauberformel*). Following

a federal poll, 66.9% of the voters refused
to grant political equality to women. The
canton of Vaud agree to allow women to
vote on cantonal or communal issues.

1971 Women obtain the right to vote at a federal level.

1979 Creation of a new canton, the Jura.

1990 The federal Tribunal grants the right to vote to the
women of Appenzell, in the half canton of
Inner Appenzell Rhodes which is the last
remaining to exclude women from
exercising their political rights.

SEARCHING FOR THE DEMOCRATIC HABITUS OF THE LOW COUNTRIES (HOLLAND AND BELGIUM)

Willem Frijhoff

In the Low Countries' collective memory, both north and south in Holland (*The Netherlands*) and Belgium, the *state* is a recent creation: 1813 for the Dutch and 1830 for the Belgians — the rest is pre-history. Also, in both cases, the state was built around a constitution which despite inevitable reforms and modernizations over the past two centuries, has by and large remained intact. In reality, these two recently created states are still motivated by the oldest constitutions in Europe, largely going back to the time when they were founded. The existence of a state and their democratic constitutions are intertwined. Before, prior to the era of revolutions, political structures did of course exist: a minimum of autonomy in Belgium and formal independence in Holland. Yet these federations of the Ancien Regime are not taken to be states in the strict sense of the term. As for Belgium, it is not clear how the state will survive in its current form, even without the problem of how Europe might change the status of Brussels.

In contrast, *democracy* was used in the Low Countries well before there was any question of a state in the modern sense of the term: the political structures worked on the principle of representation and it was precisely attacks on this founding principle of

176

collective freedom that motivated the massive revolts against the absolute monarchs of the 16th Century or the enlightened despots of the 18th Century. There is therefore nothing surprising in the fact that, in the national heritage of both countries, liberty should be perceived as a founding and long established right. The revolt of the Bataves against the Romans in 69 AD, as told by Tacitus, played an essential role in rebellious republican Holland. From the *Traite sur l'antiquite de la Republique batave* of Groitus (1610) to the *Batave* Republic created in 1795, the myth of Batavian freedom gripped the national consciousness, illustrated a national destiny and justified political structures where people would play a leading role. In Flanders, the battle of the Golden Spurs (1302) and the start of the real democratization of town councils had a similar influence on the 19th Century. Although the term *democracy* was not used much, in terms of historical reality — the whole population of the Low Countries were convinced — there are few parts of Europe where democratic practices are so well established or so ancient, characterized by representative institutions or nourished by such a profound need for freedom, as in those seventeen provinces that Emperor Charles V joined together in 1548 to make the Circle of Burgundy.

REPUBLICAN FREEDOM AND TRADITION
IN HOLLAND

The precedence of fact over law might explain why these ancient democrats had so few theoreticians whose books would survived the passage of time. The theoreticians of Dutch democracy were republicans, from the Ancien Regime. Three names stand out and represent distinct currents of thought: Johannes Althusius a Calvinist ideologist, defined the theory of the contract through which free men organize themselves into hierarchies of constituent parts, going from the family to the state (*Politica methodice digesta*, 1603); the lawyer Hugo Grotius, a moderate protestant who did not reject Catholicism out of hand, based freedom on natural law (*De jure belli ac pacis*, 1625); the Jewish philosopher Baruch Spinoza, finally, showed that it was only through democracy that the natural sovereign rights of the individual could be safeguarded (*Tractatus theologico-politicus*, 1670). Then came Locke and Rousseau whose influence was enormous. Yet the basics were already in place.

These discussions over the rights of the people occurred in the context of buttressing a Republican regime, and scarcely contemplated a democratic state structure. The Dutch Republic of the Ancien Regime suffered in fact from a congenital illness: that of corporatism — indeed a shrewd observer might still observe it even today. As for the institutions, Dutch democracy has always stressed the intermediate (in-between) structures; in terms of the direct involvement of the individual. The present-day exclusive political party machineries whose conflicts with their grassroots regularly burst forth into the public arena and whose popular credentials are continuously questioned, are the direct descendants of the coopted town regencies of the Ancien Regime — bodies representing the people while at the same time holding sovereignty themselves and therefore keeping quiet about "popular sovereignty."

At regular intervals, against this tradition of indirect democracy, there were outbreaks (hiccups) of direct democracy. During the popular revolts at the start of the 18th Century, known under the enigmatic name of *Plis*, for the first time the word *democracy* was used and unquestionably raised the demand for direct democracy: the protesters demanded the principle of election of governors by the people, or at least by their freely elected representatives, rather than the coopting of regents approved of by the ambiguous figure of the *stathoulder* — legally a public servant but in reality the monarch. The Patriots who from 1781-1787 tried in vain to restore the old batavian freedoms, assimilated this new meaning of the word and opposed both the representative oligarchy of the constituent parts and the monarchic principle that supporters of the stathoulder tried so hard to emphasize.

DEMOCRACY AND MONARCHY

It could be said that to be an irony of history that the two oldest representative democracies in Europe, the northern and southern Low Countries, should both end up as centralized monarchies. Yet this is no secret. Democracy and monarchy were never really antagonistic to each other. Monarchy was grafted onto an existing body of democratic practices, while at the same time translating them into state structures. In both cases the monarch embodied the principle of unity rather than that of power. Clearly the case of contemporary Belgium, it was no less true for Holland at the start of the 19th Century. The political system of the Dutch republic was in fact characterized by a continuous oscillation between two concepts of what the state should be: a federative centrifugal corporative pole of urban oligarchic power, as opposed to the popular centralizing unifying pole of monarchic power represented by the stathoulder. In the face of bourgeois *Realpolitiker* merchants, the stathoulders symbolized — often despite themselves — the myth of a united Holland; the *Dutch Israel*, a Calvinist people elected by God to accomplish a shared religious mission. The stathoulder embodied the landowning unity of a "Caesarian democracy" (from the expression used by the historian Pieter Geyl) against the proponents of federalism tinged with indirect democracy; in other words a populist regime under the guidance of a prince, but without direct appeal to the active participation of the people. Through the various political experiments and many reversals of alliances which followed the Batavian Revolution, a compromise took shape and proved in the end to be workable: the monarchy. In this country characterized by its individuality of thought, centrifugal tendencies and religious divisions, the founding of the monarchy, without a strong state, was the price to pay for guaranteeing unity in an authentically democratic regime. It would however be a "low profile" monarchy — even though William I, king from 1815 to 1840 meant to wield, over both countries entrusted to him by the Congress of Vienna, those personal powers allowed for by the constitution prior to its revision in 1848.

Consequently it is easy to see why this experiment of a united kingdom of the northern and southern Low Countries was doomed to failure. Too many things had happened since their separation in the 16th Century for their reunification in 1815 to have any real short-term chance of success. Besides the Batavian revolution, faithful to the principles of 1789 had been very different to the Brabantian Revolution. In the southern Low country 1780 was in a way a continuation of the failed revolt of the 16th Century: the same opposition to the emperor's centralizing and modernizing policies, the same reaction to a religious dispute, the same internal tensions between traditional defenders of the representative regime of constituent parts (the *statistes*) and the progressive advocates of power to the emergent classes (the *vonckistes*). Only the principality of Liege in 1789 rallied without hesitation to the ideas coming from Paris. For according to the analysis of Henri Pirenne, following the long experiment in "absolute monarchy moderated by local autonomy," the question of unity was no longer so important for the future Belgium state. For the south the problem was less the exercise of centralized government than the balance of power and corresponding interests of the two (Belgium) territories; whose traditions, culture and language were so fundamentally different. While in the north the province of Holland had progressively become a center of attraction for the whole Republic and had brought about a real cultural unification, which is an essential component for political unity, nothing comparable took place in the south. The diversity of regions and the duality of languages and cultures would from the start mark the political life of the young Belgium state. More so than in Holland, the monarchy traditionally symbolized in Belgium the unity of the state, which meant that the monarchy had the difficult duty of remaining aloof from all cultural issues. On the other hand each infringement of this duty risked provoking a veritable crisis for the regime since it went to the very heart of the question of unity. The question of the monarchy, during its most critical phase in 1945 to 1950, was an extremely prickly issue.

DUTCH DEMOCRACY: A SYSTEM OF PILLARS

In strictly constitutional terms the history of Holland is unremarkable. The 1814 constitution was twice amended: in 1848 parliament and ministers regained ascendancy over the king and obtained constitutional guarantees for a number of freedoms; in 1917 universal proportional representation was introduced, following a rapid extension of the vote over the preceding decades. The legislative body tried to accomplish two things at once: they wanted to involve the working classes and by introducing full proportionality at the same time hoped to break the traditional power of local potentates whose power was rooted in their districts (as had been the case two centuries previously with members of the oligarchies under the Republic). Clearly they did not understand that in a country where intermediate institutions were all-powerful and provided a necessary link for every initiative, they were in fact lighting a time-bomb under the parliamentary regime. Ultimately power failed to be transferred to the electors but went to new more diverse coteries who nevertheless still retained real power. It was the intermediate levels of the party apparatus that became empowered.

Full proportional representation gave birth to a multi-party system which worked relatively well as long as the political parties opposed each other on the basis of clearly defined principles: the anti-revolutionary party (a strictly protestant party) proclaimed itself against the principles of the French Revolution, the socialists were for etc. Yet these divisions were anchored in a social reality that had already had its day; meaning of the bizarre system of socio-cultural partitioning that occurred in public life, usually represented through the image of a *system of pillars*: Calvinist, catholic and socialist — three enormous ideological sections roughly equal in numbers — making up as many self-sufficient mini-states, pillars that supported a state structure, itself virtually powerless. Each of the "pillars" was a complete organization with amenities, schools, hospitals, associations, media as well as a political party to defend its interests at the national level. This sectionalization heralded by the evolution of social groups prior to the end of the 19th Century really came into its own during the conflict over education pitting the state against religious interests and resolved in favor of the latter by measures introduced between 1917 and 1920 to mollify them.

The *system of pillars* was to play a crucial part in the political democratization of the country: protected against the danger of too rapid secularization or modernization, and also from the demands of competing interests, large sections of the population, who up until then had been ignored, managed to free themselves of their second-class citizenship by learning to become involved. It was only well after the Second World War that this system ground to a halt: the gradual modernization of Dutch society unravelled old alliances and militated for the first time in favor of the development of real state power. Consequently, it is easier to understand the shocks and problems that since the 1960's have been the object of much discussion: the *provo* movement, the affair of the Dutch Church, permissiveness in education, sexual freedom, a tolerance of the use of soft drugs and Dutch pacifism.

This path from "pacifying democracy" (according to the much debated vision of Lijphart) to "democracy of agreement" did not destroy either the political cadres (the oligarchic tendency) nor the intermediate structures (the technocratic temptation). On the contrary they were to emerge with further power. Freed from the tutelage of the Church and the parties, the "mature" citizen would see their hopes thwarted. Hence a real crisis of confidence — less in Dutch democracy itself, (in 1990 73% of the population stated they were satisfied, as opposed to 63% in Belgium and 57% in the whole of Europe) than in the political apparatus. Since 1966 the need to thoroughly reform political democracy has been clamored for by a party called D'66 (Democrats 66) who proposes to replace the existing indirect democracy with a stronger direct democracy. The emergence of this neo-democratic opposition at the same time as the "cultural revolution" at the end of the 1960's was of course not unconnected.

In fact there are two problems. First of all the electorate have lost political power, if in fact they ever did have it. They delegate it to bureaucratic parties who discuss and seem to prefer procedure over contents and harmony of the system over questions of principle which are only meant to rouse the crowds at election times. As was pointed out by the report of the Deetman Commission on the possible reform of the political system in November 1990: "The electorate decide the numerical balance but not the balance of power, at least not directly." In fact they hardly even decide the main principles of government since the programs of the big political parties have become virtually identical, and the minor differences are generally pasted over in negotiations which in the multi-party system are supposed to result in viable coalitions or else correct the aim in the process.

There exists a real conflict of interest between loyalty of the elected representatives to their electorate and their party: failing a direct link between the elected representative and the electorate normally it is the party that wins. Hence the repeated calls for the reintroduction of an electoral regime based on districts, in the direct election of the Prime Minister and of mayors, and the possibility of referendums (which does not exist in Holland). However the political consensus of the intermediary bodies is continued caution; so the proposition to introduce the possibility of referendum was rejected by a disinterested parliament without any real debate.

The elected representatives sometimes seem to be more acutely aware of this problem which after all touches them directly, even though the big political parties clearly continue to prefer representative democracy above all other form of direct democracy. On the other hand parliamentarians clearly are burying their heads in the ground in relation to the second problem: the repeated hijacking of legislative power by the executive (ministers or their major generals). The increase in the power of the state since the Second World War has led to a massive increase in interventionism greatly reducing the relative decentralization instituted after 1848. Also the "pillars" have switched their moral preoccupations over politics to the state. Consequently the state was given a virtual mission, that quickly changed to the idea of a welfare state: the "Democratic Leviathan" to echo R.A. Dahl. Hence the impatience of the executive with the uninitiated who fail to understand the benefits they want to give or the harsh realities of the management of the country — and the scarcely hidden care with which they short-circuit the troublesome National Assembly. There is a disturbing logic in the mandatory law voted in 1974 by the Den Ulyl government following the energy crisis, to resolve socio-economic problems without referring them to parliament — the "choking law" — which fifteen years later was openly imposed on Parliament. It clearly shows a complicity between the larger political parties and ministerial cabinets that some people feel is a real threat to control by the electorate of the running of the country. As a consequence we come full-circle back to constitutional democracy in Holland; while in the 19th Century there was an increase of the parliament's influence in relation to the executive the 20th Century will end with the opposite trend.

The possibility of political choice for the citizen is hence formalized rather than real. Does this mean that democracy does not work in the Low Countries? One should not have an exaggeratedly institutional view of reality and forget the ideals and practices which are central to collective living. In this respect one should mention the change in ideas resulting from the framing of the Dutch constitution adopted in 1983. It no longer begins with a list of state structures, from which the citizens rights derive, but begins with a long catalogue of 23 articles that lay down the fundamental rights of man (political, social and cultural) before considering the citizen as a subject of the state. Significantly all forms of discrimination are denounced by article 1: for centuries a fundamental aspiration of the practice of democracy in Holland despite the difficulty of putting it into practice in reality.

BELGIUM: A KNOT OF CONTRASTS AND DIFFERENCES

Much of what has been said before is also true for Belgium. Once more the problems of democracy today come mostly from a few basic unresolved questions following the birth of the modern state. Yet while Dutch democracy is characterized at every level by a consensual style overlaid with pragmatism that tries to reconcile differences in a middle ground acceptable to all, Belgium democracy shows itself via opposition — even though, in the end, the solutions adopted are not always fundamentally different from those in the North. In any case it is easier to analyze the evolution of Belgium democracy in terms of contrasts; starting with the conflict between clerical conservatives and secular francophile liberals in 1830 that resulted in the compromise of constitutional monarchy, while the Brabant revolution of January 1790 chose to establish a republic.

It is astonishing to discover, while looking at the chronology of institutions and social change, how closely the stages of Belgium democracy coincide with those of Holland. Yet it would be a mistake to see the same mechanism at work in this. In both countries for example the partition had an important effect on the organization of social and cultural life during the first half of the century. In Holland "pillarization" (an English expression) was used by the various ideological sectors as an internal defence strategy against others, without too much harking back to the past and even resulting in a measure of political emancipation for the poorer classes. In Belgium the instrument of partition privileged an extremely conservative church opposed to a similarly militant secular arm. It also resulted as a direct consequence of a major division that had been present in the Belgium state since its genesis: the opposition separating the Catholic Church from the slightly anti-clerical Liberal state over their respective roles in the organization of political and socio-cultural life.

Further opposition emerged, also much more clearly than in Holland. Let's take the division between proprietors and workers: it was at the junction of this conflict between state and church that the Belgium organizations and parties would form. So the latter institutionalized this dual rivalry which was so characteristic of Belgium democracy and which despite broadly comparable developments was so clearly absent from consensual Dutch democracy. If one also accepts the analysis of Xavier Mabill there were two further cleavages: between the industrial and agricultural destinies of Belgium, between the center and the periphery. This last cleavage immediately expresses itself in an inability of the young Belgium state to deal properly with the duality of language and culture within its territory. This prolonged impotence of the state (also the insensitivity of the middle classes in power) ultimately would conspire with other fundamental divisions to provoke a serious institutional crisis.

Nothing of the sort happened in Holland where nevertheless religious disagreement clearly existed, where the problem of language surfaced and might have become a major actor, where the cultural duality between the 70 provinces and the southern provinces (large rivers drawing the line of demarcation) were a reality yet even so rarely became a political pawn. Political conduct, alliances, everyday values, in short the whole style of Dutch democracy — *the political habitus* to use Pierre Bourdieu's expression — rejected outrageous solutions. This is perhaps the fundamental difference with Belgium. In Belgium it proved impossible to avert the reform of political structures. Then with an implacable logic it was to occur, attacking several cleavages at the same time. No doubt it is too soon to assess the outcome of this process Belgium federalization. Seen from abroad and bearing in mind the historic importance of the problems that have to be resolved, it does seem just possible that in the end the goals and style of Belgium democracy itself could be affected. If of course Europe were to allow this.

CHRONOLOGY

Holland

1781-1787	Patriotic anti-oligarchic movement.
1786	Utrecht gives itself a democratic constitution.
1787	Military repreqsion, restoration of the House of Orange.
1794-1795	Batavian revolution: it proclaims a representative republic with a federal structure.
1795	Declaration of Human Rights (31 January).
1796	First National Assembly (1 March); separation of the church and state, and emancipation of the Jews.
1798	Coup d'etat by radicals who set up a centralized unitary state; vote of the first constitution.
1801-1806	Education laws: public schools become common.
1806-1810	Kingdom of Holland under Louis, Napoleon's brother.
1809	Unification of legal statutes, inspired by the Napoleonic Code.
1810-1813	French occupation.
1814	*29 March*: following the return of the Prince of Orange who was proclaimed "sovereign prince," a new constitution begins a period of constitutional monarchy with a single chamber elected through indirect poll tax and by district; executive power lay in the hands of the king; the provincial estates, who elect the deputies were composed of three estates: the nobility, the towns and the countryside.
	22 July: "the total and close union" of the Low Countries and Belgium, under the same adapted constitution: there would be two

chambers, the first decided on by the king,
the second by the Provincial Estates (55
northern members and 55 southern).

1815   William of Orange takes the title of king of the
Low Countries.

1818   Ban on the slave trade.

1828   Agreement on a union between the Catholics and
Belgium Liberals against the Dutch
oppressor.

1830   Secession of Belgium.

1830-1870   Single crop system introduced into the Dutch
Indian territories.

1848   New constitution with Thorbecke a Liberal who
sets up a parliamentary democracy: the two
chambers of the Estates General were
elected by district through direct poll tax;
the privileges of the three estates were
abolished and freedom of speech
guaranteed.

1851   Towns and the countryside given equal status with
a law over the organization of villages.

1853   Restoration of the Catholic hierarchy.

1857   Start of the conflict over education.

1859   Abolition of slavery in the East Indies (1863 in the
West Indies).

1870   Abolition of the death penalty (in times of peace).

1871   Aletta Jacobs, the first women to go to university.

1874   Law covering factory child labor: start of social
legislation that would be pursued from
1897-1901 and 1911-1919.

1879   Founding of the *anti-revolutionary party.*

1885   Founding of the *Liberal Union.*

1887   Revision of the constitution: poll tax replaced by
conditions of knowledge and wealth but
still only for men.

1888   Domela Nieuwenhuis, first socialist member of
parliament.

1894	Founding of the *Social Democrat Worker's Party.*
1896	Founding of a federation of Catholic electoral committees (that in 1926 would become a political party).
1898	Introduction of individual military service.
1899	Start of an "ethnic policy" in the colonies which was intended in the long-term to insure their autonomy.
1900	Law for compulsory education.
1917	Revision of the constitution: active and passive universal suffrage for men (1919 for women), proportional elections on a national level, compulsory vote (abolished in 1970) and fiscal equality between public and private schools.
1918	Attempted revolution called off by the leader of the Social Democrats Troelstra; founding of the Dutch Communist Party.
1920	De Visser Law ("Pacification Law"): total equality of public and private schools.
1922	The colonies become "parts of the kingdom" with their own structures set out in legislation.
1931	Founding by Mussert of a National Socialist Party.
1944	Benelux treaty setting up a customs union (1948 the actual start of this union) between the Holland, Belgium, and Luxembourg.
1947-1966	Vote of a number of laws dealing with social coverage which heralds the welfare state.
1949	Independence of Indonesia recognized.
1950	Law dealing with the corporate organization of institutions and branches of the economy.
1954	New status of the kingdom: its "parts" (Surinam and the West Indies) achieve complete autonomy.
1957	Founding of the pacifist Socialist Party.

1958	Treaty of Economic Union of the Benelux countries.
1965-1967	*Provo* movement in Amsterdam with anarchist features.
1966	Founding of the (center) *Democrats 66 Party* striving for a transformation of political institutions.
1968-1969	Student movements.
1969-1970	Democratic experiment with the Catholic pastoral council.
1970	Law on the democratization of universities.
1974-1975	Setting up of a National Commission for the emancipation of women and the creation of a National Council for women.
1975	Independence of Surinam; acts of violence by Moluccan refugees demanding independence.
1980	Treaty of Linguistic Union between Flanders and Holland.
	Amalgamation of the main religious parties into a single *CHRISTIAN DEMOCRAT PARTY*.
1983	Remolding the constitution placing strong emphasis on human rights.

Belgium

1780-1788	Political reforms of a centralizing, enlightened and secular nature, imposed by Joseph II.
1789	Liege revolution (18 August) followed by the Brabant.
1790	The Congress of Sovereign Insurgent Brabantians set up the federal state of the Republic of United Belgium states (11 January); Emperor Leopold II regains control (December).
1792	First French occupation following Jemappes.

1793-1795	First annexation (1795 final) of the Austrian Low Countries and Liege to the French Republic; creation of nine departments; secularization.
1795-1814	French regime.
1814-1830	See *Holland*.
1830	November: reunion of a National Congress that declared independence (18 November) and puts in place a "representative constitutional monarchy, under a hereditary leader," while at the same time rejecting the house of Orange.
1831	*7 February*: the new constitution established a two chamber parliamentary democracy elected by poll tax; the house of Saxe-Cobourg was invited onto the throne.
1836	Law on regional organization.
1839	Treaty recognizing the independence of Belgium which pledges everlasting neutrality.
1842	Education law that gives advantages to the public Catholic schools.
1846	Founding of the Liberal Party (anti-clerical tendency).
1862	Start of political action by the Flemish: founding of a political party at Anvers.
1863	Founding of the Catholic Union of electoral committees (political party in 1884).
1873-1883	First laws on bilingualism in Belgium.
1879-1884	Unrest in education following the Van Humbeeck Law which gave advantages to secular public schools.
1880	The first women allowed into university.
1885	Founding of the Belgium Worker's Party.
1887-1889	First of the social legislation under the Beernaert government; continued from 1900-1903 and 1920-1924.

1893	First revision of the constitution: poll tax replaced by "multiple universal suffrage"; election of the first socialist members of parliament.
1894	Quaregnon Charter (socialist manifesto).
1898	Full legal equality of Dutch and the French language.
1899	Introduction of proportional representation, but only within the jurisdiction of districts.
1907-1908	Leopold II renounces personal sovereignty over the Congo which becomes a colony of the Belgium state.
1909	Introduction of personal military service (extended to all men in 1913).
1914	Law making education compulsory.
1914-1918	Flemish unrest encouraged by the German occupiers.
1919	Rwanda-Burundi placed under Belgium mandate.
1920-1921	Founding of the Belgium Communist Party.
1921	Second reform of the constitution: this brings in one vote universal suffrage for men (in practice since 1919).
1922	Treaty on economic union between Belgium and Luxembourg.
1929	Publishing of the *Compromis des Belges* by K. Huysmans and J. Destree, in favor of speaking a single language in Flanders and Walloonia, with a special status for Brussels.
1930	The University of Gand made completely Flemish.
1931	Founding of a Flemish fascist party *Verdinaso*, followed by a National Socialist Party "Rex Christus" (called "rexists" by Leon Degrelle in 1935.
1936	The *Union Catholique* splits into two tendencies, one Flemish the other Walloon.
1938-1944	Compulsory insurance against illness and unemployment.

1945-1950	Energetic punishment of war criminals and collaborators (the "inciviques").
1945-1951	The question of monarchy: abdication of Leopold III in 1951.
1948	Universal suffrage for women (from 1919 in local elections).
1954-1958	Second education unrest, resolved with an agreement that set public and private schools on a par as well as funding.
1960	Independence of the Belgium Congo.
1962	Independence of Rwanda-Burundi.
1962-1963	Final settlement of the linguistic barrier.
1968	The French section of the Catholic University of Louvain transferred to Walloonia.
1970	Third reform of the constitution: creation of three partially autonomous regions (Flanders, Walloonia and Brussels) and three cultural communities (Dutch, French and German); recognition of four linguistic regions (Dutch, French, German and Brussels as a bilingual region).
1972	Creation of a large consultative committee for the emancipation of women.
1977-1978	Community agreement (named Egmont pact) aimed at drawing to a close the reform of institutions.
1979	Creation of minor partial governments within the central government.
1980	Fourth reform of the constitution: expanding the attributions of the Flemish, German and French speaking communities and extending the powers of the Flemish and Walloon regions.
1988	Fifth reform of the constitution: this sets out the region of Brussels as capital.

THE NORDIC COUNTRIES:
A TYPE OF DEMOCRATIC SPIRIT

Guy De Faramond

The Nordic democracies have often been seen as models by foreign observers which must mean that they are on the one hand perfectly well-balanced, and that on the other it is possible to export them. In fact each nation has adopted a political system that suits its own particular situation; the Scandinavian balance of institutions and democratic practices being subject to differing interpretations and even fierce argument. Let us therefore take the Nordic countries for what they are: democracies that have tried to reconcile social justice with political realism, while at the same time remaining aware of the shortcomings of their systems.

Monarchies, ruled by wise kings conscious of the profound changes taking place in society, lacking any colonial empire and spared the blood-bath of the First World War (also the Second World War for Sweden); the three Scandinavian countries: Denmark, Norway and Sweden, would experience relatively peaceful "revolutions." *Evolution* marked by strikes and tension but without violence; apart from in Sweden in 1931 and the tragedy of Adalen when five workers were killed by an unimportant officer who had miscalculated the situation. Such an unusual tragedy shocked public opinion and contributed to the landslide victory of the Social Democrats in the 1932 elections. In the same way, if a historian peruses the history of the Scandinavian countries over the last two centuries, she/he would find very few instances where the violence of an event warranted even temporarily the suspension of liberal and subsequently democratic governmental and institutional rule. The evolution towards parliamentary democracy took place between 1860 and 1920 under the impetus of the parties, public debate, the unions and above all the ballot box. This aversion to violent change has been a long-standing tradition and resulted in the political practice of consensus and democracy. Nevertheless there have been two occasions when violence has also come to the fore. The assassination of Olof Palme on the 28 February 1986 profoundly shocked the Swedes. It was the first murder of a politician since... the assassination of Gustav III at a masked ball at the Opera, in March 1792. The reaction of the Swedes was unanimous: "How could such a thing happen here? It is a terrible thing in itself but also an attack on our peaceful democratic traditions." Between these two dates in fact the history of Scandinavian democracy was gradual and "natural."

A DEMOCRATIC HISTORY
ENACTED BY QUIET INTERLUDES

We should emphasize three stages in this history although this might possibly be slightly too schematic. The first at the end of the 18th Century and two thirds of the next, and the broad *liberal reform movement.* Sweden's Gustavus III, since 1772, had been one of Europe's most "enlightened despots." A francophile who surrounded himself with philosophers and founded the Swedish Academy; he was also keen on buttressing his own absolute power. His assassination in 1792 by a young liberal nobleman who opposed him for his absolutism, paradoxically launched the kingdom into a process of reform that in the long run would lead to Charles XIII's (1809-1818) acceptance of a liberal constitution in 1809. This would remain in place until 1975; enshrining over this period the separation of powers and acting as a prelude to the increased hold of the parliamentary legislature during the second half of the 19th Century. So under Charles XV, between 1859 and 1872, there occurred a rapid political, economic and religious modernization: tolerance of religious dissenters (1859), reform of local administration and the increase of power of town councils (1860), the Criminal Code of 1862, setting up of free exchange in 1864-65 and finally in 1866 the forming of two Chambers voted by poll suffrage, the *Riksdag*, that would soon be dominated by the Peasants Party *Lantmannapartiet* led by Arvid Posse — Prime Minister at the beginning of the 1880's.

Denmark and Norway, with a few slight differences, followed the same line of development, though slightly different in the latter case because of the question of national independence from Sweden, finally achieved in 1905. The liberal movement became active in Denmark relatively early on at the end of the 18th Century, initiated by a widespread reform of education and above all the crucial abolition of serfdom and the redistribution of land in 1788. Putting his seal on this process King Frederick VII (1848-1863) promulgated a constitution with a democratic flavor that would operate in Denmark, Sleswig and Holstein. Finally a constitutional amendment voted in 1866 set up two chambers, the *Landsting*, elected on a limited basis and the *Folketing* where the popular mass political parties would dominate because the amendment also extended the right to vote to all men "of good repute and who have lived in the constituency for over a year." Consequently, in a country at peace and with little migration, the Folketing would have been voted by virtual universal male suffrage.

In Norway, following the Act of Union, signed with Sweden in 1815, Prince Bernadot, who would soon be king of Sweden and Norway with the title of Charles John XIV (1818-1844), was forced to agree to the liberal constitution of Eidsvoll that gave full legislative power to a *Storting* elected on a broad poll suffrage and left the king only with the right to dissolve the house. Further political developments confirm the liberal nature of the regime. A law in 1836 set up the system of municipal councils, voted by almost universal suffrage. Then in July 1884 the threshold for national elections was lowered significantly. Civil servant or former civil servants were also given the vote, a graphic example of the great esteem in Scandinavian countries of public service.

Even in Finland, under Russian administration since 1809 (because the Tsar had the title of Grand Duke of Finland) there was a clear liberal evolution. The country was in fact self governing and through a decree issued in 1869, the Tsar made the Diet into a parliament meeting every three years also granting autonomy to rural villages.

By the end of the 1880's the Nordic nations had clearly entered the epoch of parliamentary monarchy: their chambers generally elected on a broad electoral basis and their sovereigns respecting the political balance of power. Above all democratic practices were already well established in a type of government that allowed initiative at a local level. This practice was tied to a dual tradition that Sweden illustrates well. Firstly social: *bruk*. In the same way as the *mir* in Russia, the Scandinavian *brik* gave society a physical organization and linked it to political myths of idealized communal life and harmony, where true democracy could exist in the context of a defined area and close ties between all producers of wealth. The *bruk* means a small industrial concern created far away from the towns. There were about a hundred all over the center and south of Sweden. These small isolated colonies gave birth to a very strong collective spirit and were the nursery ground of various community institutions of modern Sweden. The workers of the *bruk* labored in return for what the owner of the business, their employer gave them: a house, a pension for the elderly, medical care and schooling for the young. A cooperative spirit and paternalistic caring, at the core of this type of collective enterprise, evolved from this form of organization of life and work, together with the political tradition of the importance of the village council. The widespread autonomy of municipal organizations as well would contribute in a significant way to the development of Scandinavian political culture that favored the election of national assemblies; the Swedish Riksdag, the Danish Landsting and Folketing, the Norwegian Storting or the Finnish Diet. Hence it was through three successive phases — constitutional/ municipal/ parliamentary — that the process of political liberalization would gently unfold. There still was to remain a fourth stage that would finally crown the Nordic democratic institutions: universal suffrage and the organization of political life through national political parties.

The end of the 19th Century and the two thirds of the next century therefore form the second cycle of modern Scandinavian political history and could be given the title *domination of the social democrats.* As has been seen above Denmark was the first to obtain almost complete universal suffrage with the establishment of the Folksting in 1866. Its development between 1866 and 1924 serves as an exemplum. Up until that time J.B.S. Estrup, a conservative, had governed the country (1875-1894) supported by the king and the Landsting, a sort of upper chamber. Yet a democratic dynamic was gathering force under pressure from the parliamentary opposition in the Folksting, under the leadership of Ch. Berg and then J.C.Christensen. An agricultural crisis and a serious workers' conflict in 1899 helped the moderate left to gain power following the 1901 elections who implemented in 1915 constitutional reform which gave women the right to vote and instituted elections by universal suffrage for the Landsting. From then on, apart from a few exceptions, the country was governed up until the 1970's by the social democrats. Initially led by Torwald Stauning the party quickly developed a policy of social intervention: health insurance, unemployment insurance, pensions, paid holidays and educational reform, all in place by the 1920's.

The Swedish evolution is similar since by the end of the 19th Century a Social Democrat Party and a workers' Central LO (1898) had been formed who rapidly took on a crucial role in the management of social conflicts. Despite a spirited resistance by the conservatives the Social Democrats succeeded in forcing economic reform (pension rights in 1913, eight hour working day in 1919) and constitutional change (universal suffrage in 1907 and the vote for women in 1921) prior to becoming the largest party in the Riksting in 1920 under the leadership of Hjalmar Branting. The latter got into parliament in 1896 and had a seminal influence on the party; fighting vigorously against, in both Sweden as well as in European congresses, the tide of Bolshevik ideas and methods which during the 1920's were being portrayed as an international model. At the Berne Internationale in February 1919 Branting defined the social democrat approach to politics in the following terms: "We have to stay rock-solid in the field of democracy. Social reorganization, always more thoroughly penetrated by socialism, can not be achieved nor above all given stability, if it is not based on the conquests of democracy nor if it fails to remain rooted to the principles of freedom. The constituent institutions of all democracies: freedom of speech and of the press, the right of assembly, universal suffrage, the parliamentary system with its institutions that guarantee the involvement and decisions-making of the people, the right to form coalitions etc., are for the proletariat, both at the same time, the instruments of emancipation and the class struggle." Branting therefore saw in the concept of democracy an instrument of liberation which his Bolshevik opponents qualified as "bourgeois" and "formalist." So by having the Swedish Social Democrat Party accept the involvement of the working classes in the democratic institutions and practices of the bourgeois state, the socialist leader attempted to portray the "Red Party" as a credible political organization capable of playing its role in government and power in a non-violent and consensual manner. He succeeded, either through coalition or else with a solely social democrat government, and Branting held power from 1920 to 1925 when he died. From 1932 onwards the social democrats held an absolute majority in the chamber and were to remained in power up until the present with a small interruption from 1976 to 1982. Both Tage Erlander (1946-69) and Olof Palme (1969-76/1982-86) would continue implementing the social program and political philosophy of Branting.

Norway confirms the Scandinavian political process: universal suffrage in 1898, vote for women in 1913, then Labor got to power in 1935 leading to a period of more than 30 years of government marked by a policy of strong social intervention under the leadership of Gerhardsen.

The Finnish evolution, though following the same general direction, was nevertheless more stormy, marked by the struggle against its mighty neighbor Russia and subsequently the Soviet Union. Finland also elaborated its own path to democracy, wresting universal suffrage and the vote of women in 1906 from the Russians, who in the last decade of the 19th Century had become increasingly more overbearing; obtaining finally independence after a violent civil war between whites and reds from 1918 to 1920. The national question, and the distrust of the socialist that ensued, believed to be in league with Moscow, hindered for a long time the establishment of a social democrat party on the model of the other Nordic countries; on the contrary favored the agrarian and conservative parties who from General Mannerheim and P.E. Svinhufvud in the 30's and Urho Kekkonen (agrarian) between 1956 and 1981 together with President Paasikivi, were to hold power almost continuously.

During the 1960's and 1970's the social democrats were to experience an unprecedented political crisis and crisis of identity; which forced the parties, in the face of their first electoral defeats, to question the limits of social intervention. This crisis of the *Scandinavian model* forms the third historical stage of the Nordic nations' democratic evolution. The facts are clear: the elections of 1965 in Norway marked the first serious defeat of the Scandinavian social democrats; a coalition led by Per Borten, formed of conservatives, agrarians and liberals were to beat Gerhardsen the Labor leader. The new government of course implemented the draft legislation left over by the Labor party (complementary pensions and raising the school-leaving age); a prime example of the Nordic spirit of consensus. Yet this initial setback was confirmed by further social democrat electoral defeats. Olof Palme fell from power in Sweden in 1976 leaving the center party of Thorbjorn Falldin victorious, while in Denmark the post of prime minister in 1982 went to the conservative leader Poul Schluter. Finland, which as previously stated was an atypical Nordic country, was the exception that goes somewhere to confirming the rule with a social democrat, Mauno Koivisto, becoming president in 1982.

Even though the conservative experiment was not always a success (I refer to the Falldin parenthesis in Sweden) it is still obvious that the social democrat model had reached a crisis-point. Especially as one of the key issues during these crucial years had been the problem of European integration. Should they turn their back on a social model that had taken 50 years of intervention to build? Had the side-effects of this model taken over from the beneficial elements? Several books pose this sort of direct and controversial question. Roland Huntford, long-time Stockholm correspondent for a quality British newspaper, denounced the *New Totalitarianism* in his best seller, translated into French in 1975, in which he compared social democratic Sweden to Huxley's *best of all worlds*. In other words a world where "a population of slaves, without being forced, love their slavery." Economic security, isolation in a cocoon of well-being, total submission to collective authority, love of state, the power of bureaucrats; these are the symptoms of a "gentle totalitarianism" stigmatized by Huntford with the brazen intention of shocking the reader and of dismantling this much vaunted model.

Is the Swedish model, weakened and given a rough ride by critics, dead? It is true its citizens have less respect for the law, that fiscal fraud has reached great heights, that collective negotiations are no longer centralized as before, that public esteem has been diminished following among other things the sale of Bofor arms to Iran and other countries. Furthermore "Nordic Pudjadism" that emerged in the late 1970's with the anti-taxation parties indicates of more profound problem. At the same time these movements existed in Denmark under a lawyer M. Glistrup, in Norway with A. Lange, in Finland with M. Vennamo defending the corporate demands of the small farmers. These groups, apart from in the Danish Parliament where in 1975 Glistrup's Progress Party was the third largest political group, have never disturbed the smooth functioning of the Scandinavian democratic process. Yet they do underline the fact that although the egalitarian spirit is deeply anchored it might be corrupted by a strictly corporatist movement; that the "blissful Swedish need" (*Kungliga Svenska Avundsjukan* to echo an expression that Strindberg once used) might be open to protecting sectarian interests over and above the collective good.

Whatever the case, it is obvious that the system has come to a political dead-end: a deficiency of democratic vitality when, since 1932 in the case of Sweden, less than half the electoral body have governed the country through their exclusive representatives, the social democrats. The latter have only held an absolute majority in 1932, 1940 and 1968. This last date was Tage Erlander's "leaving present," the quiet father of the social democrats, a victory such as will doubtless never be had again. Yet it should also be stressed how learning democracy in everyday terms: the high respect for the views of others, the search for consensus, the strength of associative life and the originality of some of the institutions, these are vigorous forces within Scandinavian democracy.

In 1991, Sweden was faced by one of the hardest challenges of its history: European integration. In the autumn of 1990 the four largest parties in the Riksdag — after years of hesitation — in effect crossed the Rubicon by voting on the principle of requesting to join the EEC, the request would then be sent to Brussels in 1991.

Of course it was the upheavals in the Soviet Union and in Eastern Europe that changed the basic elements of the question: Swedish neutrality no longer has the same sacrosanct quality that it had during the cold war. The government announced in March 1991 a referendum in 1994 following negotiations with the EEC. The deal is not yet a foregone conclusion since the Swedes are not yet ready to totally abandon their neutrality. Nevertheless over the months they are steadily realizing that they can no longer remain outside this community which is being built. However there is a definite problem of identity: do the Swedes feel European? The other major event of 1991 was of course the September elections. Never have the social democrats been so low in the opinion polls: 30% in March. This loss of support can be explained by the wearing down effect of being in power, the terrible economic situation, the covert arms sales by the government, but also by the lack of charisma of Ingvar Carlsson and the dithering of the social democrats on the European Community — prior to those first steps of autumn 1991 — which look very much like face-saving solution in the face of general disaffection.

A PARTICULAR DEMOCRATIC CHARACTER

To what might be termed a "shared inheritance" of democratic practices and institutions in western Europe, the Nordic countries add a few distinctive features, still making the Scandinavian order, despite its shortcomings, a distinctive model. I want to briefly describe them and put them into three groups: the openness of political decision-making, the art of conciliation and adult education. The *openness of decision-making*, first: "A tendency to secrecy is a characteristic of all authoritarian regimes," wrote a Finnish professor of law. This candid opinion is worth looking at because it emphasizes the extreme importance of freedom of information in a democratic regime: the authorities must not hide their actions or methods from the people from whom all power emanates. In this sense six countries can now claim to be fully democratic: the four Nordic countries — Finland, Sweden, Denmark and Norway — as well as the United States and France. These alone in fact guarantee constitutionally the right of their citizens to see documents held by the different state organizations, above all the administration. Yet whereas in France for example the law of 1978 intended to improve relations between the administration and those administered to (LARA), it does allow the perusal of "unnamed" documents, yet it is not widely known and the resources are seldom used. In contrast in Sweden, this possibility is not only anchored in tradition since the principle of "transparency (the glass house)" goes back to the 1809 constitution, but also and above all since it has become a usual and widespread process.

This publication of administrative documents has two complementary roles. It contributes firstly to the forming of public opinion: the press makes extensive use of this right, allowing the media to involve the citizen by initiating far-reaching debate on future social plans, a dialogue resulting in an informal way — since the Scandinavian countries do not have the right of referendum nor of initiative — in direct involvement in the political debate. It also has a role in those practices supposed to oversee the smooth running of state organs, since this publicity maintains control not only *a posteriori* but equally concomitantly: a strict watch can be kept on classified events as well as those in progress, allowing at any time the end, change or return of public debate. Administrative transparency is allied to and introduces a further practice: the re-opening of discussion which the Swedes call *remiss*.

The drawing up of laws is, theoretically, in effect the domain of the administration. In practice the latter hands this task over to commissions fielded by experts whom it appoints (*Kommitteer*). At present in Sweden nearly 300 commissions are at work, presenting a hundred or so reports or draft reports each year. But once handed back to government each report is not only made public but also subject to a long procedure where consultation with various organizations occur. The procedure called *remiss* is where a long list of administrations, union, professional or collective organizations are asked by the minister concerned, to express to him — in writing and publicly — their views and ultimately put forward counter proposals or amendments. This stage of *remiss* is on sensitive subjects accompanied by a broad public debate following which any person is allowed to send the government their own contribution.

One might think that such a decision-making process involves *the art of conciliation* to a high degree and demands a unique cultural mentality. Indeed, even though tensions have increased over the past few years consensus remains at the heart of social policy. This for example is expressed in the "rules of negotiations" between employers and employees, who in Sweden, ever since the agreement of Salstjobaden in 1938 results in negotiations between the two parties and the inability of strike actions as long as negotiations are running. This art of conciliation, strictly practiced, is not just a question of marrying fire with water but of effectively controlling the decision-making process — several other commissions and individuals are exemplary. Let us look briefly at the quite widespread role of the Constitutional commission *Konstitutionsutskottet)* — a sort of Constitutional council — and the delegation of twelve deputies who form the parliamentary commission with far-reaching powers of investigation, at the request of a member of parliament, into the workings of the Riksdag. Let us linger rather over the role of the four judicial *ombudsmen.* They are recruited by Parliament from career judges and oversee both the administration of justice and judicial proceedings, judging the legality or opportuneness of decisions already taken or about to be taken. Without binding powers, the *ombudsman* are only able to apportion blame or appeals. Yet they have considerable weight: public opinion. Every citizen in fact can request a judicial *ombudsman*, without too much trouble or cost, and the latter are held in great esteem by the public. The number of cases viewed each year (about 4000) shows the ever increasing importance of their role. They are helped by two more recent figures: the chancellor of Justice who is a sort of government *ombudsman* referred to by public services to negotiate agreements with businesses or to control them; there was also in 1971 an addition to the system, a consumer *ombudsman* who fights at the request of individuals against unfair trading or misleading advertising.

The basis elements of Scandinavian democracy would be incomplete if we ignored one essential element; one which in a way, links all the rest; initiating the involvement of citizens and also limiting their conceits. *Education,* above all adult education has the function of laying the civic foundations of society. Sweden for example, where compulsory education goes back to 1841, draws its spirit of democracy from the popular movements of the 19th Century, driven by thousands of teachers in a fight against alcoholism, prostitution, to educate adults so profoundly irrigating the nation, even in the smallest of villages. So, in Denmark another example, in 1844 a clergyman named Grundtvig created the first "public school" meant for peasants. In Sweden the "public high schools" came into existence from 1868 onwards. These movements have continued adapting to political and social change: even today one person out of six goes to "evening classes." Subsidized by the state and the village, schools are open to all: there are 107 "écoles superieures" where teaching takes place above all during the winter, giving out additional general information. Each school decides on its program which of course includes Swedish, literature, history, civic instruction, psychology, chemistry and hygiene. These are strictly organized and subsidized. Furthermore there are "study circles" which are less formal but are recognized, completing the education of adults either at work or elsewhere. There are about 200,000 study circles and over two million people participate in civic, literary, historic or manual activities on offer...

Olof Palme might provide us with the final word, comparing the study circles with "mini-democracies." Throughout his life he retained a strong awareness of the role that continuing education plays in the civic life of Scandinavia. Did he not say at the 1969 social democrat congress: "Sweden is a democracy based on the study circle. It is due to the circles that generations have trained themselves in critical analysis, so as to be able to make reasonable decisions and to work together without abandoning their ideals. It is often in the study circle that proposals for social change are first airing." In the end it is a veritable "democracy of circles" that the Swedish model illustrates, which could also be seen as a *democratic social spirit.*

CHRONOLOGY

1788	Abolition of serfdom, redistribution of land, education reform (Denmark). Some officers try to set up a republic in Finland (Anjala plot).
1789	Gustavus III of Sweden restores an absolute monarchy, but gives equality in law to all his subjects.
1792	Banning of the slave trade (Denmark).
1809	Tsar Alexander I conquers Finland which becomes a Grand Duchy of the Russian crown. Sweden adopts a constitution which sees to the separation of powers and the disclosure of administrative documents.
1814	To gain Norway, Marshal Bernadotte, regent and then king of Sweden, invades this country. This was to be the last war for Sweden, a country with a military tradition up until then. The Eidsvoll Constitution is adopted by the Norwegian Assembly on the 17 May. It gives legislative power to a Storting elected by poll tax whereas the King has a right of veto. The two Kingdoms, united by the act of union, share only the royalty and a minister of foreign affairs.
1840	Bernadotte, ruling under the name of Charles-John XIV, agrees to reform the Swedish constitution of 1809 by giving the Council of State the form of a ministry.
1842	Law concerning primary education (Sweden).
1848-1863	During the reign of Frederic VII Denmark gives itself a constitution. Uprising in the duchies

of Slegvig and Holstein by separatists
helped by the Prussians.

1862 Law on religious tolerance (Sweden). Law over the
village organization (Sweden).

1864-1865 Setting up of free trade (Sweden).

1866 Appointment of two chambers elected by poll tax
in Sweden: the Riksdag, and in Denmark:
the Landsting and Folketing (for the latter
virtually universal suffrage).

1869 The Tsar authorizes the Finnish Diet to meet
regularly (every three years) and grants
autonomy to the country villages.

1889 Creation of a Swedish Social Democrat Party.

1897 Dictatorial power under a Russian general
Bobrikov in Finland (policy of intensive
Russification under Nicholas II).

1898 Adoption of universal suffrage for men in Norway.
Creation of the LO Worker's Confederation
in Sweden.

1901 Defeat of the Danish conservatives: the moderate
left comes to power.

1904 Assassination of Bobrikov in Finland.

1905 (Peaceful) independence of Norway. Tsar Nicholas
II stops his policy of Russification in
Finland and agrees wide autonomy for the
diet, replaced from 1906 by a chamber
elected by universal suffrage. Women take
part in this election (an innovation for the
whole of Europe).

1907 Hardening of Nicholas II's policy in Finland:
opponents are deported to Siberia, the
chamber is dissolved and Russian is made
obligatory.

1907-1909 Universal suffrage for men in Sweden. Women
obtain the right to vote in Norway.

1913 Law governing pension rights in Sweden.

1915	Universal suffrage and right to vote for women in Denmark.
1917	Finnish independence.
1918-1920	Civil war in Finland: the "reds" are beaten.
1920	Social Democrat (Branting) government in Sweden.
1921	Right to vote for women in Sweden.
1922	Law governing religious freedom in Finland.
1924	The Social democrats in power in Denmark (T. Stauning).
1930	Conservative governments in Finland (Kivimaki).
1931	Tragedy at Adalen in Sweden: 5 dead during a strike.
1932	The Swedish Social Democrats obtain an absolute majority in the Riksdag.
1935	The Labor Party in power in Norway.
1939-1940	Russo-Finnish war. Denmark and Norway are invaded by Germany.
1946-1969	Successive governments under Tage Erlander in Sweden: the social democratic "model" is finally put into place.
1953	Constitutional reform in Denmark: a single chamber, the Folketing. The right to succession to the throne is granted to women.
1956-1981	U. Kekkonen is elected president of the republic in Finland.
1962	Helsinki convention of cooperation between the four Nordic countries.
1963	Fall of the Labor government in Norway.
1969	Olof Palme is successor to T. Erlander as leader of the Swedish Social Democrat Party and government. Failure of "Nordek," the Nordic common market after pressure by the USSR on Finland.
1972	Denmark confirms by referendum its entry to the EC (Norway refuses).

1976	Defeat of the Swedish Social Democrats in the elections. They lose power for the first time since 1932.
1976-1981	Return of the Norwegian Labor Party to power.
1982	Conservative government in Denmark (P. Schluter). Return of the Social Democrats to power in Sweden.
1986	Assassination of O. Palme (28 February).
1990	In Norway a Labor government under a woman, Gro Harlem Brundtland.

THE LONELY DESTINY
OF THE RUSSIAN DEMOCRATS

Caroline Ibos

If one were solely to follow a liberal and institutional definition of democracy, it would be fruitless to search for its existence in Russia in its intellectual or political past. First of all historical reality only shows ephemeral and incomplete experiments in democracy. Following the 1905 revolution in April 1906 a *Duma* representative of all the social classes was elected, and was dissolved in June of the very same year. It had no constituent power and very limited legislative powers. In February 1907 a second *Duma* was elected without any change to the electoral procedure and sat until the 3 June 1907 when Stolypin staged a coup d'état, dissolved the assembly and unilaterally changed the basis of eligibility. Secondly, opposition ideas in Russia were characterized from the beginning by an unwillingness to compromise, and as a result pouring scorn on bourgeois freedom as a substitute for "absolute freedom." Finally, in Russian for most of the 19th Century the word *democracy* had a pejorative sense and was only later rehabilitated through its misuse, to legitimize the communist system (socialist *democracy* and *democratic* centralism).

In view of this it might be more apposite to theorize on the lack of democracy. Yet such a procedure would mean falling into several pitfalls: first of all, concocting a reality that reduces the differences between the Russian revolutionary movement in the last century and the totalitarian Soviet regime — which would amount to obscuring the excessive nature of totalitarianism; secondly, arguing over (suspect) cliches such as: the absence of a bourgeoisie which precluded the development of liberal ideas, the geographical setting of Russia on the edge of Europe and Asia or even the endemic mysticism of Russian intellectuals; finally, failing to understand that democracy can not be reduced to just procedural political solutions (republican or parliamentary) but is, more generally, a desire that troubled history, a desire to break with tradition and set mankind free.

It also seems more apposite to examine Russian social thought, at least up until the break of 1917, as the main thrust of a strategy that wanted to free the people from a rule that set itself up as sacred and everlasting. Born of the Enlightenment, aggravated by the French Revolution, opposition thinking was aroused by the realization of a minority of enlightened aristocrats of the intolerable suffering of the majority of the peasant masses. Alexander Nikolaievich Radichtchov, an obscure civil servant at the time of Catherine II, was first to express the cultured man's crisis of conscience and challenge to tradition.

BIRTH OF THE RUSSIAN *INTELLIGENTSIA*

Indeed, in early summer 1790, Radichtchov published, thanks to a strangely slack censorship, *A Journey from Saint Petersburg to Moscow*; and this both isolated and anguished action anticipates in three ways the (tragic) fate of the Russian *intelligentsia*. On the one hand, hiding under a Romanesque title this text was an acerbic critique of absolutism, counterbalancing this with rapturous glorification of liberty, heralding the preoccupation — later to become a mission — of intellectuals with the people's cause. This responsibility in both moral (because of compassion) and concrete terms (sacrificing their lives) — would socially distinguish over the next two centuries the uniqueness of Russian *intellectuals*, a founding member of the *intelligentsia*: their demands were based, not on the defence of class interests, but on the level of ideas and morality. Furthermore, a century after Peter the Great, Radichtchov raised the question of the Europeanization of Russia, precisely to challenge the basis of Petrogradism itself; in other words autocracy, orthodoxy and nationalism. In reality, leaving aside any reassessment of the destiny of Russia in the light of the inroads made by the Enlightenment, leaving aside praise for freedom tempered by the formula of the social contract, Radichtchov was the first to identify a Russian identity, distinct from his understanding of Europe. Finally if one bears in mind the fact that the publication of the *Journey* resulted in the author's imprisonment, internal exile and death, then one can understand why ideas and survival were always linked with danger; so historically the fight against unjust authorities, from Radichtchov to Solzhenitsyn, was inextricably bound to the realm of ideas as well as action, and hence a long list of ill-fated biographies. The experience of democracy in Russia was linked to secrecy: not just a question of simple parties but clandestine plots by lone individuals.

Radichtchov might be seen as a precursor to the *intelligentsia*; precursor because to be an *intellectual* it was not enough for a writer or publicist to devote himself to the people's cause but would also need, at least until the total destruction of society, to be in essence a revolutionary. This begs further clarification: firstly the *intellectual* was a martyr, as a consequence of his refusal in the name of the people to reject a belief in certain universal values, which condemns him subjectively to hardship and objectively to violence. Yet we are quite right to then ask ourselves where this violence comes from, and furthermore who is the hangman: the state? The people? (For instance, in the summer of 1874, the peasants failed to understand the actions of the students when they "went to the people" and handed them over to the Tsar's police!) A tacit alliance between the authorities and the enslaved people? The democratic dream came about in Russia through a narrow entrance: the *intelligentsia* only briefly triumphed when they succeeded in allying themselves with the people against the autocracy, in other words when they triumphed over their idealism and reappraised as educated men their ethical relationship with the people. The second question concerns the birth of the *intelligentsia* as a social category. Indeed it was the revolt of the Decembrists on December 14,1825, that gave birth to the *intelligentsia* not least because by then the *intellectuals* had assumed their revolutionary character, to such an extent that the terms were to become synonymous. The birth was also a liberation: the failed coup d'état in 1825 ended any interlude there may have been for the *intellectuals*, in terms of limiting their contribution (like Radichtchov) only to criticism and at the same time gave birth to a social category. The sole free beings in a society of slaves, they were fated to enlighten society and reveal the uncertainty and fragility of the authorities, moving from the intransigence of the political system to specific situations. The *intelligentsia* therefore broke with tradition following the example of the Decembrists, at the same time giving up their own past (sacrificing themselves) and tradition.

A break with tradition, to shake the existing world to its very foundations, questioning the legitimacy or existence of all institutions be they political, economic, social or religious. So the Russian *intelligentsia* condemned the actual authority of the Tsar, the Church and the landed nobility with the intention of uniting government and the people, through the tautological slogan: government of the people. The synchronism of schism and unification signified upheaval resulting in revolution, the founding of a new world. The people, through revolution would emerge as a political force; the sharp change through revolution would make everything clear (revelation), in other words apocalypse in the strictest sense of the word, encompassing the destruction /foundation/ construction sequence of a break (a single short sharp action) with tradition (a series of quasi-ritual actions which by definition are handed down).

They needed a break with tradition in order to free themselves from specific locations which undermine the struggle; tradition in essence betrays one because it keeps the people in ignorance and darkness: the deep rich darkness of fertile ground (*tchernozioms*) that limits the Moujik's conscious universe because he loves the earth. So that the people might accede to this "moral threshold" of understanding, the *intelligentsia* undertook to dispel the darkness and clear the horizon — to Europe. It is no coincidence that the Decembrists were those very same officers who ten years before their failed coup, had beaten Napoleon and been to Paris; at the same time discovering Europe and the fact that Russia was a great European power. They refused to accept a "Russian reality" separate from the rest of the world, isolated in time, replacing this "Russian myth" with the dynamism of modernization. This would mean initially dragging Russia step by step out of its backwardness. Necessity and the obsessive lure of a new world meant that upheaval would occur through amalgamating into one strategy progress and the Labor of the masses as a political force.

According to this analysis there were three periods and events that mark uncertainty and changes in direction; periods that demonstrate the contribution of the *intelligentsia* in developing the people as a political force; events when Russia, on the point of dissolving (or escaping?) takes its place in history and joins the history of Europe. Hence in the mid-18th Century, overshadowed by the repression that followed the Decembrist outburst, there took place the "incredible decade" of Herzen, Bielinsky and Bakunin inaugurating the theory of a just relationship between the authorities and the Russian people and allowing them to rise up from political oblivion. Then, the 1905 revolution which coincided with the blossoming of Russian philosophy under the influence, above all, of Piotr Struve the founder of the first legally permitted liberal newspaper and shortly after of the Constitutional Democrat Party. In 1917, Lenin in the tragic role of *deus ex machina* harnessing the popular revolt and hijacking, through Bolshevik alchemy, their aspirations for political change into the Soviet regime. And finally, the instigator of *perestroika*, appealing to the older generations of dissidents, and the new generations of *intelligentsia* to discard the more dogmatic delusions, vanquish popular apathy and convince a battered society of the correctness of his reforms.

1848: THE PEOPLE AS A THEORY

In 1848, the European revolutions dominated events; the "remarkable decade" with its Herzens and Bakunins evaluates this with analyses of the philosophy of history, which in fact were the origin of populism (*Narodnichestvo*). Populism was the intellectuals' ideal of peasant socialism, at the forefront of political protest from 1848 up until the economic upheavals of the end of the century. It never had the form of an organized political party, nor a coherent doctrinal system. A broad radical movement, from it sprang factions and tendencies, for example the Nihilists, the anarchists and the Social revolutionaries. Yet it also demonstrated unity, showing the revolutionary commitment of the whole of the *intelligentsia*. Indeed leaving aside their rivalries, the populists drew together key principles advocated since 1848 by Herzen and Bakunin; Jacobin principles that criticized the western liberals and radicals for unsuccessfully prosecuting their own revolutions; a dual slogan summarizes these eclectic principles: populism is revolution without history and society without a state.

In 1848 Herzen, who up until then had been strongly Hegelian, drawing from the failure of the European revolutions rejected any inherent superior guiding principle of history. This volte-face led to a reappraisal of all his most fundamental theories: first of all "inevitable progress" which assumed a model of historical progress that linked technical and human progress meeting ultimately some time in the future; progress as an absolute; finally the conviction that the west, at that time in the midst of an industrial and political revolution, provided the broad guidelines of a model of civilization that backward Russia should aspire to.

Herzen drew populist opprobrium with his precept of a non-mechanistic evolution — telluric — a sort of unpredictable and indomitable rise of human freedom. He argued against the notion that technical progress automatically conditioned human progress or that man's domination of the natural and human world through increased knowledge, does not necessarily lead to achieving liberation, morality or the end of oppression and the arbitrary. On the contrary, according to him, technical progress leads inexorably to the unhappiness of man who thus destroys all hope of freedom, equality or social morality. So Herzen denounced the barbaric vanity of industrialization, of capitalism and hypocritical liberalism; holding that the only just and worthy revolution would be one which destroys the perverted social structures, so as to discover the truth about the people, and human nature until then buried or veiled. He claimed that in the face of this decadent Europe, with its bourgeois mirage of degrading democracy, Russia should save the world from lies and achieve real human progress by revealing the real nature of man.

If this were the case then a different civilization would emerge that would restore man to himself. To this end Herzen looked to the natural harmony as it had existed in the *mir*. The *mir*, a medieval Russian institutional myth, was defined as the free association of peasants, entrusted with the periodical redistribution of arable land and through its decisions giving every member an equal say. The *mir* therefore would form the criteria on which federal, autonomous socialist units would be based. For Herzen and his successors this original society would be enough to guarantee a *humanist* system based on the absence of private property and true equality, since it incorporated the most profound moral instincts and universal values. At a stroke the anonymous, remote and considerable power of the state would be removed, since its continuation would pose a threat to this delicate balance. In the safe world of popular proceedings (the village *mir*) order would never again be imposed by the violence of raison d'état but because of justice, which only needed a suitable environment to flourish spontaneously, and through solidarity, compassion which in many ways resembles the Greek notion of *filia*. This type of populism, illustrated by the protection of the people in the *mir* by the *mir*, leads towards a social ethic that is antithetical to a European democratic archetype.

The populists therefore tried at one and the same time to bring the people out of political oblivion and fire Russia with a different force than the European enlightenment. But they dreamed of a dogmatic socialism that emphasized practical equality over equality before the law, which complicates rather than rationalizes pressure mechanisms on the individual. Even Herzen, who reflected on the fate of the individual, failed to foresee the precariousness of their situation when weighed against the general good but would emphasize first and foremost the indomitable nature of inner freedom, the desires of the soul and the individual's responsibility in relation to the community. The populists fought against serfdom up until it was abolished; they condemned social and economic inequality; they proclaimed their love of the people; yet in general they made individual freedom subject to wider exigencies. Most of them, above all the intransigent generation of "sons," paid scant attention to the individual. They felt it was demonstrated that the place of the individual in society would be directly related to the social transformation — the overriding objective.

In short Russian populism far from resolving the break with the past maintained this vague past with a vague myth; building syncretic and messianic utopias that detracted from the modernizing dynamism of progress and mixed their mythological origins with the myth of their destiny. They considered the "people" through rose-tinted glasses, and endowed them with qualities that made the reassuring illusion of the *mir* credible. It was only in the 1890's that the industrial revolution and its political consequences — the rise of Marxism and liberalism — freed the committed *intelligentsia* from its obsession with the *mir*.

1905-1917: THE PEOPLE BROUGHT OUT INTO THE OPEN

The turn of the century almost unexpectedly complicated this picture of an archaic Russia, and was at the root of uprisings that painfully showed the unreasonableness of the Imperial autocracy. Structural changes were focused classically along three main axes. An economic axis: Russia of blast furnaces, business banks and commercial companies. A social axis: the application of a process of social distinction illustrated most clearly by the rise of the unions and the bourgeoisie. A cultural axis with the artistic and spiritual renewal of the "age of money," rejecting the aesthetic and moral guidelines fixed by the *populist intelligentsia* during the "age of lead": in other words atheism, materialism, realism and the absolute value of social utilitarianism. Yet these changes took place within the constraints permitted by the Ancien Regime, still clinging to its hold on power despite the reforms of Alexander II. Furthermore the gap between old-fashioned institutions and social aspirations of a society on the verge of becoming modern, was widening. To such an extent that the disturbing contradictions of this budding civil society ended up overpowering the repressive machinery which was in place. They also served to organize and define a specific political domain in which to express conflicts. On the threshold of the 20th Century the state was increasingly under threat from society: a protest movement started by territorial assemblies, supported by the bourgeoisie and mirrored by the peasants and the urban proletariat highlighted an anti-establishment social democratic tendency rather than a liberal current, and demonstrated the possibility of different social classes joining together to stand up for their rights. In contrast to 1848 when a revolutionary movement anticipated a revolutionary event — dooming it to a return to sterile precepts — in 1905 everything came together to highlight the power of the people; to wrest power away from and bid farewell to the anachronistic Tsarist regime.

To get rid of the Ancien Regime would take two attempts (1905 and February/October 1917) — by two different movements: two self-consciously "responsible" revolutions (i.e. ready to justify themselves), staunchly modern, European, with a sustained will and fired by a democratic spirit. The 1905 revolution aspired in the same way as the 1917 revolution to build a just and free world; a similar intuition of the symbolism of revolutionary action would twice occur and notwithstanding the skepticism of some, the suffering or enthusiasm of others, would go from insurrection to revolution. Nevertheless these two revolutionary sequences can not be simplified to a single double triggered mechanism: each was the opposite of the other since they were the framework and implementation of a project that resulted in a choice of societies.

The 1905 revolution was an overtly referential revolution while the 1917 revolution an absolute revolution. The Cadets at the start of the century, led by Piotr Struve and Miliukov, envisaged taking advantage of the increased flexibility of the autocracy to break it and set up a Constituent Assembly. Their idea of revolution had two meanings; a pragmatic view: revolution was the more extreme way of dealing with the autocracy; but also a more symbolic idea: revolution is a historical marker of an irreversible break between the past and modern times. The prime movers of 1905 based their actions on an existing political playing-field; they used the western experience of revolution and the modern state, whether it be a republic (Miliukov) or constitutional monarchy (Strouve) as a paradigm. In contrast the Bolshevik revolution that was triggered by Lenin and Trotsky was scatological and unprecedented; the last trial that would plunge the iniquitous Empire into the burning fire of the people's power and the law. In freeing history from the past both the culmination and starting point for the post-revolution were reached — the new world dawning— as it was already implicit in the revolutionary epic.

This distinction modified both in time and place the scope of the two revolutions. The former tried to align itself with a European situation, retaining notions that came from the rights of man and the citizen — notably the inalienable right to private property and individual freedom — as intangible principles and vehicles of progress. It attempted to unite an already constituted world. The latter wished to increase the speed of the tide of history and according to Marxist dialectics make the "historical leap" spawn an unparalleled universal civilization. Finally the liberal revolution projected the model of the urban citizen onto the individual whereas the Marxist revolution claimed the proletariat to be the precursor of the new man. Proletarian/citizen people: in the 1905 and October 1917 revolutions the people did not have the same role, the same face, actions, nor the same energy. It would therefore seem clear that in their respective analyses the revolutionaries should have attributed them with varying degrees of effectiveness or even symbolic values — one might even speak of aesthetic values. On the other hand it could seem paradoxical that it was precisely in the October revolution that an exhausted and disunited population would play such a minor role, viewed by some American historians as nothing other than a coup d'état that inspired and sustained, through its portrayal in books and images, a popular ideology.

The events of 1905 were initially a huge spontaneous popular uprising subsequently guided by the Cadet Party, driving force of the constitutional movement. The urban masses, with their externally visible density and internal strength, exerted a peaceful pressure on the authorities to demand initially a National Constituent Assembly and ultimately popular sovereignty. The nation is the political status of the people during their fight against those who appropriate ultimate power; the Constituent Assembly is therefore the mechanism that embodies popular sovereignty. Yet the National Assembly could only represent all the people by means of elections. But the election that the Liberals demanded in 1905, a mixture of universal and secret suffrage, marks the moment when the ideal of full popular representation gives way in the polling booth to so many individuals as numbers of votes. So the people becomes a thing that can not be represented yet is necessary if one is to believe that power does not belong to anyone in particular and that it exists independently of those who govern. Power is inviolate, with the sanction of revolution giving the people as a whole a positive menace. This was the meaning of the 1905 revolution when the people were not at the behest of a mythical notion but were the principal players in the power struggle; a player that could always come into its own.

In October 1917 the emancipation of man also acted as a trigger. But the Bolsheviks who ordered the revolt for the good of humanity assumed for themselves exclusive knowledge of the nature of social relations and claimed exclusively to be able to free man of a condition that expropriates him from himself. The party, in other words the avant-guard of the proletariat, in other words again a fraction of a part of society, understood the truth about the people and expresses the desires of the people. The party acts, rather ambiguously, *for* the people, assuming both the ability (after all it did dedicate itself to the cause) but also acts as substitute for the people (acts in its stead). The party line looks for and expresses popular truth; the dividing line between good and evil, right and wrong, and the people from the enemy of the people. It determines the make-up of *us*, the *us* of the people whose only opponent are

those who do not conform; and this popular *us* synthesizes unity
and plurality and is identified with the *us* among the proletariat,
who identify with the *us* of the party, who identify the *us* of its
leader. Through the body, voice and face of the leader the people
are embodied. It not only becomes embodied but also tangible,
ever-present, in speeches and posters, in icons (to be worshipped)
and in performances where the leader plays his own role; after the
1917 revolution the unrepresented Soviet people were represented,
in other words an idealized representation or again in formal rules
of ideological conformity.

1986-1990: THE PEOPLE CONFRONTED BY REALITY

The Soviet regime, born out of a founding violence and under
the sign of a blood-red flag, wished to destroy the "old world." *At
any price* they had to avoid the brutality that weighed down the
west — guilty of imperialism. The price in question was totalitarian
ossification, a modern and sophisticated version of barbarity. From
the setting up of war communism up until 1985, the regime kept
itself in place despite the commotion of the Khrushchev thaw. At
the time, neither the report of the 20th Congress nor the lessening
of censorship symbolized by the publication of Alexander
Solzhenitsyn's novel *A Day in the life of Ivan Denisovich*, nor
again the decrease in diplomatic tension, altered the leading role of
the Party or replaced the legality of its way on a permanent basis.

In the implacably levelled Soviet society, the smallest aspect
of human life could not escape the control of the authorities, with
its hold over the whole social fabric. The Party, its derivatives (the
many official organizations) and the idiocratic bureaucracy had
invaded social life and laid down customary yet still restricting
norms, regulating definitively the way people thought, their
behavior and values. The authorities congratulated themselves that
they had pacified a society where all the proletariat, the unchang-
ing human value, now marched to the same tune towards the same
goal: communism. Doubtless the dissidents marred this fetishistic
illusion of a society without internal contradiction, yet all it needed

was for their treachery or madness to be put on display in a long trial to preserve the balance of the Soviet anti-world.

On the other hand, the spasm that under the banner of *Perestroika* shook the Soviet Union in 1986 was clearly of a different order. An event giving meaning to the news. An unforeseen event even when in retrospect signs are discovered that narrow the gap between the unexpected and the inevitable. An unquantifiable event that in its wake returns Europe to itself and no less raises the slightly embarrassing question of universal principles having a positive force in the intensity of history; with its corollary of democracy as the implementation of these principles.

In December 1986 the First Secretary of the Party, Mikhail Gorbachev himself informed Andrei Sakharov, in exile in Gorki, of his freedom which preceded that of 200 other dissidents. This act meant much more than an attempt to woo the west. Implicitly it was a recognition of political opposition as such, and as a result made a mockery of an order that portrayed itself as eternal. Gorbachev agreed to lift the spell over a society supposedly impervious to disorder, and to scramble the catechism of an unshakable power. Nevertheless this sanctioning of protest needed a regular forum for criticism. Comment in the press added to the lowering of censorship, showed an end to empty phrases and the liberation of previously mesmerized thought. So the objectivization of conflict tore Soviet society apart, engulfing the triumphant ideology with its idealized images in a storm of self-blame and uncertainty.

The "big" literary and social reviews such as *Novyi Mir* or *Ogoniok*, inheritors of an editorial tradition inaugurated by Herzen's *Kolokol* worked toward a "cultural perestroika." Until the 1989 parliamentary elections which established a legal forum for debate, the press had the role of agora (market-place). Each review became the tribune of one or other political tendency (*Ogoniok* the voice-box of democrats; *Neva* of aesthetes; *Nash sovremennik* of nationalists) and together they established an unprecedented pluralistic machine to seize on civil liberties and analyze the transition from totalitarian society to civilian society. But above all the reviews searched in the past for a solution to the identity crisis of society: in proclaiming a right to memory they joined the political future (democracy?) to the question of history.

By digging out works that until then had remained hidden by the censor, showing archive documents — for example of the German-Soviet Pact — by correcting the imbalances of official histories — for example on the massacre of Katyn —, the reviews began the process of reclaiming history for society. This drew attention to the ambiguity of the break with the past that Gorbachev's reforms had accomplished. Indeed this break can be seen, on the one hand, as a way of reconquering the Soviet past; felt as a liberating and perhaps even salutary collective catharsis. On the other hand, through renewed ties with the pre-Soviet past, it was felt to be an attempt to anchor social identity to a point of reference and do away with myths — not in the general sense of representing things but precisely of the great communist epic discourse. In the present confusion the break with the past is ambivalent since it results in ideological control being replaced by other mythological organizations: for example the illusion of "true socialism" which would delegate "all power to the Soviets." In other words the "self-management of the uncorrupted" embodying the rejection of controlling structures; or else a modification of the populist legend, underpinned in different ways by both Rasputin and later by Solzhenitsyn. The reoccurring variations of a Golden Age that might be rediscovered in the Russian village, with its natural sense of community and spiritual freedom. Any democratic overtures that might have existed in the Soviet Union has had less impact than society's attempt to free itself of the *enchanting* idea of an all-embracing solution. The situation seems paradoxical when at the same time as all the balances were crumbling (economy, politics, food distribution) the pace of change increased. Precisely because of those initial reforms. Because of the clash with reality, because of attempts to replace the system of distribution with one of production, the lowering of censorship and the regulating of free enterprise. Yet freedom of information was the only real obstacle to reform of the system. The policy of restructuring is now rejected because in many people's minds there has been a sort of concertina effect, with on one side the widely held view that democracy would be a miraculous palliative (a thaumaturgist or magician appeals to the people's way of thinking) and on the other side the real concrete demands that give democracy a harsh image, at odds with the sort of ideas and images that were portrayed all over the place.

Social uncertainty which is a basic element of democracy, appears unappetizing to former Soviet public opinion. The millions of letters of protest against public policy that are sent every weeks to the newspapers and reviews bear witness to this. Looking at this society in agony because it does not understand itself any more, emphasizes the need to get away from the determinism of a mythical representative and elemental community. In its initial phase *perestroika*, seemed a threat, embodying the danger of imminent chaos, somatized by the possible disintegration of a major part of the Empire (the nationality crisis). Having opened a breach in the system, it destroyed the idea of a strong communist people, without actively nurturing responsibility of the individual in the city or the struggle of the people in relation to the question of sovereignty. And the people, a present-day illusion, is thrashing about without really trying to take hold of power. As if itself diminished by this systemic crisis, the people seem unable to do anything other than lay the seeds of their own self-destruction. The Soviet nation, thrown off balance by the death-throes of totalitarianism that previously had shaped history, seems to have disappeared apart from in official speeches. Lacking the necessary optimism or imagination to think of progress or relinquish its image of itself as a whole it still trusts in the force of destiny. Why should one look to divisions that spell uncertainty in the future and pose a threat to the very heart of the social edifice; why should the polyphony that is a symphony of difference be heard as other than cacophony; how can the future be seen in other terms than a self-justifying mess: the Soviet Union faced by its own weakness questions the outside world as much as itself, not so much over the victory of democracy but over the pitfalls of contemporary democracy.

CHRONOLOGY

1825	Decembrist uprising in Saint Petersburg.
1861	19 February: abolition of serfdom.
1864	Creation with an imperial oukas of territorial assemblies (zemstva); they fostered a constitutional movement which would result in the end in the forming of the Cadet Party.
1873-1874	Peak of the student movement "out to the people," violently suppressed in 1875.
1877	Start of terrorist plots by the revolutionary populists to disorganize the forces of the despotic state.
1879	26 August: forming of a secret group *"Will of the people"* who had as their goal the destabilization of the regime through terrorist actions and the overthrow of the Tsar.
1881	1 March: assassination of Tsar Alexander II by Rysakov a member of the terrorist group *Will of the people.*
1898	Founding of the Social Democrat Party of Russia which was immediately dismantled by the authorities.
1901-1902	Founding of the Socialist Revolutionary Party.
1905	*9 January*: Red Sunday in Saint Petersburg. *October*: General strike; forming at the same time of the Constitutional Democrat Party and the Leningrad Soviet; imperial manifesto promising a constitution.
1906	27 April-8 July: first Duma (National Assembly), dissolved by a coup d'état by Nicholas II's Prime Minister Stolypin.

1917	*23-27 February*: Revolution in Petrograd.
	3 March: Abdication of Tsar Nicholas II.
	25 October: Armed uprising of the Bolsheviks in Petrograd.
	27 October: Lenin elected President of the Council of People's Commissars by the Congress of Soviets; forming of the Soviet government.
1918	*February-March:* Peace of Brest-Litovsk; decree on the socialization of land.
	August: Start of the civil war and war communism; setting up of a single party, marginalization of the Soviets and formation of an effective political police force.
1922	*March*: Stalin became General Secretary of the CP.
	30 December: Forming of the Union of Socialist Soviet Republics.
1924	*21 January*: Death of Lenin.
1929	Expulsion of Trotsky.
1934	Assassination of Kirov; start of the terror.
1936	Show trials; purges.
1953	Death of Stalin; Khrushchev elected General Secretary of the CPSU; revolt in the Gulags.
1956	XX Congress of the Communist Party; Khrushchev reads out the "secret report".
1964	*14 October*: Following a plenum of the Central Committee, Brezhnev replaces Khrushchev.
1968	April: Demonstrations in Red Square against intervention in Czechoslovakia.
1974	Solzhenitsyn expelled from the USSR.
1980	Sakharov, Nobel peace prize-winner in 1975, was expelled to Gorki.
1985	*10 March*: Gorbachev is Chernenko's successor at the head of the CPSU.
1986	*19 December*: Sakharov is permitted to return to Moscow.

1987   *27 January*: Plenum of the Central Committee of the Communist Party; start of the policy of *Glasnost*.

10 February: The Soviet Minister for Foreign Affairs Edward Shevernadze confirms the release of 140 dissidents.

1988   *1 January*: The law on autonomy of companies is applicable.

23 May: The Central Committee vote for the enforcement of "Socialist Rule of Law."

1 October: Mikhail Serguievich Gorbachev is elected head of the Soviet state by the Supreme Soviet.

1989   *25 May*: Opening of the session of the Congress of People's Deputies. the first Soviet parliament resulting from partially free elections (with multiple candidates).

1990   *13 March*: The Congress of People's Deputies agrees a series of constitutional amendments that result in a presidential regime, political pluralism, and private property.

14 March: M.S. Gorbachev elected president of the Soviet Union for 5 years.

2-13 July: XXVIII Congress of the Soviet CP; M.S. Gorbachev reelected Ist Secretary of the Party following a speech in favor of speeding up reforms.

20 December: Edward Shevernadze, Minister of Foreign Affairs for Gorbachev, resigns due to "inescapable dictatorship"; on the 25 December M.S. Gorbachev had the Congress of Deputies approve increased presidential powers.

POLISH DEMOCRACY TESTED

Marcin Frybes and Michel Wieviorka

Polish people feel that they have always been democrats. Yet all one can say is that they have had very little opportunity over the last two centuries to experience democracy. Deprived of national sovereignty and of an independent state since the end of the 18th Century up until 1918, all that many generations of Polish people could do was dream of it. It was the same post 1945 until 1989 when the system of "people's democracies" that the communists had built was shaken and finally collapsed. Today Poland, together with other countries of Eastern Europe, is emerging from communism. Yet is it not faced by the same problems that it faced in the past. Marcin Krol, a Polish historian, is conscious of this when he ponders the reasons for the failure of democracy in independent Poland between the two wars: "The rebuilding of political parties and the election of a parliament following the restoration of freedom was in fact quite easy. [...] Yet the rebuilding or even perhaps the fostering of a basic democratic culture will take much intellectual and educational effort." Krol was a well-informed democrat, founder of the significantly named review *Respublika*, author of a *Dictionary of Democracy*, and his words still remain true for Poland in 1991.

It is not surprising that when there is foreign domination, or with a past where this has been an important or major factor, that

229

the main thrust of the Polish people's actions should have been the expression and defence of the nation and its culture. Yet would it not be possible to promote a mix of these and arrive at a democratic national culture? Although during the last two centuries the democratic issue has not had much importance in Poland as a distinct issue, on the other hand it is most of the time associated with the struggle for national independence, the debate over a definition of the Polish nation and also with the search for an ideal of social justice.

A TRADITION OF DEMOCRACY OF THE NOBILITY

Poland, be it only in history books, likes to portray itself as one of the first democratic countries of Europe. Yet the system of "democracy" of the nobility that operated erratically in Poland during the 16th, 17th and 18th Centuries corresponds to a very narrow understanding of democracy, open only to a section of society, the *Szlachta* (nobility), who represented only 10% of the overall population (25% if only the Polish population is counted, excluding the many various minorities at the time: Jews, Ukrainians, Lithuanians, Germans and others.)

In the 18th Century Poland experienced a steep decline. The social gap between the nobility and the peasantry widened. The growth of towns was slight, in any case mostly brought about by a foreign bourgeoisie. "Democracy of the nobility" initially based on the good graces and patriotic responsibility of the *szlachta*, progressively became archaic, the principle of *liberum veto* (unanimity) resulting in an absence of government. In 1772 its powerful neighbors Russia and Prussia decided to divide it up. Following this national disaster an enlightened minority under the leadership of Hugo Kollataj (1750-1812) and Stanislaw Staszic (1755-1826) tried to initiate a plan of reform. Their efforts in support of King Stanislaw August Poniatowski, resulted in the calling of a Great Diet. The meeting was held in Warsaw (1788-1792) and in 1791 it adopted the celebrated 3 March Constitution that stated: "All power in society has its source in the will of the people." The 3 March Constitution retained the power of the king, which displeased the French Jacobins. Even so it did try to remain true to the ideas of the French Revolution: "This revolution, both joyful and peaceful, Poland owes it to you," the message sent to the Paris National Assembly points out. Looked on with favor by European democrats precisely because of its unrevolutionary nature, the 3 March Constitution is one of the most well-known expressions of Polish democratic thought and would become a symbol for future generations to refer to continually.

Tadeusz Kosciuszko (1746-1814) a hero of the War of Independence in the United States and honorary citizen of the French Republic, staged an uprising in 1793 in which many peasants took part. However the support of revolutionary France, which was keenly expected, failed to materialize.

At the precise moment when the great European nations were entering the modern age of the industrial era, when they might freely question their political system, their institutions and the principle on which they were run, Poland as an independent state would disappear (in 1795) for a period of more than 120 years.

DEMOCRACY AND THE STRUGGLE
FOR NATIONAL INDEPENDENCE

The Congress of Vienna (1815) finally dashed Polish hopes that independence might be restored fighting for Napoleon. This had proved futile even though the Emperor gave the Grand Duchy of Warsaw in 1807 a new constitution that abolished serfdom and introduced the Napoleonic Civil Code. Henceforth the main aim became the struggle for national independence. The failure of the January uprising (1813) led to a tide of emigration to France where all through the 19th Century free Polish thought evolved, often mixing the themes of nation and democracy. It was influenced by Joachim Lelewel (1786-1861) one of the founders and first theoretician of the Polish democratic thought. A respected historian, Professor at the universities of Warsaw and Vilnus, he published in 1836 a manifesto in which he questioned how far values of liberty, fraternity and equality had been respected in Poland in the past. He concluded: "While remaining faithful to tradition we must think of a different Poland where the social order needs to be changed."

Under his influence in 1832 the Polish Democratic Society was founded in Paris, gathering together the cream of democratic and liberal Polish exiles. The *Great Manifesto*, published in 1836, proclaimed the sovereignty of the people, equality and freedom, independent of their origins or opinions, for all the citizens of Poland: "The new Poland will be democratic. [...] Power will come back to the people; the party which in the past had exercised dominion will forever be disbanded; all men will be free and equal, sons of the same mother — the motherland."

How could one fail to mention the poet Adam Mickiewicz, one of the luminaries of the Great Emigration, who in 1832 wrote: Every struggle for freedom is a struggle for Poland's inspiring generations of Polish people to engage in a multitude of struggles for freedom all over the world, join the Carbonarists or participate in the Paris Commune. Mickiewicz himself took an active part in the 1848 Revolution and edited *La Tribune des peuples*. The motto "For your freedom and mine own" became the catch phrase of Polish democrats.

The debates which took place among the exiles influenced the stance of the provisional governments thrown up by successive uprisings (1846 and 1863), above all over the question of the abolition of serfdom which was an essential factor to get the peasant classes engaging in military actions. The insurrectional government of 1863 abolished serfdom and contemplated granting land to the peasants, yet Tsarist Russia by announcing the same sort of measures on March 2, 1864, undermined its impact on the insurgents and on Polish democrats.

After the failure of the 1863 uprising, plans for armed action and revolution were dropped, to be replaced by more pragmatic ideas emphasizing "organic work." One of the leading lights of this reassessment was Alexander Swietochowski (1849-1938), a supporter of gradual economic and cultural evolution. In his *Wskazania Polityczne* published in 1882 he explained: "The dream of external independence now must be replaced by striving to gain a form of internal independence. This can only be seen in terms of the end-product of buttressing intellectual and material forces, [...] together with a democratization of society." Democratization which the positivists understood to mean trying to civilize the country, develop its industry and reflect on the relationships between the various national communities living in Poland. However in a general way, conditions in Poland itself were far from favorable for the development of independent political ideas.

So it was still up to the exiles to prepare plans for a free and independent Poland. In 1892 a meeting of socialist activists was held in Paris where the PPS (Polish Socialist Party) program was adopted, later known as the "Paris program." It foresaw a "democratic, sovereign republic" in Poland. Edward Abramowski (1868-1918), a supporter of the cooperative movement, saw the question of democracy within the framework of a wider notion of "social cooperativism." It is not by chance that a century later he was seen as the precursor of ideas that *Solidarnosc* would defend: "Democracy can only come as a consequence of an actual need on the part of the social masses. It is in fact a reaction to the omnipresence of the state, an essential defence of social organizations against bureaucracy." For Abramowski democracy was inconceivable without the existence of a form of democratic culture. "The Polish people does not have a modern society, organized in various associations or free unions. [...] Lacking social institutions that they could freely develop and improve, the Polish people have got used to waiting, above all for policy reforms. This deadening of an autonomous sense has become so ingrained in the national character, that even the intellectual elites or the political parties have become used to drawing up programs that can be summarized thus: What can we demand from the state."

Among the supporters of a democratic Poland, let us finally mention Boleslaw Limanoski (1835-1935), author of a remarkable *History of Polish Democracy*. This former insurgent in 1863, was elected to the Polish Senate, before he died, to represent the interests of the workers. A true patriot, he was nevertheless hostile to all chauvinistic ideas. He cherished the dream of a future united democratic Europe: "Every nation, whether they be large or small should enjoy the same rights. [...]. We must hope that if the principle of universal suffrage becomes the political basis of relations between different countries, then Europe will become a federation of national states, joined to each other like the Swiss cantons, with a shared parliament and a court with power to sort out national conflicts. A federation with an executive which is strong enough to implement the decisions and decrees of the confederation. Then wars within Europe would not, or need not, happen."

AN INDEPENDENT POLAND

In the end it was as a result of war that Poland recovered its independence. The end of the First World war, brought the simultaneous defeat of the three old powers that had divided it up, and saw the birth of a sovereign Polish state. Political discourse no longer needed to concern itself with independence. Even so it continued to be dominated by the theme of the nation. Against the overtly nationalist concept put forward by Roman Dmowski (1864-1939), Jozef Pilsudski (1867-1935) favored, at least initially, the idea of the nation as a shared destiny.

The first years of independence seemed favorable to the setting up of a democratic state. The *Manifesto* of the first provisional government, dated 7 November 1918, proclaimed the "total equality of all citizens independent of their origins, religious beliefs or nationality; as well as freedom of conscience, the press, of assembly, protest, trade unions and strikes."

The main task of the new parliament that gathered for the first time in February 1919, was to draw up a new constitution. Two main tendencies emerged. The left-wingers wanted a modern law which took into account the social problems of the country, while the right-wingers called for a constitution based on that of the French 3rd Republic.

The debate continued. In the end a compromise meant that the new constitution was adopted on the 17 March 1921. The text, while referring to the "hallowed tradition of the 3 May Constitution," recognized the principles of the Republic and returned to the idea of the nation. This was inspired by the principles of 1789 and seen as the political embodiment of all citizens, independent of their ethnic or national origins.

Meanwhile the political situation remained very unstable. The problem of frontiers, the large presence of national minorities and an economic crisis conspired to make the situation ever more critical. Many doubts were raised about the prerogatives of the Diet, deemed too extensive, and divisions among the numerous parties resulting in a lack of coherent policy. On May 12, 1926, Marshal Pilsudski at the head of part of the army entered Warsaw. Jakub Wotjtiuk a communist representative commented: "The guns of Pilsudski not only overthrew the Witos government but also buried parliamentary democracy with it." Despite the opposition of left-wing representatives, the Diet on August 2, 1926, adopted changes to the constitution that considerably strengthened the powers of the presidency. The new authorities above all tried to strengthen the power of the state, which led directly to a dictatorship. At the same time the social climate was getting worse. Anti-Semitism spread, fed by nationalist forces and the global economic crisis.

The struggle between supporters of Pilsudski and the opposition parties (centered on the *Centrolew* alliance) increased. The latter organized in Krakow in June 1930 a meeting of the Congress in defense of the rights and freedom of the people. The declaration that was adopted during this meeting, the text of which was banned by the censor, was applauded by more than 30,000 workers and peasants who came to Krakow to show their loyalty to the principles of democracy: "The representatives of Polish democracy gathered in Krakow declare: Poland for 4 years has been under the dictatorial power of Jozef Pilsudski; the different governments do nothing more than put his orders into practice." Pilsudski's reaction was immediate. In the night of September 9 and 10, the police arrested the main leaders of the opposition. They were then tried in what has since become known as the Brzesc Trials.

Henceforth it was no longer possible to claim that the Polish military regime was parliamentary, even though a parliament did continue to exist and there remained a forum for criticism of the arbitrary rule of the authorities. The authorities' policies became increasingly authoritarian and openly fascist. On the 24 September 1930 the president of the Diet, Igancy Daszynski (1866-1936), appealed once more to Pilsudski "to stop the course of events which risk throwing Poland into anarchy and paralysis" and reminded him that "only free and legally organized elections" could bring a solution. The elections organized in the autumn, but rigged by Pilsudski's supporters within the BBWR, led to the triumph of antidemocratic forces. Finally in 1935 a new constitution was adopted that enshrined the principle of authoritarian government. The years preceding the Second World War were indeed dark for supporters of democracy. Those that were to follow, in a very different way, would be as dramatic.

Indeed, the war was not yet over when a communist regime, the Lublin government, was installed, for whom democratic projects and ideas were of little importance. The country had suffered greatly and incredible shifts of population were implemented to match the new national borders. The rebuilding of the country was the main objective and allowed the government to mobilize the population, however keen they might have been. Above all the opposition, dropped by the west due to the Yalta agreement, concentrated more on the nation and religion, and had greater support from the Catholic Church and the conservative and peasant forces than the socialists or the political center, who generally became marginalized, aligning themselves with and becoming a tool of the regime.

By 1947 Poland had firmly entered the totalitarian era. The Catholic church itself, apart from Cardinal Wyszynski who was imprisoned, agreed to make many compromises, and the democratic ideal was no longer aired in public. The death of Stalin in 1953, as everywhere else in the Soviet Empire, brought hope of change. This was expressed not in terms of democratization but revisionism; the idea being that it was possible to reform the regime from within. In 1956 the events in Poznan (a riot on the 28 June) seemed to open up the possibility of the workers' social movement joining with political forces, and the possibility, if not of democracy, then at least of greater openness. Gomulka was the leader and a new wind of change seemed to blow over Poland, attested to by the heightened vigor of those who for the last time in Polish history believed that there could be a renewal of the Jewish community with its cultural and economic activities. The intellectual milieu once more benefitted from relative autonomy, new reviews were started as well as discussion clubs among them the KIK (Catholic Intellectual Club) and the KKK (Twisted Circle Club).

During the 1960's the major development was the gradual abandoning of revisionism among intellectuals in favor of open dissent which increasingly included the theme of democracy. An early expression of this transformation, auguring the end of the intellectuals' involvement not only with the regime but with communism and even socialism, is found in Jacek Kuron and Karol Modzelewski's *Open Letter* of 1964. The phenomena gathered impetus and became more organized in 1968 when dissent joined together intellectuals and students in the same rejection of foreign Soviet domination and absence of democracy. This protest made no attempt to build bridges with the world of the workers, and it was vigorously suppressed, above all through an anti-Semitic campaign that resulted in the departure of the majority of Polish Jews.

Nevertheless a general evolution had begun against which repression would be powerless and which had two distinctive features. The first was that democratic ideas have become widespread within intellectual and student circles who believed less and less in the ability of the system to reform itself, but also among powerful sections of the Catholic Church, above all within the tendencies such as the ZNAK group in Krakow and the review *Wiez* in Warsaw. Adam Michnik, with his book *The Church and the Left*, was clearly one of those who first sensed the change in the Church's attitude, henceforth able to hold discussions with the lay authorities but also hostile to the communist regime.

The second characteristic of this change, which became more apparent by the end of the 1970's, was the rapprochement of the three main resistance or dissident movements opposed to the totalitarian authorities. The worker's movement, national and religious consciousness, and action for democracy, up until then disparately expressed, appeared to be converging, underlined by the establishment of KOR (committee for support of the workers) in 1976 following workers' riots in Radom and Ursus.

Elected Pope in 1978, Cardinal Wotjtyla not only made a triumphal tour of his native country in 1979, but also showed his desire for democracy. The birth of Solidarnosc in August 1980, as we pointed out at the time, brought a dramatic expression to this fusion, in a unified movement, of workers awareness, national and religious beliefs, ethics and a political wish for democracy.

The 1980's were for Solidarnosc, an era of clandestine activity and repression; but for the regime that had turned more into a military junta that a Party-State, it was an era of decline which was to become terminal with the rise of Gorbachev to power in the Soviet Union. Afterwards Solidarnosc became less structured at the same time as the democratic process, initiated by the 1989 round table, became more secure. In the space of a few months Poland gave itself democratic institutions, went on to hold elections, discovered Tadeusz Mazowiecki, the first non-communist Prime Minister in Eastern Europe, and in December 1990 chose a president, Lech Walesa, by universal suffrage.

Today democracy is strong in Poland if one looks at its institutions, the existence of a political system and the workings of that system. Yet its limitations are also glaring. These stem above all from the terrible economic problems that the country is experiencing, which strengthen populist tendencies, frenzied and sinister nationalism and anti-Semitism even though there are virtually no Jewish people. Poland has never wanted democracy more than at the start of the 1980's when Solidarnosc managed to embody this wish, at the same time as working class consciousness and a national identity. Yet the time when these different elements joined together against a common enemy, the totalitarian Party-State, has now passed, and even though the Polish institutions seem well and firmly established within the rule of law, nothing guarantees that in the future there might not be a drift towards an authoritarian regime. This is indeed the sole response to populism which has increased steadily since the start of the disbanding of Solidarnosc in 1981.

CHRONOLOGY

1772	First division of Poland by Russia, Prussia and Austria.
1791	The Great Diet adopts the 3 May Constitution and abolishes the *liberum veto*.
1793	Second division of Poland.
1794	Tadeusz Kosciuszko organizes an uprising appealing to the peasant masses.
1795	Third division of Poland. The Polish state disappears from the map of Europe.
1797	J. Wybicki, with the permission of Bonaparte forms the Polish Legions in Italy whose command is given to General J.H. Dabrowski.
1807	Napoleon created the Grand Duchy of Warsaw.
1815	The Congress of Vienna created the Kingdom of Poland, a dependency of Russia.
1830-1831	November Uprising against Russian dominion. Following its defeat, the former insurgents emigrate to Paris to avoid punishment.
1832-1845	Development of the "Great Emigration" in France. Paris becomes the center of Polish cultural and political life (J.Lelewel and A. Mickiewicz).
1846	Krakow Uprising against Austrian dominion.
1848	Anti-Prussian uprising in Greater Poland.
1848-1849	The Poles take part in the "People's Spring."
1863-1864	January Uprising. Fighting continued until 1864. The Tsarist authorities deported more than 30,000 rebels. New wave of emigration to the west.
1914	Start of the First World War. Jozef Pilsudski forms a Polish Legion.

1918   Forming of a provisional People's Government in
                Lublin, led by a socialist Ignacy Daszynski.
                Pilsudski becomes Commander-in-Chief.
1919   The Treaty of Versailles recognizes the
                independence of Poland without however
                outlining the exact position of Poland's
                borders.
1920   Soviet-Polish war.
1921   The Diet adopts a new democratic constitution.
1922   Legislative elections to the diet results in a
                politically unstable situation: 29% for the
                right wing parties, 30% for the center, 22%
                for the left and 20% for national minority
                representatives. On the 16 December the
                President of the Republic Gabriel
                Narutowicz was assassinated.
1923   Jozef Pilsudski resigns from his position of
                commander-in-chief of the army and
                withdraws from public life.
1926   Jozef Pilsudski stages a coup d'état. Wincenty
                Witos' government resigns as well as the
                President of the Republic Wojciechowski.
1928   Legislative elections give victory to the left parties
                (30.9%) yet the supporters of Pilsudski,
                gathered into the BBWR (an non-party
                alliance collaborating with the government)
                obtained 29.3%. The center parties only get
                12%, the national minorities 19.3% and the
                right only 8.4%.
1929   Worsening of the economic crisis. Strikes in the
                industrial and agricultural sectors occur. On
                23 August Pilsudski became head of the
                government and asked President Moscicki
                to dissolve Parliament. Several days later
                the main leaders of the opposition were
                arrested and imprisoned in the Brest
                military fort.

1930	Early elections resulted in victory for Pilsudski supporters (46.8%).
1931	Trial of the political opposition leaders.
1935	The April constitution is adopted. It reinforces and legalizes dictatorial practices. Death of Pilsudski. New elections bear witness to the bankruptcy of the post-Pilsudski authorities (54% abstentions).
1939	Hitler's Germany invades Poland on 1 September. On 17 September of the same month Soviet troops enter into Poland. In line with the Ribbentrop-Molotov Pact between Stalin and Hitler, Poland once more disappears from the map of Europe. The Polish government leaves for exile in London.
1944	Warsaw uprising. Creation of a provisional government in Lublin dominated by the communists.
1945	At the Yalta Conference Stalin, Roosevelt and Churchill decide on the "fusion" of the Polish government in London and the provisional government in Lublin.
1947	"Elections" on the 19 January gave a majority of 80% to the pro-communist bloc.
1948	Union of the Polish Socialist Party and the Worker's Party. Start of the Stalinist period in Poland.
1953	Arrest of Cardinal Wyszynski, the primate of Poland.
1956	Worker revolts in Poznan. Stanislaw Gomulka becomes Ist Secretary of the Party.
1964	Publication of an open letter by Jacek Kuron and Karol Modzelewski.
1968	Following the banning of a play by Adam Mickiewicz student demonstrations took place in all the large towns of Poland.

	Repression of intellectual circles and an anti-Semitic campaign.
1970	Workers strikes in the Baltic ports (Gdansk and Szczecin). Edward Gierek becomes Ist Secretary of the Party.
1975	Letter by intellectuals against the outlined bill for constitutional reform. These reforms would enshrine the "leading role of the party in society" and of the "friendship between the USSR and Poland."
1976	Workers riots at Ursus and Radom. Creation of KOR (Committee for the Defense of Workers).
1977-1980	The opposition movement begins to organize. Signature in 1977 of a declaration by the Democratic Movement. Start of a clandestine press.
1979	First trip of John Paul II to Poland.
1980	Worker's strikes all over Poland. Signature on the 31 August of the "Gdansk agreement." Creation of the union Solidarnosc [*Solidarity*].
1981	The Ist Congress of Solidarnosc, which was held in Gdansk in the autumn, adopted a program for "a self-governing Polish Republic." On the 13 December General Jaruzelski decreed martial law. Arrest of Solidarnosc leaders.
1982-1988	The underground Solidarnosc movement organized itself and split. Surfacing of underground political parties.
1988	New worker's strikes. General Kiszczak suggests to Lech Walesa holding round table discussions.
1989	Agreement of the "round table." The union Solidarnosc would be legalized once more. Legislative elections brings a resounding

victory for the anti-communist opposition. Tadeusz Mazowiecki, adviser of Solidarnosc, forms a government.

1990 The Mazowiecki government introduces radical economic reform. Fall of 30% in the standard of living. Presidential elections give victory to Lech Walesa.

THE DEMOCRATIC CHARACTERISTICS OF CZECH IDENTITY

Antoine Mares

A few initial comments, ranging from the geopolitics of a troubled area to the mythical identity of a people, are needed to gain an appreciation of a Czech democratic model. The Czechs live on a crossroads of Europe, in a quadrilateral called Bohemia which is both at the same time a frontier state in the heart of Europe and a permanent strategic objective. The Czechs have always had to live with this ever present external threat. This uncomfortable location has resulted in unstable government, a characteristic of the whole of central Europe. Following the kingdom of Bohemia of the Premyslides (10th Century-1306) and the Luxembourgs (1310-1436), the crown of Saint Wenceslas fell into abeyance followed by a brief noble interlude at the hands of the Jagellons (1479-1526), and then the Hapsburgs. The arrival of the house of Hapsburg on the throne was a prelude for heightened tension between the new sovereigns and the Czech lands, leading to open conflict at the start of the 17th century. The Czech crown lands were defeated on the 8 November 1620 at the battle of the White Mountain. Afterwards their political rights were restricted and whittled away until all that remained was a form of internal autonomy. The end of the Thirty Years War did nothing more than confirm the situation established in the 1620s. The Catholic reconquest was launched and following the flight to exile of the Protestant elite, the whole country returned to Catholicism either through conviction, seduction or force. The horrors of these events were to leave a very strong impression on the Czech identity itself. They had lost a large number of their noble elite, which was replaced by a cosmopolitan nobility resulting in the Czech language being socially devalued while at the same time a sumptuous baroque civilization, which still adorns the Bohemian landscape today, flourished.

Finally the profound historification of a Czech identity needs to be mentioned, linked to the need to compensate for the instability of the state, via models and points of reference that recur throughout the centuries. For a Czech the European roots of *Czechness* goes without saying — from the conversion to Christianity in the 8th and 9th centuries to the start of the Thirty Years War — being part of a shared European heritage that is constantly reaffirmed: of values inherited from a Christian culture, the western relationship between the individual and government and art with a universal vocation (Romanesque, Gothic, Renaissance and Baroque). Some of these points of reference were often so firmly anchored that they do not even need to be expressed or mentioned. However these European origins arise from several singular mediums. Charles IV, who was at the same time King of Bohemia and Emperor of the Holy Roman Empire, a descendant of the Premyslides through his mother and a very cultured man, raised the Czech lands to the same level as western Europe in the 14th century. A few decades later Jan Hus (1372-1415) was the first reformer whose arguments won over the majority of the population of a Catholic kingdom. While at the same time keeping faith with the ideals of early Christianity, he was a precursor of the reformation. The surprising thing about the Czechs was that they overwhelmingly agreed with his critical teachings, stamped with a desire for purity and truth, summed up by his assertion (echoed ever since by Czechs throughout the ages) that "truth will prevail." The third symbolic figure was Jan Amos Komensky, the last bishop of the Union of Brethren, a church which rose out of the Hussite movement. Komensky embodies Czech sadness and hope:

the sadness of defeat and exile and hope in faith and the enlightenment of education. Forced to leave his motherland he wandered around protestant Europe, finally dying in the Low Countries and leaving behind him a body of literary and educational works. Komensky created the model of the citizen who chose exile and defended freedom abroad. So while Charles IV, following the initial efforts of Premysl Otakar II, led the medieval Czech kingdom to its apotheosis, the Hussite reform introduced the idea of equality of faith with a new ecclesiastical teachings while Komensky advocated strongly egalitarian education for all.

The consciousness of a specific identity arises out of these elements. Although it is impossible to speak of democracy in a feudal system, that in Austria would survive until 1848, Czech society was marked by egalitarian tendencies inherited from the past, as well as by its own social structures making it different from its neighbors within the Hapsburg Empire.

A CZECH MODEL

When the French Revolution took place the Czech lands had already experienced an evolution that resulted in them readily accepting Joseph II's reforms; scientific or secret societies had developed, and the libraries of the aristocracy would have included Voltaire, Rousseau and above all Montesquieu. But the French Revolution was not the starting point for a democratic model. The decade from 1773 to 1782 — with the suppression of the Jesuit order, the publication of the *Defense of the Czech Language* by Bohuslav Balbin written a century earlier and remaining in manuscript form, and Joseph's reform *patents* — had important repercussions. The Revolution even had a rather negative effect because it brought with it the counter-revolution. On the other hand only the "spirit of the age" could have permitted the "liberation of thought" that Joseph Jungmann observed and which would lead to the blossoming of romanticism. Frantisek Palacky the future political leader of the Czech nation, was of course influenced by the beliefs of Herder and the philosophy of Kant, but also by the

De l'esprit des lois, Condorcet's faith in knowledge and the sensitivity of Rousseau.

If there is a particular Czech model of democracy, or rather a model of political action, it was developed during the 19th century. The Czechs at the time were experiencing the consequences of erratic government. They would invent, or rather build a new identity, enthroned at its heart the "Czech nation." This vision would inspire the national movement throughout the century.

In 1819 a young Palacky, carried away by the atmosphere of romanticism, spoke of a new "spirit of our time." He felt Franklin, the Polish patriot Kosciuszko and Lafayette were role-models and reflected continuously on the legitimacy of revolutionary force. In his opinion freedom relied on the constitutional guarantee of the rights of the citizen. His philosophical and historical studies convinced him that it was necessary to avoid confrontation through reform. His *Study of the Changes in the Czech Constitution* written in 1846 at the request of Count Deym, shows clearly his position: the authorities should be aware that "in accordance with the eternal law of polarity, the steady growth of central power has aroused an even stronger counter-power, that of public opinion." Under such circumstances, it seemed to him, feudalism would inevitably disappear.

Palacky was at the same time the creator and the embodiment of the Czech model. A Moravian Protestant, he studied in the Presburg (Bratislava) evangelical high school and symbolizes the role and rise of the *intelligentsia* in the Czech lands. That a "bourgeois" should be the founder of modern Czech political activity is important. Since the defeat of the lands in 1620 the Bohemian nobility had become much more cosmopolitan. Territorial patriotism no longer fulfilled its function once national appurtenance had been defined in terms of language in the 19th century. A turning point was reached when Josef Jungmann categorized national identity with linguistic identity. Yet Palacky himself started publishing his major study in German. His life therefore reflected the state of the whole of society, at its core incipient industrialization attracting to the mainly German towns the Czech peasantry, who slowly but surely were taking over the urban centers and changing the balance of national forces.

Palacky also drew up an overall model that would work for the Czechs: a mixture of patriotism and universalism, with on a national level binomial Germanic-Slav antagonism. Palacky erected a veritable philosophy of Czech history that, like Herder's, pitted peaceful democratic Slavs against conquering Germanic warriors. With the Hussites and the Church of Unity of Brethren, the Czech nation had reached its apex and democratic values that were defended legitimized its existence. Their punishment was in proportion to the extent of their betrayal. Having such a vision of history, on rather similar lines to Michelet, Palacky should not be seen as a blinkered nationalist. He was above all a liberal who would push his compatriots to mobilize national forces around the idea of a moral restoration.

While he might not have been the originator of the idea of an Austro-Slav, he was its most famous standard bearer and his reply to the Congress of Frankfurt, which invited the Czechs to participate in preparative work in 1848, is famous: "I am Czech of the Slav race" and then..: "If an Austrian state had not for a long time existed, we would have had to create it as quickly as possible, in the interests of Europe and even of humanity." Yet in 1867, following the Austro-Hungarian compromise, Palacky stated that Bohemia and Moravia existed prior to Austria and might last longer. The Czechs, while being Slavs, right up to the First World War oscillated between the two extremes of being part of Austria and refuting it.

What Palacky achieved in terms of historical study and national politics, Karel Havlicek-Borovsky, a very different character, achieved in the press. He breathed a refreshing wind of change on Czech intellectual circles, with rationalist and sometimes ferocious criticism. Shaped under the triple influence of the liberal theories of the young Germany, of Slav ideas and popular poetry, he would rescue his compatriots from the rut in which they had fallen; of petty provincial patriotism which although necessary was out of date at this stage of their development; a sentimental Slavism that had become blind pan-Slavism, a jumble of emotions that ignored the political realities of tsarism. Havlicek is emblematic of the Czech condition both as a martyr of liberty —

his *Tyrollean Eulogies* are a moving complaint over the Austrian reaction — and for his satirical wit which he turned on the political scene. Yet Havlicek was the very opposite of a revolutionary; in 1848 he raised his voice against destructive "cafe politicians" whom he condemned in the same way as he rejected reactionaries. He therefore was as opposed to extremism as to sentimental patriotism, remaining the father of Czech democracy impregnated with moderation, justice and social awareness.

Even though Havlicek rejected the revolutionary movement, 1848 nevertheless was to be a starting point for Czech politics. Having had this experience together with the models that Palacky and Havlicek provided, the Czechs would proceed along the road to democracy within the framework of the Austrian Empire, and after 1867 the Austro-Hungarian Monarchy. This democracy was fed by a feeling of solidarity, all the more powerful because Czech society had its roots in peasant life which still had an influence. The majority of people was literate and the economic development of the Czech lands was rapid. There was however one obstacle, also sometimes a trump card: the coexistence of different ethnic groups and the growing competition between Czechs and Germans. An obstacle when nationalism separated allied social groups but a trump card when emulation became a factor of dynamism for the whole of society. The *Sokol* movement, founded in 1862 by Miroslav Tyrs and Jindrich Fugner, belonged to the twin notions of promoting national identity and universal values which were its justification and made it important.

The character of Tomas Masaryk, essential in my opinion, was equally important. Son of a coach driver and a servant, of Slovak and Moravian origins, he was an apprentice smith prior to secondary schooling and further education. He is a good example of social climbing through education. This morally upright intellectual with startling ideas would be at the avant-guard of the struggle for democracy, largely inspired by the Anglo-American reality. Fighting against all forms of conservatism, he first of all argued against those reflex- actions behind which his compatriots sometimes hid. As a Catholic sociologist, soused in French (especially Auguste Comte), German and English philosophy, he was at the heart of the struggles of his time. Fighting against Marxism, anti-Semitism and the unbridled exploitation of labor, and even though his supporters saw themselves as "realist" he had a religious streak which made him stand out.

To speak of Masaryk's democratic spirit would require much discussion. Overall moral and ethical considerations intrude into all his political thinking. History for him was characterized by the antagonism between myth and science, organically linked to theology and philosophy, between aristocracy and democracy. With scientific entropism of this kind he was led to humanism, which does not rule out religion but a religion of tolerance, such as the Czech (Hussite) reformation that had taken the country to the heights of European humanism and of humanitarian democracy. On a more singular note, for him the national awakening (of Dobrovsky, Kollar, Palacky and Havlicek) was linked to the ideals of the Hussite reform and the Unity of Brethren being universal values. The sense of Czech history consists precisely in this idealization of humanity forming a central tenet of Masaryk's beliefs and as a result of which he would reject both political romanticism and extremism.

The 1914 War was for him the confrontation of western democracy and the theocratic aristocracies of the central European powers: the Czech and Slovak preference was a foregone conclusion. Masaryk chose exile and linked his personal fate with the victory of the Western Allies, to whom the Czech and Slovak communities abroad (emigrant from 1880-1914) lent their support. It was therefore as a consequence of the First World War that the Czech state was born. In some peoples eyes it was the legitimate child of the right of peoples to self-determination, while for others it would be the illegitimate child of history and of the powerful interests of the western powers and again for others it would be the monstrous progeny of imperialism and capitalism.

This new state in fact was the fruit of a *desire to separate* from the Austro-Hungarian Monarchy that had proved incapable of becoming a federation and granting the various nationalities a legitimate role thus compensating for its internal contradictions. The war acted as a huge accelerator for national and social demands, a sign of its breakup rather than novel forms of solidarity. After the Russian defeat, the stalemate of the Tsarist army offensives and the October "revolution," an alternative Czech system could only be seen in terms of the west, for which T.G. Masaryk had opted in 1914, being joined in 1915 by Edward Benes. In their view the victory of the Western Allies meant the triumph of western democracy over German theocracy. Democracy would win at the level of countries in the same way that it had won in terms of the individual: there was a historical inevitability, but not the Marxist one, which Masaryk criticized for its materialism and concept of the class struggle.

THE FIRST CZECHOSLOVAK REPUBLIC

Czechoslovakia, born on the 28 October 1918 was democratic and republican. Universal suffrage was immediately introduced (including women) and proportional representation. The constitution, passed on the 29 January 1920, established a parliamentary system firmly rooted in its egalitarian tradition. This regime was not changed until the autumn of 1938, unlike *all* its neighbors. Czech democracy in the 1930s would remain the exception in central Europe.

Constitutionally the legislative was dominant, but proportional representation produced so many parties that there was a shift of decision-making to coalition party managers and it was at this level that compromise was reached, that ministerial portfolios were shared out and that the balance within the civil service was agreed to. The second shift was towards the presidency of the Republic, known as the "Castle" because it was based in Hradcany Castle, the seat of the Bohemian kings. Masaryk, president from 1918 to 1935, had such a strong personality that he won the admiration of virtually everyone. The Czechs were grateful for his political service, for the creation of the new state and held him in such high esteem that he had powers that do not appear in any of the constitutional texts. Some have said that he exercised a "dictatorship of respect," or even that he was a sort of "king without a crown." He had supporters in each of the various parties which meant that he was able to resolve crises as and when they arose. A *Deus ex machina* behind the scenes, yet with a tendency to intervene at the heart of a problem, he was at the same time the tutor and the teacher of the nation.

Czechoslovak democracy, which was to last for 20 years, was not restricted to politics. It had a moral and ethical dimension that the Czech citizens would hold up with nostalgia, as a beacon, during the subsequent painful experiences. For there exists for the Czechs a social and moral feeling that in part might be a substitute for religion, following the horrors of the Catholic counter-reformation. In Masaryk's eyes tolerance, morality and spirituality not only had to be found at the heart of the republic but in the hearts of each citizen. The republic taught once more pride and seriousness, duties rather than rights and respect for pluralism. Social interaction in such a heteroclite society; the cafes, brasseries, clubs, parties, unions, cultural organizations and the press were also forums for discussion where the likes of Jaroslav Hasek, Karel Capek or on another level, Jaromir John, Adolf Hofmeister or Milena Jesenska could voice their views. Intellectuals could develop their ideas in a law abiding society where fashion, ideas of beauty and aesthetics all had a part to play, expressed in a world where Czechs, Germans, Russian and Ukrainian refugees cohabited with each other. In the face of officialdom incarnated by "T.G.M." (Thomas Garrige Masaryk) who shored up the heteroclite state, the likes of Ferdinand Peroutka could express a very young modernity, even more western but charged with fundamentally the same values, although it wished to break with the past. Openness to the great humanist causes were not the sole province of the left wing parties; Czechoslovakia was the country of asylum for the Germans, Austrians and Jews fleeing from Nazism. It was shocked by the Spanish Civil War and sent humanitarian aid to the republicans. To speak of a culture centralized around Prague however would be an exaggeration. Naturally the state structures and the weight of Prague did influence the rest. There were different regional and local cultures; the working class was also sufficiently long established to have their own roots and traditions which parties and unions were careful to develop. Elsewhere, deeply rooted religious cultures also coexisted.

Czechoslovak democracy also had some clear shortcomings: it wanted to provide itself with the means to fight against those who might wish to destroy it. When the minister of finances (Rasin) was assassinated, Parliament adopted a law for the protection of the republic. When the leaders of the minorities acted against the integrity of the state they were pursued and punished. When the communists tried to take advantage of social unrest for political ends they were hunted down.

Furthermore, and especially with the countries that followed the Austro-Hungarian Monarchy, Jacobin centralism held sway over the promise or attempts at federation. Centralizing Czechoslovakia held sway over regional autonomies. Nationalism was vigorously fostered. Yet it would be a mistake to judge this by today's criteria. In Slovakia the strong Protestant minority that was influential among the elite had been won over to the idea of Czechoslovakia, allowing the Slovaks democratic development, which had not existed under the Hungarians. The Slovak-Czech question was above all a Slovak-Slovak problem that, in broad terms, pitted the catholic majority against the protestant minority. Czech supremacy was only possible because of the lack of a Slovak elite capable of taking control of the administration and leadership of the nation in 1918. In regard to minorities the Czechoslovak government tried to respect international agreements reached at the peace conference. In Europe, since the first decade of the 19th Century, international politics had been dominated by the contradictions of belonging to a state and that of ethnicity. The peace treaties of 1919 -1921 settled some of these, but in so doing gave birth to a new opposition between the principle of self-determination of peoples and the permanency of minority problems. It was at times painful and sometimes unacceptable for Germans, Hungarians and even Poles to find themselves under the guardianship of Czechs or Slovaks, who until then had been ruled by them, even though the latter had been in the majority. Here again we must refrain from simple judgements. The attitude of the Czechoslovak state should be compared to that of its neighbors and seen in the context of other European states. The German minority that made up 22%-23% of the population, were won over in their majority to the new state by about 1922, and remained so until their radicalization in the 1930s. In terms of foreign policy Masaryk was very careful not to offend *our* Germans as he would call them. It was only with the economic crisis — industrial production falling by 40% — and the advent of Hitler to power, that the Germans were attracted in large numbers to National Socialism. The democratic model and majority rule had had the effect of satisfying some and alienating others. Only a system of autonomy —such as the one put forward by Otto Bauer at the start of the century — would have been equitable for the different nationalities that made up the country. Yet would it have been strong enough? Masaryk's view is well known. That it would need "fifty years of peace" to stabilize the situation and establish the new European reality.

Unfortunately society was splintering by the end of the 1930s. The values that it represented had been defeated in Europe. The generation who emerged at the end of the 19th century (Masaryk, Kramar, Pekar, Salda, Capek, Fischer...) were gone. The nation no longer had an intellectual leader. They were followed by a new generation of "realists" who were to experience the realities of the economic crisis, new developments with confrontation with Germany and the Allied "betrayal."

A "NEW DARKNESS"

Henceforth Czech society would be divided between opportunism, to suit the moment, and attachment to moral values, between calculated cowardice and striking courage, between collaboration and resistance. The history of the protectorate of Bohemia and Moravia and the Slovak state has usually been told in heroic terms and it is a present task to write about the concrete reality, uncluttered by thoughts of justification. First of all Slovakia should be distinguished from the protectorate of Bohemia and Moravia, where some layers of Slovak society, although deprived of democracy, found nationalist compensations in a pseudo-independent state. While the Bohemians and Moravians, who were mostly democrats, found themselves deprived of their independence and freedom. This freedom was therefore defended abroad by exiles who were inspired, with President Benes, by the experience of the First World War. Their struggle was at the same time both political and military, the latter distinguished by many Czechoslovaks. About the six years of occupation, beginning in the Czech lands on the 15 March 1939 and ending in the Spring of 1945, we can only say that they were fundamentally no different from what happened in other occupied countries. Conservative organizations were put into place, drawing on clericalism, sometimes influenced by fascism or Nazism, tending to anti-Semitism based on their own beliefs or those from Germany. Resistance initially came from students, soldiers, the nationalist center and right-wing parties and the national socialists. These forces were successively decapitated and all higher education institutions were shut from the 17 November 1939 for the duration of the war. The martyrdom of writers is also quite astonishing. The elite consequently were exterminated or unable to develop. Others would develop in the underground, in touch with the stark reality and responsibilities. The map of war in Eastern Europe and familiarity with clandestine operations (acquired since October 1938) would work in favor of the rise, together with non-communist groups, of a communist force that up to then had been relatively marginal. The struggle against Nazism gave it a new national aura that previously had been tarnished by the German-Soviet pact. This certificate of good civic conduct gained during the resistance was not something particular to Czechoslovakia. Yet through it they were to gain fundamental influence, for on this fertile ground the idea of a national way to communism took root, in which patriotism and communism could join together.

Whatever attachment the Czechs — and the Slovaks — might have had for a western style democracy, as people such as Vaclav Cerny or Jan Patocka still remained committed to, the shock of the Munich agreement, of occupation and war were to leave their mark. The special alliance with the Soviet Union, sealed in December 1943 and the positive image that they had as liberators meant that there was a reawakening — fostered — of the traditional idea of Slavic solidarity. On a local level the communists had the ascendancy, to such an extent that the restoration of the state would become largely confused with the setting up of a social order that would redistribute land and property. How far would it be possible to integrate these new currents with a continuing attachment to those ethical values that T.G. Masaryk had promoted, and that his successor E. Benes declared himself equally attached to? Czechoslovakia would enter a decade of *limited democracy*, defined in outline in the Kosice governmental program of April 1945.

Those drastic measures taken against collaborators and the repression of minorities were broadly accepted because they corresponded both to national as well as social considerations. In the political field the communists henceforth had a dominant position, confirmed in the elections held in May 1946. Already exercising a sort of ideological dictatorship the CP made use of its widespread support to gain its own ends. Nationalized businesses, their hold on local councils, hijacked state functions and closed-shop unions were all used as leverage. In the face of these strong forces the other parties, which to a large extent had been infiltrated, above all short on the ground and largely incapable of action, could only fight with limited means. They proved unable to respond to the mobilization of the communists in February 1948. The country was once again a victim of its geographical position. The idea that Czechoslovakia might play a role as bridge between East and West crumbled. All that remained was for it to be integrated into the Soviet bloc. The illusion of a Czech road to socialism vanished as the satellite states were progressively brought into line. Czech democratic traditions only survived in as much as they legitimized a communist society, fast becoming trapped in its own schizophrenic double-talk.

Between 1948 and 1989 the Czechoslovak political system developed closely following the interests of Moscow, yet this did not mean a complete alignment. Although control of the Czechoslovak Communist Party was total so as to avoid a break up, augured by independent Yugoslavia, it had been essential first to eradicate all possible tendencies that might have become "deviationist;" hence those who had fought in the Spanish Civil War, local resistance fighters or "westerners" were eliminated. The very people who had taken part in bringing their former comrades to trial (for example the trial of Rudolf Slansky) were themselves crushed by the party apparat. One of the functions of the purges had been to institute a reign of terror to insure the obedience of the leadership.

There does not seem much point in rambling on about what was "democratic" in the Czechoslovak "People's Democracy," which in July 1960 became a "Socialist State." Yet one should not forget that this state did bring material benefits, paid for by the loss of freedom itself. The reverse side of the coin was that all independent social interaction had to disappear. Fear and indoctrination spread. All forms of assembly were controlled. The police was everywhere through a vast network of either paid or voluntary informers. Intellectual thought was censored, channelled and directed. And yet Czechoslovakia would retain specific characteristics, with its own particular phases, late de-Stalinization, its liberalization during the Brezhnev era between 1963 and 1968 and above all with its own system of references. It was only due to compromise that the authorities managed to survive. It came to terms with the glaring difference between official discourse and reality. Tolerated a parallel economy and bad workmanship, which insured a tolerable supply of goods. Accepted that at times parts of society might escape the totalitarian regime.

In 1968, over a period of a few months, helped by a weakening of censorship, the traditional values of Czechoslovak society surfaced again. The 1st Republic and its key leaders were rehabilitated, national pride rediscovered. The economic crisis of 1963, the starting point for these reforms, became secondary in the face of society's demands for freedom. Once again it was the students and writers who were the mouth-pieces for this deeply felt need, which for some would be satisfied by reform but for others only by the demise of the regime. How can we explain the reemergence of a democratic model in such a muzzled society? Was it a consequence of the survival of old ideas, hidden but still present in the domain of family or friends? Or was it the conclusions drawn from the failure and inefficiency of the system? For let us note that under the vocabulary of "socialism with a human face" there lurked the possibility of a return to a pluralistic society. In other words western European society. Society rapidly overtook the authorities who had been aware of the need for change. The personality of Alexander Dubcek, a Slovak, who was liked for his integrity and sincerity, was indicative of the hopes that had been awakened within the communist party itself. Even then more limited than those of society at large.

The intervention of Warsaw Pact forces on the 21 August 1968 stopped this process and restored the never really "total" totalitarian regime. The process of "normalization" that came into effect in the spring of 1969, was stifling during Gustav Husak's reign. Czech sociologists have just finished an analysis of their society using the triple stratification: officialdom, dissidence and "gray area." The dissident movement from 1 January 1977 revolved around *Charter 77* and determined to act on a legal basis for respect of human rights. A comment on this group was that there were "Few mouths but many ears." There were roughly 1,700 signatories, from all fields of life, ready to confront the authorities clandestinely. Officialdom was incarnated by the mediocre leadership, grown old in harness, who clung on to their jobs and emoluments. Their inability to dominate the situation and introduce political reform became glaring in the 1980s. Increasingly, voices were raised critical of this paralysis, fatal both for the authorities and for society in general. In between theses two poles there was a heterogeneous "gray area" made up of millions of citizens, unwilling to suffer through dissidence or compromise themselves with the authorities, preferring to continue working in their own fields and often in low-ranking jobs. It is in this latter area that society today is remodelling itself, redistributing power in a way that recalls the republican "revolution" of 1918.

VELVET DEMOCRACY

Czechoslovak democracy, in as much as it can be character-ized, is imbued with some unique features that are now seemingly "spontaneously" reemerging. It would like to be truly European, however it attains this dimension via historical roots. Leaving aside the mythological view of the peaceful Slavs of yore, those traditions established by Jan Hus, the exiled Jan Amos Komensky, by Joseph Dobrovsky and Frantisek Palacky, feed the Czech imagination in a society where democracy is inseparable from the exercise of sovereignty. Masaryk also takes his place among these lofty figures whose common feature was to imbue their actions with *truth* and *morality*.

A non-violent tradition, inherited from Petr Chelcicky and the peasant society left to its own devices, is also a characteristic. Revolutions are peaceful in the Czech lands. Spilling blood was so rare that it fuelled the myth of heroic actions — the Hussite wars, the June 1848 Revolution, the epic odyssey of the Czech Legion in Siberia, the Slovak uprising in August 1944, the Prague uprising of May 1945.... In comparison to events in Hungary in 1956, the Prague Spring of 1968 was revealing. Also the "velvet revolution" of 1989. In fact isolated violence, sometimes self-inflicted, takes on disproportionate symbolic importance. Personified as sacrificial metaphors, such as the murder of Saint Wenseslas or Jan z Nepomuk of Catholic tradition, or the death of Jan Hus burnt at the stake, of the leaders of the Czech lands beheaded in 1621, Jan Opletal killed by the Nazis in November 1939, of Jan Masaryk dead in March 1948 or of Jan Palach who in January 1969 burnt himself alive.

Another tradition: the leaders of the nation were intellectuals, men of letters, who tried to answer the fears of their compatriots. Whether it be Palacky, Masaryk — even Benes — or Havel, the leaders of public opinion have justified the existence of Czechoslovakia at the center of Europe by giving it a meaning, wider than mere provincialism — that Czechs are wont to hide behind. Politicians see themselves as educationalists: teachers are often at the heart of public life.

The events of November 1989 that appear more as a *restoration* or *liberation* than a revolution, more a collective exorcism than a brutal upheaval of society, bring together and add to this heritage. The moral rectitude and ethical integrity of a few hundred individuals defeated the logic of a seemingly omnipotent state. Czech citizens themselves speak of a "miracle," which comes *a posteriori* from a sense of having been nothing more than objects manipulated by history. The symbolic roots of the November 1989 events are in time — the 50th anniversary of the shutting of higher education colleges by the Nazi occupiers on the 17 November 1939

— and in space — from the historic Slavin cemetery to Wenceslas Square, via the National Theater.

Democracy has resurfaced remarkably fast and vigorously for those who forget how tightly intertwined are national and democratic values. Vaclav Havel donned the clothes of T.G. Masaryk. Some parties look back with nostalgia to the 1st Republic. Former political traditions show themselves in the massive participation in elections (96% in the legislative election of June 1990, 74% in the local elections of November). Yet democratic debate has not been seen in 50 years. The social fabric is deeply split and judging from economic portents one might fear for the dangers that threaten democracy in Czechoslovakia. Those in favor of autonomy have gained ground and regional aims are often different, or even diametrically opposed.

For even though in the 19th and 20th centuries the Slovak democratic experience has often matched those of the Czechs, they are not the same and have often differed in time and aim for they have often felt that the affirmation of a Slovak identity is more important than the democratic ideal. Today one of the challenges that Czechoslovak democracy faces is the exact relation between the two parts of the new Federal Republic. In contrast to the 19th century and the first six decades of this century, the socio-economic gap between the Czech lands and Slovakia has narrowed. Shall it be a guarantor of entente or will nationalist passions carry the day?

One thing however is certain. The Czechs have regained control over their own destiny. The events of November 1989 have followed the Masaryk tradition that holds that the Czechs only become a force when they follow the "Hussite truth." This heritage of Jan Hus and Jan Amos Komensky has nourished an internal messianic streak that is expressed in fraternity and humanism. Masaryk's concept of service cut the nation from its Catholic past. Today as a consequence of the role it had in the struggle for freedom, the Catholic Church has regained legitimacy once more and has become integrated. Hence moral and Christian values are joined and form, often in a secular way, a peaceful ideological undercurrent that appeals to the Czechs.

CHRONOLOGY

1781	Patent of tolerance and patent for the abolition of serfdom.
1789	First Czech paper edited by V.M. Kramerius.
1818	Founding of the Patriotic Museum in Prague.
1831	Founding of *Matice ceska* to foster Czech culture.
1843-1844	Ludovit Stur lays the foundations of Slovak literary style.
1848	*11 March*: Start of the 1848 revolution in Prague.
	11 April: Letter by Palacky to the Frankfurt parliament.
	12-17 June: Uprising of Prague radicals, stamped out by General Windischgraetz's troops.
	31 August: Abolition of the corvée.
1849	*10 May*: Arrest of radicals who were planning an uprising.
1849-1859	The reaction raged under the regime of Alexander Bach.
1860s	Renewal of Czech and Slovak political life.
1867	Austro-Hungarian compromise.
1878	Birth of a Czech Social Democrat Party.
1880	Czech and German are put on an equal footing in Bohemia and Moravia.
1881	Opening of the National Theater in Prague.
1905-1907	Struggle for universal suffrage.
1907	*14-23 May*: First elections with universal male suffrage.
1915	Desertion of Czechs from the Austro-Hungarian Army.
1917	Patriotic radicalization of Czech parties and increased action by the emigration led by T.G. Masaryk, Edward Benes and M.R. Stefanik.

1918	*28 October*: Proclamation of the independence of Prague.
	30 October: Declaration of Turciansky-Svaty-Marth by which the Slovaks join the new state.
1919	*16 April*: Beginning of agrarian reform.
1920	*29 February*: Adoption of the constitution of the Ist Czechoslovak Republic.
	14-16 May: Formation of a Czechoslovak Communist Party on a pluri-National basis.
	20 May: First reelection of Masaryk as President of the Republic (second in 1927 and third in 1934).
	10 December: Call for a general strike started by the far left: violence with security forces resulted in 13 dead.
1924	*25 January*: Franco-Czechoslovak treaty of alliance.
1929	Bolshevisation of the CCP with Klement Gottwald.
1932	Trial of Nazi organizations.
1935	*16 May*: Signature of the Soviet-Czechoslovak pact follows the Franco-Soviet pact.
	19 May: Third and last legislative elections of the 1st Republic.
	18 December: Benes succeeds Masaryk as head of state.
1938	*29-30 September*: discussions by the 4 Great Powers in Munich and an agreement that carves up Czechoslovakia.
	5 October: Benes resigns, the 2nd Republic begins and Slovakia from then on is autonomous.
1939	*15 March*: The II Republic is invaded by the Wehrmacht, replaced by the Protectorate of Bohemia and Moravia and a Slovak state.
1941-1942	Heydrich is entrusted with governing the Protectorate in September 1941. The first

	transportation of Jews from Prague begin in October.
1942	*27 May*: Attack on Heydrich followed by the destruction of two Czech villages (Lidice and Lezaky), symbols of Nazi barbarity.
1943	*12 December*: Signing by Benes in Moscow of a Soviet-Czechoslovak treaty of friendship, aid, and mutual cooperation.
1944	*29 August*: Slovak uprising.
1945	*5-9 May*: Uprising of the Prague citizens and liberation of the capital by the Red Army.
1945-1947	On the basis of plans established at Kosice (5 April 1945): Purging and expulsion of Germans, nationalization and increasing control of the authorities by forces linked to the CCP.
1946	*26 May*: Legislative elections.
1948	*25 February*: The communists seize power. *7 June*: Resignation of Benes, replaced by Gottwald.
1949	*28 January*: Death sentence for General Heliodor Pika. *23 February*: Law governing cooperatives (first congress in February, 1953).
1950	Milada Horakova trial (June) and trial of Catholic prelates (December).
1952	*20-27 November*: trial of Rudolf Slansky.
1953	*14 March*: Gottwald dies upon his return from Stalin's funeral. He was replaced by Antonin Zapotocky. *21-24 April*: Trial of the "Nationalist" Slovak communists, including Gustav Husak.
1957	*19 November*: Antonin Novotny, Ist Secretary of the CCP, is also made President of the Republic following the death of Zapotocky.
1960	*11 July*: Czechoslovakia becomes a socialist republic, once collectivization was implemented.

1962-1963	Economic and demographic crisis. First rehabilitation of some of the communists victims of the Stalinist purges.
1967	*27-29 June*: Congress of Writers, marking the start of open protest.
1968	*5 January*: A Slovak, Alexander Dubcek, replaces Novotny at the head of the CCP.
	5 April: Action plan of the CCP.
	21 August: Military intervention of 5 countries of the Warsaw Pact.
1969	*25 January*: Funeral of Jan Palach.
	17 April: Gustav Husak replaces A. Dubcek at the head of the party. Normalization begins.
1971	*25-29 May*: The XIV (official) Congress of the CCP marks a pause for normalization. Political trials begin.
1975	*29 May*: Husak accumulates the leadership of the party and of state.
1977	*1 January*: Proclamation of Charter 77 which follows the death of the philosopher Jan Patocka following police interrogation.
1983	The first mass petitions were signed in April.
1985	*July*: Pilgrimage to Velehrad to mark the 1,100th anniversary of the death of Methodius.
1987	*17 December*: Milos Jakes succeeded Gustav Husak as leader of the CCP.
1988	Opposition movements and demonstrations increased.
1989	*21 February*: Vaclav Havel was sentenced to 9 months in prison.
	17 November: 50,000 people demonstrate to mark the 50th anniversary of the closure by the Nazis of Czech higher education colleges. The next days, hundred of thousands of people march daily. The government collapses.

> *7 December*: Marian Calfa forms a government of national reconciliation.
>
> *29 December*: Following the resignation of Gustav Husak (on the 9), Vaclav Havel is elected President of the Republic by the Federal Assembly.

1990   *8-9 June*: Legislative elections. Civic Forum backing Vaclav Havel obtains 53% of the vote in the Czech Federal Republic.

THE UPHEAVALS OF
HUNGARIAN DEMOCRACY

Pierre Kende

Modern ideas of democracy first began to filter through to Hungary at the end of the 18th Century to a restricted audience of literate nobles who latched on to the message of the Enlightenment, even using it for subversive purposes, although one can not speak of a cultural revolution on a national scale. The first real democratic upheaval happened in the middle of the 19th Century and would have a lasting impact. The instigatory events occurred in 1848-49, therefore modern Hungarian democratic ideas have developed over a period of 150 years.

Nevertheless, democracy in its wider sense goes back to Medieval times for the nobility in the form of freedoms and institutions of self-government. Since the 13th Century (the golden Bull of 1222) the kingdom of Hungary's constituent charter had indeed recognized some "inalienable freedoms" for the king's subjects, that were also curbs on royal power. These principles of freedom, continued to apply and were even reaffirmed under Hapsburg rule, aspiring to absolute rule. These principles would later leave their mark on Hungarian 19th Century liberalism but in a retrograde way, hindering social development. To such an extent that democracy in its full sense would only come with the advent of the short-lived republics of 1918 and 1945.

However, in the collective memory these two dates spell disaster rather than initiating periods of promise and change. 1918 was mainly associated with defeat, humiliating peace terms and the terrible carving up of historic Hungary. 1945 marked the start of 45 years of occupation by Soviet troops. Moreover these two dates, far from being stages of a gentle ascension, are either side of one of the most unhappy periods: the authoritarian regime of Admiral Horthy. As for the democratic interlude of 1945-47 it was expropriated by the communist sequel and today's generations have trouble in remembering it at all. They also find it hard to accept the inheritance of 1956 which was too socialist a revolution for the tastes of the 1990's... The arrival of democracy in Magyar lands can not really be said to have been linear!

The fact that until 1989, every advance of democracy was immediately followed by a fall, has had clear psychological repercussions. Hungary does not have a democratic *tradition* in terms of a savoir-vivre handed down from generation to generation and also in terms of tangible certainties. Hence public anxiety and the mistakes of the new leadership, as well as a tendency for everyone to see every disagreement as a precursor of a terrible crisis.

THE NOBLES' DEMOCRACY

In the same way as in Poland prior to 1795, Hungary prior to 1848 was a "Republic of Nobles." It is true that at the end of the 17th Century, under the rule of the house of Austria, the royal position once again became hereditary (as it had been under the ancient founding Arpad dynasty). Yet notwithstanding this restriction, the Hungarian political system was not run by a monocracy. Against the power of the crown were pitted the weight of the law (to which the king submitted explicitly when he took his oath) and the jurisdiction and self-government of the *comitats*; sorts of noble mini-republics that elected their own magistrates and made laws applicable within their territories (roughly as big as a modern French department). The Hungarian Diet made up of representatives of the most powerful families and high dignitaries of the kingdom, together with delegations from the *comitats* and representatives of the lesser nobility, would continue even when Hungary was incorporated into the Hapsburg Empire (16th -19th Centuries), with the king the key partner for all legislation and even voting of new taxes. Only laws duly approved by the Diet were deemed legitimate by the nobility of old Hungary, who were very attached to their *rights*. Several sovereigns of course tried to break the rules but the pressure of obstruction of the comitats was so great that they generally ended up giving in to them (the example of Joseph II is the most famous occasion). Thus the Hungarian nobles several times forced the Hapsburgs to overtly recognize religious tolerance and successfully defended all their privileges — the most noble as well as the meanest — until 1848.

The 19th Century marks the end of this happy balance. By the end of the 18th Century the most far-sighted of the nobility recognized that the time for civic equality — in other words the emancipation of the serfs — had come. Yet the majority of the nobles, the sole political class in existence, remained reluctant to implement radical reforms while accepting the principles of moderate liberalism tinged with patriotic and nationalist overtones directed against Austria. It was only with the March 1848 revolution that the Diet finally conceded to the radicals what they had in vain been asking for decades.

The 1848 revolution, under the *leadership* of Lajos Kossuth and against the house of Austria (dethroned in April 1849), resulted in the restoration of Hungarian sovereignty and at least in theory marked a shift from noble to the modern era of equal rights for all. In reality this shift would take some time to occur. The main reason was not the reconquest, in the summer of 1849, of rebellious Hungary by the Austrian Emperor (supported militarily by Tsar Nicholas I) and although extreme harshness was applied against those who remained loyal to the idea of an independent Hungary, the Viennese Imperial government itself implemented much of the 1848 plans for modernization. The liberation of the serfs as well as the emancipation of the Jews were to become reality well before the 1867 Compromise that would mean the restoration of a national entity and Hungarian autonomy. And even though it was the emperor who between 1849 and 1866 (Sadowa) passed legislation in Hungary, following the 1867 Compromise (granted reluctantly because of the stubborn resistance of the Magyar nobles and also the quiet wisdom of their liberal leader Ferenc Deak), Hungary would recover its own internal sovereignty. Yet at the price of restraints placed on it by union with Austria, although broad enough to "forge its own history."

Yet 1867 was also a lost chance for democratic modernization. Some important changes did happen. As in 1848-49 Hungary had a government that was "responsible to the representatives of the electorate" in the context of a pluralistic parliamentary system, accompanied by a freedom of the press that was virtually total and a rule of law that was essentially liberal. Theoretically, there would no longer be a privileged class, or restrictions on freedom of trade or of assembly. But in practice equality in law was contradicted by the huge inequalities of wealth, above all in terms of land, and democracy would remain paralysed by the exclusion from the right to vote of the great majority of the popular classes (virtually all the working class, about two thirds of the peasantry and at least half the bourgeoisie). Right through the period of Compromise with Austria (1867-1918), in the Hungarian part of the monarchy, "popular representation" was monopolized by the noble classes; a closed elite who occupied all the key posts of government and were unwilling to share their privileges with anyone. Existing at the edge of the political system, the rising bourgeoisie of the capital — largely of German or Jewish origin — had influence on the cultural climate but not in terms of social intervention which remained marked by the lord-peasant cleavage.

The failure of noble liberalism to become democratic can largely be explained by the problem of nationalities. The Hungarian rural masses, prior to 1914, were mainly made up of Slav (Slovaks, Serbs, Croats and Ruthenians) or other non-Magyar elements (Romanians and Germans). Therefore a complete democratization of the political system held the fear that the administration of the villages or even comitats might escape from Magyar control. In the long run they could count on the Magyarization of the Slav and Romanian elements (a process that did indeed take place in the urban context) but in the meantime, in so far as they wished to retain their national character in the strict sense of the word, the Hungarian state preferred to rush slowly forward. In any case in the eyes of the political classes — unanimous on this point — the adoption of universal suffrage risked giving political power, or at least parliamentary power, to anti-nationalist forces; to supporters of the Romanian and Slavic cause. Potential representatives of an internationalist socialist proletariat. Representatives of an urban bourgeoisie who were not Magyar enough ... Universal suffrage was introduced at the start of the 20th Century (in 1907) in the Austrian part of the Dual Monarchy but not in the Hungarian part, despite the appeals by the Emperor who on this point was more modern than the Budapest Parliament.

Economically Hungary was in full expansion during the Dual Monarchy. Politically, however, it was petrified by the insoluble equation of noble liberalism. Finally, as a national state it was heading towards destruction since it refused all form of federal type compromise with the non-Magyar nations living within its territory. This Kossuth finally understood too late (following the defeat of 1849). Oscar Jaszi the leader of the nascent 20th Century democrats understood this all too well, before the 1914 war, but was in no position to influence the policies of the ruling circle. He nevertheless saw this as the essential element for democracy in Hungary.

FROM DISMEMBERMENT TO SOVIETIZATION

In the history of Hungary the years 1918-19 brought a triple failure: the collapse of noble Hungary, also the end of a phase of organic (linear) democratic evolution, and finally it was the year of the dismembering of historic Hungary.

The collapse was a result of the war — of defeat — and it sparked off a democratic revolution that was also national in the sense that it cut its ties with Austria. Under the leadership of count Michael Karoly (a friend and disciple of Jaszi) and supported by a coalition of moderate nationalists, left-wing liberals, some peasant and socialist leaders, this revolution was doomed to failure.

It did not even have the time to draw up a democratic program (agricultural reform etc.) before the whirlwind of the collapse of all former structures carried it away. Too moderate for left-wing critics — a Leninist CP had only just formed itself in December 1918 under the impetus of former prisoners of war from the Russian front — and too "red" for the likes of the victorious powers who gave it short shrift. Refusing to abase himself by the evacuation of its territories (in the north, east and south) which had been ordered by the commander of allied forces, poor Karoly, president of a republic that had lasted 5 months, resigned in favor of a coalition social democrat and communist government. By proclaiming "Hungary of the council of workers and soldiers," the government — in fact under the Leninist leadership of Bela Kun — launched itself into an impossible experiment of wholesale communism, putting the finishing touches to complete chaos throughout the country. Even so these "communards" did manage to do what Karoly had not dared; they organized an army and tried to repulse Czech and Romanian troops that had penetrated into Hungary with allied encouragement. The Hungarian communists hoped to "hold on" until they were joined by Trotsky's Red Army. But the Russians did not come and in August 1919 the army and the red republic of Bela Kun collapsed. At the same time as the east and the center of the country were occupied by the Romanians, a counter-revolutionary regime was set up in Budapest. It would last for 25 years.

These two successive revolutions mark a tragic turning point in the evolution of a democratic Hungary. They left behind some nostalgia mixed with unease and a lot of resentment (if not hatred). Above all they compromised, for a quarter of a century, the idea of democracy, synonymous for the ordinary Hungarian with left-wing extremism. Of course it was rather a sad fate meted out to the Karoly republic since it had been far from communist. Yet it had been clumsy; above all it made the unforgivable mistake of practicing the virtue of pacifism and love of humanity in a hostile environment, when from Paris to Belgrade passing via Prague all future peacemakers were resolved to get rid of Hungary. Also in the eyes of the Hungarian onlooker to these events, who was later exposed to the propaganda of the Horthy dictatorship, the transition from Karoly to Bela Kun was logical and natural, Karoly himself doing everything to legitimize this amalgamation and then going off on the road to exile to join the ranks of supporters and bed-fellows of the Stalinist Soviet Union. There were few who remained loyal to the spirit of October 1918, above all in Hungary, around Jaszi who criticized Bolshevism in the name of democracy.

The discrediting of the two revolutions, and the success of the counter-revolutionary right, were linked to a quite frightful extent to the rise of popular anti-Semitism. Even before the war, the great failure of the democrats — from the left-wing liberals to the socialists — had been to draw their support from urban Hungary and to become identified with the Jewish intelligentsia or intelligentsia of Jewish origin. So Bela Kun's communist staff had been overwhelmingly Jewish, as were the local commissars of the Hungarian Soviets. Even when it was not the case the public perceived it as such. Therefore the counter-revolution portrayed itself as "national" and "Christian" in a violently *anti* way, and "Bolshevik" in the public mind came to be synonymous with "Jew." So as to make this link even more heinous it was the "Jews" and the "Bolsheviks" who were accused of the loss of former Hungary, even though the carving up of the country had clearly been the work of the victorious powers and Bela Kun's communists had put up a fight to prevent it. The counter-revolutionary regime of admiral Horthy itself bowed to the "diktat of the victors" but which it would ceaselessly fight against ...with words.

At the beginning of this crucial period that would lead Hungary into the arms of Hitler, there was consequently a dual trauma: the unfortunate experiences of two "left-wing" revolutions and the carving up of Hungary. Let us emphasize the incredible nature of the latter: two thirds of its territory had been taken and 55% of its population, an occurrence which is almost unique in the history of Europe (leaving aside the only precedent: the triple partition of Poland in the 18th Century). Undoubtedly the majority of the territories ceded had been inhabited by non-Magyar peoples, however the new borders were very far from ethnic borders. To the extent that of the 11 million people who in 1920 had considered themselves Magyar, more than 3 million had been integrated into one or other of the successor nations (Czechoslovakia, Romania or Yugoslavia). It is therefore not surprising that for a quarter of a century *irredenta* became the main preoccupation of Hungarian politics and an obsession for several generations. The irredentist flavor of the Horthy regime was used to hide the absence of concerted policies, or to be more precise, to try and respond to the *hiatus* between the democratic hopes of the period and the staunch conservatism of the privileged classes, recovering power thanks to the counter-revolution. Avoiding the question of land reform — which would have been a prime means of getting the support of rural Hungarians (two thirds of the population) — the regime started energetically preaching traditional values (family, work and religion) sublimated by the notion of everlasting Magyarity....

Socially, Hungary between the wars, becomes more "democratic" only in comparison to what it had been previously, and to the extent that the aristocratic or noble ruling classes became more open to elements of humbler origin (mostly coming form the meritocracy of the civil service on condition that they were patriots and Christian). Politically the situation was more complicated. Following the upheavals of the counter-revolution, the country once more became, at least in theory, a country where the rule of law applied with a parliamentary regime and an opposition with full rights. In practice it was to be throughout, dominated by a majority party, with a muzzled press, an intimidated opposition and manipulation of popular suffrage. The systematic violation of civil rights was so bad that at no time were the liberals, socialists or peasant democrats represented in parliament in their true strength. Only one opposition party had the wind in its favor: the far right. Supported by the Germans, the "Arrow Cross" Party had tremendous success at the final elections of the period, in 1939.

In the same way as General Franco, Admiral Horthy tried to stay out of the new conflict between Germany and the West; but, unlike the Spanish dictator, he was unable to maintain his neutrality for internal reasons and because of the geography of his country. Hitler took the Hungarian *effort* into account and returned several pieces of lost territory. Even so, was it necessary to declare war on the Soviet Union in June 1941? It is thought that Hungary, obsessed by the question of the future of Transylvania, did not want to be outdone by Romania who had been the first of the Reich's satellites to declare war on Russia. Yet the fanatical anti-communism of the Hungarian regime no doubt influenced this decision (they had joined the "anti-Comintern Pact" that Hitler had formed before the war). Similar reasons would hinder any attempt to get out of the war and right to the end they continued to support Hitler. In October 1944 when Admiral Horthy had finally come to a decision, he was to fail totally, not just because of the Germans (who tried to put the "Arrow Cross" into power) but also because the army refused to follow him. The end of Admiral Horthy's regime was also marked by the tragedy of the large Hungarian Jewish community who were killed (500,000 out of 800,000) in 1944, with or without the complicity of the Hungarian authorities.

The Soviet Army which from 1944-45 pushed the Germans out of the territory, together with the last defenders of the extreme right-wing regime, were portrayed, in keeping with the Allied doctrine, as "liberators" of the Magyar people. This was only partially true and sometimes the very opposite of reality, yet this interpretation was also adopted by the "new democratic forces" emerging from this historic transformation. Primarily the communist party — once again legal after 25 years of illegality and persecution — as well as, due and thanks to the liberators, four other political tendencies: two peasant paries, the social democrats and the "bourgeois democrats" (descendants of the former liberals). The ambiguity of the Soviet liberation was more or less felt by these tendencies, apart from the communist party, although a minority did in fact recognize it. But in so far as the Soviets represented the Allied coalition, everyone subscribed to this thesis of liberation, either through conviction or else in the hope that the post-war order would resolve the problem. Hence the most eminent political thinker of the day. Istvan Bibo, subscribed to this convention basing himself on a line of argument —close to communist beliefs — that emphasized the immediate emancipation of the landless peasants and industrial workers, who until then had been deprived of any kind of dignity. Control of course was in the hands of the Soviets, yet the first act of the provisional government was an extensive reform of agriculture. This action, Bibo (together with so many other democrats) interpreted as a real "revolution," a social liberation, as the founding act of democracy by the people and for the people. The democrats who shared this view, or felt inclined to accept it, naturally hoped that democracy might be reinforced and reaffirmed politically; in other words that the forced *leadership* of the communists and the privileges they enjoyed (control of the police and justice system etc.) would end as quickly as possible.

Yet this was the advantage that the communists had over them. Put in place and protected by the Soviets, they were aided by two major factors: the total and irredeemable collapse of the former regime and the disarray of the non-communist parties which emerged dispersed and decimated by the war. In this vacuum the communist party made the law, by manipulating its allies and when it suited them discrediting all those it feared might pose a challenge to them (by raising the specter of a plot by the former regime). Indeed it was impossible to face up to a party that was supported by the occupation forces and more especially the Soviet Military Police.

Yet a miracle did take place. A largely free and pluralistic election, conceded by the Soviets *in extremis*, resulted in a crushing non-communist majority: 57% of the electorate voted for the so called "small holders" moderate Agrarian Party, 18% for the Social Democrats, 17% for the communists and 7% for the populist allied to the CP (November 1945). The government that emerged from these elections was even headed by a "small holder" and the first president of the Republic was also from this party. In 1946, Hungary seemed on the road to consolidating this, even though the majority party had still not managed to wrest back control of the secret police from their communist masters in the Interior Ministry. For the first time in its history, Hungary had a Republican constitution (judicially Hungary had remained a "kingdom" until 1945 and Admiral Horthy, although he had been called "governor," had been regent). However, the Republic would not survive long enough to develop balanced institutions; from start to finish it was reliant on negotiated decisions — regardless of legality — between the leaders of the parties. Political life during this period (ending in 1947) was determined by the balance of coalitions but not of institutions.

In 1947 Stalin decided to end pluralistic interaction both in Hungary and Czechoslovakia. As a consequence Hungarian democracy entered a period of deep crisis followed by prolonged death throes. The crisis culminated in the forced resignation and escape to the west of the Prime Minister Ferenc Nagy, leader of the "small holders." The death throes came to an end with the proclamation of a "Peoples' Republic" in May 1949 and the adoption of a Soviet style constitution, set in place by the actions of the Communist Party leader Matyas Rakosi.

RETURN TO DEMOCRACY

The first return was attempted in 1956 following a popular uprising on October 23, on such a scale that it resulted in a matter of hours in the collapse of the communist regime. The Prime Minister Imre Nagy, a former communist opposed to Stalinism, appointed to the post on October 24, to placate the rebels, attempted to restore social order by resurrecting the four party coalition that had existed just after the war, while at the same time negotiating with the rebels. As if it were the most natural thing, the interaction of democratic parties was established with great speed. Fearing a chain reaction, the Soviet Union brutally ended this experiment on the 4 November, returning to power *manu militari* the communist regime that had been toppled by the revolution.

Thirty three years later, on October 23, 1989, the constitution of the "peoples' democracy" was abolished and the "Hungarian Republic" (neither popular nor socialist) was solemnly proclaimed with reference to the will of the people, who this time had not needed to stage a revolt. How did this come about?

Two things have to be borne in mind about the third communist regime that existed from 1957 to 1989: 1) it owed its existence (in a way its acceptance by the people) to a political factor that the Hungarians after their misadventure of 1956 considered unchangeable, meaning Soviet domination; 2) Above all since the mid-sixties it had been ruled with a spirit of openness; the authorities refraining from controlling its population, even opening windows of opportunity towards the west. This was broadly speaking why, with the arrival of Mikhail Gorbachev, Hungary became one of the first countries to free itself from communism.

The Hungarian CP itself had its own reformers whose leading role needs to be emphasized. Anxious to soften the political actions of the regime, and fostering critical thought, these reformers contributed to bringing debate out into the open — initially limited but then more and more openly public — on democracy. The opposition which for many years had been suppressed or condemned to silence, consequently could speak out once more in public. Conservatives within the authorities of course tried to put an end to this, but their range of action was fast becoming limited under the dual impact of economic crisis (at the start of the 1980's) and a succession crisis (the number one of the period Janos Kadar was getting old) that lost them any remaining credibility. Unstable and inexperienced, the communist *leadership* of 1988 vacillated between two stances: to end all dissent using force if necessary, or try and survive by retreating and so appear as instigators of far-reaching reform.

The institutional reforms drawn up by the experts of the last communist government, went as far as possible along the road of rejecting the Soviet model; they supported the principles of rule of law and even equality of rights, on condition that all citizens respect the "socialist" framework. A multi-party system itself seemed to have the blessing of the authorities with this proviso. It was logical and even quite clever, but clearly impossible from the moment Moscow no longer made communist supremacy a condition *sine qua non*. The trigger occurred on the day that the Soviets agreed without demur to the forming of a non-communist government in Poland. This was in August 1989. Afterwards the communist taboo was at an end. There was no longer any reason to continue with limited democracy.

In Hungary the dialogue between the authorities and the opposition started in April 1989. Progress was slow because the gulf between the two positions was so great: that of controlled democracy (CP idea) and wholesale civic rights (the opposition movement's view). After five months of difficult negotiations the thesis of civic equality emerged triumphant, with the CP agreeing to free elections and necessary laws for the transition from one party rule to democracy. It is worth noting that when the regime's last parliament voted these laws, the freedoms they granted had in fact existed for some time: press censorship had ended in 1988 and political movements had sprung up in quick succession since the autumn of 1987. The authorities had tried to stop this but had initially lost the means to do so and then a justification.

In returning to democracy Hungary gave itself a constitution which was quite similar to that attempted in 1946, before the Sovietization, but adding several new elements drawn from the European experience. A parliament (National Assembly) at the center of the structure: it elects the President of the Republic, casts votes of confidence in the government or the opposite. The government is formed by the Prime Minister who is in charge of the government of the country, and not the President who is a symbol of unity and the guarantor of laws. Parliament is sovereign apart from matters relating to the constitution (and international treaties). A constitutional court is beholden to make sure laws do not contravene the constitution. The latter in principle guarantees all fundamental freedoms and sets out the organization of the civil authorities.

The first legislative elections of the new republic took place in March-April 1990; there emerged six parties of national importance and three of these managed to form a majority coalition. It is a national Christian coalition and holds (at the start of 1991) 60% of the votes. Among the opposition parties, two have liberal tendencies whilst the third is the heir to the reforming wing of the ex-CP (with 9% of the votes). During the local election in the autumn of 1990 the two liberal parties won practically all the major town councils around the country.

Yet the main political cleavage in the new Hungary is between the "nationalist" camp (some conservatives with a significant minority holding populist views) and the opposing camp of "western" liberals, with a large proportion with "modernist" or "social democrat" sympathies. The problem that faces both camps is the absence of a democratic tradition that they can now put into practice. The Hungarian parties are faced by either new or very old problems (such as relations with neighboring countries) where recipes inherited from the past are scarcely applicable nowadays.

CHRONOLOGY

1785	Abolition of perpetual serfdom during the reign of Joseph II, the Hapsburg Emperor.
1794	Some Hungarian Jacobites (Martinovics and his friends), accused of plotting, were executed.
1843	Hungarian became the official language.
1848	*15 March*: Revolution in Pest; the leading figures were the poet Sandor Petofi and the liberal leader Lajos Kossuth. Nomination of a government with the confidence of the National Assembly.
	2 December: Reign of Franz-Joseph I. The Hungarian government under pressure from the Assembly breaks with Austria.
1849	*14 April*: Declaration of independence. The Austrian army, helped by the Russian army, intervenes and crushes the Hungarian troops (surrender of Vilagos on the 13 August; death of Petofi on the field of battle). Exile of the leaders of the revolutionary government of L. Kossuth.
1866	Austrian defeat at Sadowa.
1867	Austro-Hungarian compromise ratified by the Hungarian Parliament which has much of its power restored.
1884	Creation of the Independence Party by the son of Kossuth.
1906	Victory of the Independence Party in the elections but which is unable to implement its program since it is too divided over the problem of minorities (shooting at Cernova

	of Slovak demonstrators, on the 27 October 1907).
1918	*31 October*: Michael Karolyi government.
1919	*16 February*: Law on the division of estates.
	21 March: Proclamation of the Republic of Councils, led by Bela Kun.
	1 August: Resignation of the Revolutionary Directorate. Admiral Horthy seizes power (elected regent of Hungary on the 1 March 1920).
1921	Decline of the Hapsburg dynasty and democratic constitution (free elections, parliamentary regime and a multi-party system): yet emergency laws hinder its implementation.
1937	Creation of the pro-Nazi Arrow Cross Party.
1941	*26 June*: Hungary declares war on the USSR.
1944	*19 March*: German troops occupy Hungary.
	23 September: The Soviets in turn enter.
	15 October: Failed attempt by Horthy to end the war, coup d'état of the Arrow Cross.
	22 December: A provisional National Assembly, based on communists returned from Moscow, appoints a provisional government.
1945	*April*: The whole of the territory is liberated from the Germans.
	March-April: Agrarian reform.
	4 November: Elections: victory of the Party of Independent Smallholders with 57% of the vote.
1946	Proclamation of a Hungarian Republic, with a priest, Zoltan Tildy, as elected President and the leader of the coalition government: Ferenc Nagy, the leader of the Smallholders Party (a Communist occupies the interior ministry).

1947	Pressure from the communist party led by Matyas Rakosi with a view to gaining complete power. Discovery of a "plot" which is thwarted by internal security: arrest of the leader of the Smallholders Party; F. Nagy flees to Switzerland. Early renewal of the National Assembly: the Communist Party obtains 21.8% of the vote. Other political forces are gradually brought into line.
1948	Amalgamation of the CP and SDP. Start of purges within the Communist Party.
1949	*February*: Trial of Cardinal Mindszenty.
	19 June: Arrest of Rajk, Rakosi's rival, accused of "Titoist" deviation. Trial and execution.
	18 August: Formation of the Popular Republic of Hungary.
1953	*4 July*: Imre Nagy, called to head the government, announces a new way: closure of concentration camps, halt to the collectivization of agriculture and encouragement of private craftsmen.
1955	In the spring the Communist Party, still under Rakosi, removes I. Nagy from his post.
1956	*July*: Resignation of Rakosi, replaced by Erno Gero. Intellectual stimulus around the Club Petofi in Budapest. Demand for a swift and complete de-Stalinization.
	October: State funeral for Rajk who was "rehabilitated." Demonstrations, programs and student pamphlets demanding the return of Imre Nagy, free elections and a review of relations with the USSR (22). Huge demonstrations in front of Parliament in solidarity with Poland. Uprising (the statue of Stalin is unscrewed). During the night of the 23 the Party leaders recall Imre Nagy but at the same time asking Soviet

troops to restore order. Nagy's government, during the following week, attempts to quell the troubles before Soviet intervention. On the 30 a coalition government with a non-communist majority takes power under the leadership of Nagy who announces a return to multiparty rule with free elections and request the retreat of Soviet troops.

November: A communist counter-government is set up under the leadership of Janos Kadar (4). Soviet tanks gradually occupy the whole of the country.

1958   *June*: Sentencing and execution of Imre Nagy. Since 1956 the repression has resulted in the deaths of thousands of people.

1963   Widespread amnesty of sentences relating to the events of 1956.

1968   *1 January*: General reform of the rules and regulations for how the economic system works to set up "new mechanisms based on the autonomy of enterprises."

1988   *22 May*: Janos Kadar is forced out of office. Karoly Grosz becomes Ist Secretary of the Party. The 20th anniversary of the execution of Nagy gives rise to large remembrance demonstrations.

September: Creation of Democratic Forum.

November: Miklos Nemeth is Prime Minister and soon broaches the possibility of a return to multi-party politics.

1989   *September*: Hungary dismantles the Iron Curtain.

23 October: Proclamation of the Republic of Hungary. A multi-party system is established. New political parties are formed (Alliance of Free Democrats, Young Democrats....).

1990   *25 March*: Legislative elections. Jozef Antall,
President of Democratic Forum becomes
Prime Minister and Arpad Goncz, a
Liberal, becomes President of the Republic.

ROMANIA AND THE
DEMOCRATIC MISUNDERSTANDING

Catherine Durandin

Political thought on democracy among the Romanian elite has evolved since the start of the 19th Century, initially expressed in essays denouncing the abuse of power and privilege, manifestoes written in 1848 on universal suffrage and justice, fuelling debate on the reality of popular representation in a parliamentary system and begging the contemporary question of the relationship between politics and morality. Yet the overriding experience has been of popular peasant violence — primitive jacqueries in 1888 and 1907 — denunciations when Romania became independent in 1878, infringement of peoples' right to self-determination — of Jewish people and national minorities — in 1919 when Greater Romania was formed, the inter-war crisis that led to royal dictatorship in 1938 and finally the setting up of a totalitarian communist system in 1948. In fact it does not seem that theoretical thought has led to any practical applications, reality of expression or guarantee of the rights of a citizen. Clearly, and quite rightly so, there is a feeling of despair among today's liberal thinkers searching for points of reference and a democratic tradition in Romania.

The wide gap between theoretical ideas and the history of failure of democratic experiments leads unavoidably to the question of the relationship between democracy and the nation. In other words between democracy and how a society sees itself. A paradox with Romania, that sheds light on its relationship with democracy, was that nationalism was formed around western cultural models while at the same time rejecting western values in order to distinguish and emphasize its particularity. Democratic values also came from the west and were criticized or scorned for being imported, borrowed and ill-adapted to their unique Byzantine, Orthodox and peasant tradition.

1848 OR THE FAILURE OF DEMOCRACY

In Romania, and above all Wallachia, a modern expression of the desire for democracy in fact dates back to the time of the 1848 revolutions. The abortive Wallachian uprising of June 1848 was undertaken by supporters and ideologues who came from the moneyed classes, educated in France with the ideas of Michelet and Quinet, and was supported by such well-known people as Ledru-Rollin and Lamartine. The political vocabulary of these young romantic patriots endowed democracy with a sacred aura because it was derived from the sovereignty of the people. Democracy was proclaimed in an atmosphere of fraternal euphoria similar to that in France of the first few days in January 1848.

The adequacy of the people and the nation was perfect. The Wallachian revolutionary movement's 22 point program stated: "Every Romanian is an atom of the total sovereignty of the people: villagers, artisans, merchants, priests, soldiers, students, nobles, princes, everyone is a child of the motherland and moreover by our sacred faith a son of God." The political system that they demanded included: equality of political rights, a general assembly made up of all the representatives of every class in society, election of a responsible prince for 5 years to be universally chosen, accountability of ministers, freedom of the press, abolition of the death penalty and the formation of a national guard. The appeal for unification of the nation, presupposing a general sense of citizenship and the abolition of privilege, was urgently made: "Help us," the revolutionaries exhorted the Boyars, "unite all social classes into one same body, so that we may call ourselves, without shame, a nation."

This language of a failed revolution, suppressed by the large landowners and the Russian and Ottoman authorities whose armies decimated the revolt movement and restored law and order, left a strong impression and was the seed of the development of a liberal party embodying a western Romanian tradition. In fact the Liberal party was to have a decisive role in 1878 when Romania became independent and in 1919 during the negotiations of the peace treaties which resulted in the formation of Greater Romania. Its romanticism tempered by the experience of the 1850's, it evolved along the lines of the major republican parties of western Europe: a wish to be modern, progress and order based on a modified approach from revolution to reform, patriotism channelled towards the idea of the national cause, the defense of sovereignty and increase in power. The liberals, under the ferule of Ion Brătianu who had been an active member of the 1848 Wallachian movement and proponent of links between Republican France and the Romanian insurgents, thus held political power and had control of the economy at the head of the National Bank until 1888, virtually throughout the period.

Yet the democracy they practiced was very far removed from the ideals proclaimed in 1848. First of all because the representation of the Senate and the House of Deputies was of a very small portion of the population; the peasantry, with their archaic traditions that fascinated the foreign visitor and living in overpowering poverty, remained completely outside politics. As was noted in a report sent on the 28 January by a French representative in Bucharest: "The unrest that politicians take pain to spread around the country is only on the surface and disturbs only the salons, from where it has come in the first place." Political interaction, restricted to the circles of the elite, changed into plotting and clan quarrels, at the center of which the king who tried to inject a sort of balance and after some time, following the failure of the liberals, an alternative.

During the 1880's the question of enlarging the suffrage (universal suffrage was still a minority demand) stimulated political debate and led to a dissenting current within the liberals. Ion Brătianu's brother Dimitru, gathered the malcontents around him and a coalition sprung up against the liberal monopoly of power.

The verbal abuse of some of the opposition went as far as to question the legitimacy of the Hohenzollern king, Carol Ist. The problem of reform and revision of the electoral laws, of course led to a reassessment of principles. Yet in practice the administration manipulated the suffrage with abuses being committed during voting, pressure exerted and a strong system of patronage. All this increased tension. The changeover of 1888 with the resignation of Ion Brătianu and the king's request for a conservative named Carp, took place amid violence. Scuffles and fighting broke out within the House, while a crowd that was heading for the House of deputies was charged by police on horseback. How could one speak of democracy in such a climate of violence and plots. A climate where people pondered whether Prince Bibesco might gather enough support to overthrow the regime, without even thinking of what the coup d'état's aims or ideals might be?

It would appear that the political standing of "democratic" and "conservative" wings was based essentially in terms of foreign reference — those who in the 1880's were keen on an alliance with France were labelled democrats and those who looked to Berlin and Saint Petersburg were called conservatives. So by the end of the century conservatives were almost always shown by French observers as Germanophiles and Russophiles. The political crisis of spring 1888 occurred against a backcloth of an influential foreign presence. For example on March 25, 1888, dissident liberals wanted to go to the Austro-Hungarian embassy and break the windows. When they passed in front of the French Legation they shouted "Vive la France! Vive la democratie!" Yet some analysts have commented that Brătianu's opportunism dictated, since he was a minister of a Hohenzollern king, a rapprochement with Vienna and Berlin, although he continued to vaunt his everlasting loyalty to his French friends. Others stress that Carp the conservative was an ardent Germanophile yet extremely Russophobe. The 1888 crisis that marked the end of the liberal era illustrates the weakness of the authorities despite, or as a consequence of, their firmly rooted monopoly of patronage.

How in fact did those taking over act? Fearing a power vacuum, their ideological slide characterized by the abandoning of liberal ideals was not surprising. What was of supreme importance was who held power. On May 10, 1888, the French representative wrote: "The new Romanian cabinet has not got off to a very auspicious start. It was thought that the only real problem for the minister would be to find obedient and loyal men to serve him. This small group of clever and honest men did not practice patronage. At the start their most urgent and sole concern should have been to build it up. Carp promised soon to ask the king to dissolve the House. Yet he wanted to hold elections in the autumn so as to have ample time to form an administration that was not exclusively provided by the heads of the organized coteries."

The political struggle also involved the peasants who still remained deprived of any right of expression, intervening as both chorus and spectators; yet the rival factions made extravagant promises to these spectators trying to out-bid one another. What could they promise the peasants? Land. How would they react to this? With uprisings. "In several outlying districts of Bucharest gangs of peasants armed with clubs, spades and pickaxes had gone to the mayor's house and demanded the immediate distribution of land promised them and grain to sow the land. These gangs beat up those public servants who refused, burned several barns and country houses." These uprisings illustrated the consequences of rather risky electoral strategies; for several years minor civil servants had, so as to win the vote of the farmers, supported them in their struggle against the peasants. The violence of the peasant jacqueries in 1888 illustrates, twenty years prior to the Great Revolt of 1907, what contemporary commentators called *primitivism,* in other words the remoteness of the countryside from the Bucharest political scene. Strange rumors abounded: that the son of Prince Cuza (dismissed in 1866) and the Tsar had sent the Romanian government millions of dollars so that each peasant would be given a gratuity of at least 800 dollars. The upper classes had so little control over the peasants that they already reckoned they were in the hands of a foreign power, i.e. their neighbor mighty Russia.

THE JEWISH QUESTION:
IN ROMANIA A SYMBOL OF DEMOCRATIC MALAISE

The limited nature of democratic rule, the use of force and manipulating, resulted in strong criticism of the liberals yet did not put into question the legitimacy of the system chosen in 1866. A system where the nation was sovereign and even more powerful than the prince who had sworn allegiance to the constitution. Nonetheless the fallacious nature of the democratic regime, of form without substance which served the interests of privileged groups and their clients, was vigorously condemned by nationalist ideologues who claimed to reject western orders or models. On the one hand there was debate within the system and on the other rejection of the system itself. Priorities differed. This opposition to a western style pseudo-democratic regime increased during the last decade of the century. It would find a wider audience after the disillusion following the 1914 war.

What mainly fired some ideologues against the liberal vacuum was concern for the peasant masses and their concrete development. Their strategy was similar to that of the Russians who looked for a social and political plan adapted to Russian circumstances, different from the west in terms of certain social values and the tradition of the *mir*. Romanian populists during the 1890's advocated concentrating on the people, education of the country people and integration of the peasants into the nation that would emerge. Their publications such as the review *Viaţa Reminisce* were full of optimism; hygiene programs, the need for agrarian reform, the fight against usury and peasant debt, and drawing up of new agricultural contracts to stop the peasant being the farmer's slave. Yet the weakness of Romanian populism stemmed from its inability to resolve the question of the relationship between the nation and the state. Faced with a fragile nation, deeply divided by the gap between rich and poor, by the differences between the various provinces of Moldavia and Wallachia that were part of the old kingdom; the populists stressed the need for a strong state and during the uprising of 1907 advocated the use of repression against rebellious peasants.

Furthermore, values of national cohesion underpinned by the power of the state, lessened the importance of safeguarding the rights of the individual. There was one group at the heart of society which at that time were directly affected by this vocabulary of unity: the Jews. The Jewish question became a focus, from independence in 1878 to the 1914 war, for a type of nationalism that was hostile to foreigners and whose welfare was a source of uncalled for interference by foreign powers. Democracy came to be seen as a foreign idea imposed on them. The equality of rights of the citizens also put Romania under the control of outsiders who assumed the right to interfere in the internal affairs of the country.

In Romania the perception of the Jewish question as a legal and political problem leading to outside interference by the great powers, has its origins in negotiations of the treaty of Berlin (1878) that granted Romanian independence. Article 44 of the Treaty of Berlin stated: "In Romania differences of religious beliefs or confessions can not be attributed as sufficient reason for restricting or depriving a person of their civic or political rights." But article 7 of the 1866 Romanian constitution stated that: "The qualification for being Romanian is acquired, maintained and lost according to the rules outlined in civil law. Only foreigners of Christian persuasion can obtain the status of a Romanian." Was it a choice between citizenship enforced by the west or an exclusive system linked to Romanian nationalism?

So for example while during the 1879 spring elections for a sort of constituent assembly political attention in Bucharest concentrated on review committees, Romanian representatives abroad focused on the settlement of the Jewish question. The parliamentary session opened in September 1878 with three draft bills: naturalization of groups, naturalization of individuals and the third bill against any kind of change to the constitution. The government wanted international recognition without having to conform to Article 44 *ad literam* and tried to end all argument in the fear that it would be explosive. They were forced urgently to negotiate with Germany over a financial disagreement: Romania agreed to buy back, at 9 times their value, shares in the Romanian railways invested in Germany in 1868 and that had devalued repeatedly. So with German support, bought at a high price and voted by the House, the government was allowed to speed up the legal process concerning foreigners, whereby under certain conditions, even non-Christians would be allowed to have Romanian citizenship after receiving a special and individual act of law. Naturalization, rather than being given by the prince as had been previous practice, would be obtained by a vote of the House. This was all rather extravagant since from the Congress of Berlin to 1913, the number of people who had been naturalized, apart from those who had fought in 1877, amounted to 529...

Nevertheless, the interference of foreign powers in terms of rights and the settling of the Jewish question through negotiations with German bankers, tarnished the image of democracy. The practice that applied after 1879 stemmed from prescriptions outlined in the revised constitution: for example, as a result of the April 1881 law governing foreigners, they could arbitrarily expel any Jewish citizen who they felt was undesirable. Villages protected themselves from Jews moving in by expressly stipulating in a law made in May 1887 that "foreigners who would like to settle in a village must obtain the authorization of the village." This presence that was felt to be a "danger to the interests of the Romanian people," foreign interference, western government interference, the interference of the alliance of world Jews, the successive condemnation and blaming of Romanian governments for infringements of human rights, all contributed to alienating Romania from democracy. Furthermore the economic crisis of 1889-1900 and the Jewish emigration that followed, together with the peasant jacquerie of 1907 and accusations made against the "greed of Jewish farmers" once again sparked off, on the one hand recrimination, and on the other self-justification.

The awful nature of the situation was exacerbated when the Romanian government was forced to give guarantees on the Jewish question after asking for foreign loans... The use of money as a lever was unashamedly overt: it resulted in guarantees from Bucharest, but also reinforced the stereotype of a link between Jews and the world finance... In Romania increasingly rabid anti-Semitism would have an important role in the movement against democracy, with its links abroad, and the world of finance as well as parliamentary corruption, resulting in both the democratic system and the Jewish minority being lumped together and considered untrustworthy.

HOMEGROWN TEMPTATIONS VERSUS WESTERN DEMOCRACY

This mistrust of democracy explains the paradox of the post-war period. The armistice and signing of a separate peace in 1918 brought Bucharest into the camp of the victors beside the great western powers: France, Great Britain and the United States. The United States entering the war, justified by Wilson's 14 Points, raised the military victory to one of universal rights. Yet the Romanian delegation were not from the same democratic culture, nor did it have the same points of reference when it put its case forward during the Versailles treaty negotiations. The Romanian case was basically based on ethno-historic rights, the commitments made by the great powers in 1916 and recalling the sacrifices made during the war at the request of the Western allies. Romania's western leaning and solidarity with the democracies had at that time nothing to do with human rights as Wilson would have wanted, but was due to Romania joining in an anti-Bolshevik crusade and accepting the ideology of a sanitary cordon.

Although the western democratic model did not overly motivate Romanian foreign policy, it was at the bottom of the constitutional reforms that founded Greater Romania. Universal suffrage was adopted in 1919. The unification of Romania therefore took place within the framework of a democratization of political life, even though the parties that emerged might not have had democracy at the heart of their programs. From the new provinces that were joined to the former kingdom, in fact, there emerged renewed political forces such as the National Party that had sprung up in Transylvania and voiced Romanian opposition in Budapest before the war. In 1926 the National Party amalgamated with the Peasant Party and gave birth to the National Peasant Party and vying with the Liberals for power. Popular characters in the nationalist struggle with the Austro-Hungarian Empire, for example Maniu, raised the hopes of those who wanted cleaner politics and supported economic and social policies for improving the condition of the peasants.

Yet serious weaknesses clouded the dawn of a Greater democratic Romania. The risks of derailment grew more acute during the 1930 economic crisis. The king decided to free the farmers of their debts. It was discovered too late that there was a high proportion of creditors among the peasants and that the law was forcing small agricultural banks in Transylvania into bankruptcy. The situation worsened in the countryside, an unexpected result of the royal measure. Furthermore political practices remained corrupt: intrigues and plots continued to be deplored by foreign observers. Liberalism was waning during the 1930's , undermined by divisions within the party and by a narrow political philosophy which restricted itself to safeguarding the interests of the ruling classes without a thought for the rest of the population who were experiencing in their everyday life the economic crisis. The feeling of mistrust of "western democracy" once more became prevalent and the most serious danger had its source in the radical reappraisal of the fundamental values that the victorious west had imposed in 1919.

The anti-democratic campaign was suffused by nationalist resentment and indignation at foreign interference in the name of the defence of national minorities. Of course French or League of Nations requests to respect the law were not always altruistic. This is clear from reading a report by General Berthelot in November 1918 that concerns Romania: "I stated by telegram the desperate state of affairs in terms of food, clothing, linen and shoes throughout Romania. We must make a humanitarian gesture. We will lose nothing by doing so, on the contrary. Our influence in this country is already greater than we could have imagined. We shall have a veritable colony that will give a hundredfold return on our expenditure. Already petrol resources and its derivatives can easily pay for what we send." This balance of power that portrayed Romania as the underdog explains to some extent the rejection of demands for better treatment of the minorities, who in a sense exemplify the impossibility of achieving an ethnically united Greater Romania.

The Romanian political classes were deeply irritated by complaints from people of Hungarian origin to the League of Nations, confirming this minority's continued attachment to their privileges; large Transylvanian landowners of Hungarian extraction were also accused of hindering, under the pretext of misappropriation of funds, the implementation of land reform passed in 1920 and which would have harmed their interests. Furthermore Bucharest's need after the war to negotiate a concord with Rome, due to the size of the Uniate Church in Transylvania, was felt as a further betrayal — a reassessment of the idea of Romanian and Orthodox meaning the same — a sort of forced opening up to the west that would weaken the Byzantine heritage, one of the pillars of national identity. This resentment and fear of the denaturation of national tradition and the failure of liberal economics that plunged the population into the consequences of the 1930's economic crisis, goes some way in explaining why Germany with its anti-liberal, anti-capitalist and anti-democratic ideology should hold such an attraction for Romania.

So, almost immediately after the war, there was a violently anti-democratic current espoused by several well-known people from the intellectual and university elite. Philosophers such as Nae Ionescu and Nichifor Crainic glorified the concept of being Romanian, rejecting the elderly and decadent West, and drawing strength from native values linked to the land and Orthodox beliefs. Orthodoxy is consubstantial with the Romanian identity. One of the most important essays by this group was Nichifor Crainic's *Ethnocratic State*. He published regularly in the magazine *Calendarul* and expressed simple concepts in a compendium *Germania și Italia*. On May 18, 1933, one can read: "The Romanian government is hemmed in by the international ideology of the League of Nations. In our country the persecution of the idea of being Romanian is a sad necessity for every government..." According to Crainic international policies would lead to the destruction of the state's Romanian nature. The Legionary Movement found these ideas a source of inspiration: the democratic ideal would be rejected as being hypocritical and destructive of popular values. Quite large numbers of the Orthodox clergy joined this revolutionary culture which claimed to represent the true nation.

The commitment of Romania in 1941 to support Hitler's Germany was the fruit of an ideology that wanted to establish a new Romania in a new Europe. The war took on the hues of a national struggle against the Soviet Union, whose vocation was international and Bolshevik, and who in 1940 had also taken from the Romanians the region of Bessarabia...

More than 40 years of Stalinist Communism has led the Romanians to a different appreciation of "democracy." The points of reference and values of the interwar period have also been swept aside as elsewhere in the Soviet Empire. An end to private property, rapid industrialization and regimentation of the intellec-tual elite to be used as tools for propaganda, this was Gheorghiu-Dej's plan, to be taken over in 1965 by Ceauşescu. A few anti-fascist idealists believed in 1945 that a new era was starting. They were quickly brought down to earth and purged, in the same way as the romantics of Bolshevism in the Soviet Union had been purged ten years after 1917. Others, believing that the west was powerless to do anything, in 1968 wanted to believe in the salvation of country that Ceauşescu had been talking about and this hope of reform justified supporting the regime. They quickly realized that the nation that Ceauşescu wanted was above all a totalitarian island. Many therefore chose exile.

For a few days in December 1989, from the 17 to the 25, there was an impression that the people had won the initiative. The crowds gathered in Bucharest booed the tyrant, who fled in a helicopter... Yet the euphoria went away, poisoned by suspicion. The team that had emerged from the street revolt was none other that a group of anti-Ceauşescu plotters, neo-communist technocrats who had staged the removal of the old tyrant and his clan while leaving the nomenklatura in place. The ordinary people had been manipulated in a clever, dramatic and bloody stage-managed act. The communist illusion was followed by post-communist disillusion...

A year after the fall of Ceauşescu, the political scene is faced by a difficult inheritance. There is great uncertainty over the readjustment of values. Several sources of violence are joining together: fear of being duped, the wish for quick and radical change and fear of losing social privileges, gained by some from collaborating or complicity with the former regime. The democratic path, that was a component of late 19th Century political culture, although deeply mistrusted for bowing to the west, might provide the energy for rebuilding society through a social contract. Yet today's society is radically different from what it was earlier on. Forty years of monolithic communism and totalitarian ideology did not preclude a deep transformation of society, which has thrown up new elites: a large middle class bureaucracy and a worker's universe heralded as the privileged object of history. This society broke from its archaic past and was forced into brutal modernity. Ceauşescu's plan for the systematic ordering of society, launched at the start of the 1970's and re-launched in 1988, bears witness to this ambition to destroy all vestiges of tradition.

The democratic model that is put forward for this society comes from the outside world. Once more the democratic plan is synonymous with the west and carries with it dreams of development and prosperity. Once more one stumbles on the link between socialism and democracy. Constraints imposed by the outside world, ideological as well as economic, might appear unjust. In a conference held at the French Institute for International Affairs on 21 November 1990 the Romanian minister of Foreign Affairs compared Romania with a child playing in a courtyard while the west looks down from a window without interfering. The symbol of the adult-child relationship, above and below, evokes a real feeling of crushed innocence, or at least a wish to exploit reactions of this type. Therefore might not a recourse to exclusive nationalism, resentment and expansionism become the most alluring way to restore historical continuity and a feeling of power?.

CHRONOLOGY

1711-1826   Phanariot rule in Moldavia and Wallachia.

End of the 18th Century   The principalities acquired a degree of autonomy in relation to the Ottoman Empire due to the intervention of the Russian Empire.

1821   Nationalist revolt in Wallachia, led by Tudor Vladimirescu.

1848   Nationalist revolutions in Wallachia and Transylvania.

1877   Proclamation of independence in Romania.

1881   Proclamation of the Kingdom of Romania, Carol I Hohenzollern.

End of 19th start of 20th Century   Peasant revolts (1888 and above all 1907: 11,000 dead) and nationalist demands by Transylvanian Romanians (1892: Memorandum movement).

1916-1918   Participation of Romania in the First World War on the side of the Allies.

1918-1920   Creation of "Greater Romania" by the free joining of Transylvania, Bucovina and Bessarabia to the former kingdom.

1933   *January-February*: Worker's strikes in several cities (Grivița workshops in Bucharest).

1938   *10 February*: Establishment by Carol II of a royal dictatorship.

1940   *14 September*: Establishment of a National Legionary State by General Ion Antonescu (Carol II abdicates).

1941   *22 June*: Romania enters the war on the side of Germany.

1944	*23 August*: Coup d'état against Antonescu. Romania at war with Germany on the 24 August.
1945	*6 March*: First communist majority government (Petru Groza).
1947	*30 December*: Abdication of King Michael; proclamation of the People's Republic of Romania.
1948	*February*: Creation of the Romanian Workers Party by the fusion of the Communist and Social Democrat Parties.
1948-1953	Purges in the party, Stalinist repression of the population, collectivization of agriculture, 5 year plans and industrialization. Gheorghiu-Dej, main power (1952).
From 1960	Gestures of independence from the USSR; start of a Romanian-Chinese rapprochement; modest internal "liberalization" (until around 1970).
1964	"April Declaration" by RWP affirming "independence" in relation to the USSR.
1965	Death of Gheorghiu-Dej (19 March). Nicolae Ceauşescu, General Secretary of the RWP, which transforms itself into the Romanian Communist Party (IX Congress, July). The People's Republic becomes the Romanian Socialist Republic (21 August).
1967	Increase in economic dealings with the West.
1968	*14-18 May*: General de Gaulle visit.
	21 August: Strong Romanian protests over the intervention of Warsaw Pact forces in Czechoslovakia.
1969	*August*: Richard Nixon visits.
1971	*June*: N. Ceauşescu visits China.
	November: "The RCP's plan aimed to improve ideological activities [...] and the socialist education of the masses": "cultural

revolution" Romanian style and the regime
becomes harsher.

1974   *October*: Law for the "rationalization" of the
territory.

1975   *April*: The United States grants Romania most
favored nation status.

1977   First opposition movements amongst intellectuals
(Paul Goma and Mihai Botez).

August: Miners movement in the Jiu valley.

1980s   Worsening of Romania's image in the West:
exchanges and visits becoming fewer;
rapprochement of Romania and Libya;
worsening of food and energy shortages.

1980   *Summer*: Strikes in several towns and in the Jiu
valley.

November: Romania declares it would default on
payment of debt and requests a
rescheduling of its debt.

1982   *June*: Decree on rationalizing and reducing energy
consumption.

1983   *October*: Implementation of a "global agreement"
in industry (salaries calculated in relation
to "productivity"); strikes in the northern
mining area of Transylvania.

1984   *January*: Decree establishing compulsory norms of
production for the peasant plots lend out by
the farming collectives.

July-August: Romanian participation in the Los
Angeles Olympic Games that were
boycotted by the USSR and its allies.

1987   *25-27 May*: Visit of Mikhail Gorbachev.

15 November: Workers' revolt at Braşov.

10 December: Interview of Doina Cornea on
French television Antenne 2.

1988   Very serious Romanian-Hungarian tension; tens of
thousands of Romanian citizens take refuge
in Hungary.

March-April: launching of the plan for the rationalization of the countryside.

1989 *10 March*: Open letter condemning N. Ceauşescu's policies signed by six former leading figures (among them Silviu Brucan and Corneliu Manescu).

17 March: Interview with "Liberation" by Mircea Dinescu denouncing the Romanian regime.

12 April: Full repayment of their foreign debt.

Summer-Autumn: N. Ceauşescu several times speaks out at the changes in other eastern block countries and requests a reunion of an international conference for the safeguard of Marxist-Leninist Communism.

End of Summer: Appeal by the *National Salvation Front* to delegates of the XIV Congress of the RCP not to reelect N. Ceauşescu.

24 November: N. Ceauşescu reelected General Secretary of the RCP by the XIV Congress.

22 December: Fall of N. Ceauşescu during the Romanian revolution that started in Timişoara on the 16th. A National Salvation Front is formed to organize the revolution.

25 December: Execution of the Ceauşescus, husband and wife.

1990 *January*: First disagreements: Dumitru Mazilu (on the 12), then Doina Cornea and Mircea Dinescu leave the National Salvation Front.

20 May: Elections. The National Salvation Front gets 86% of the vote in the Presidential elections and 66% in the legislative elections. Ion Iliescu is President and Petre Roman Prime Minister.

13-15 June: The President asks the miners of the Jiu valley to restore order in Bucharest. The latter use terror tactics against the student protest movement led by Marian Munteanu.